THE LAZY APPROACH TO EVANGELISM

A Simple Guide for Conversing with Nonbelievers

Eric Hernandez

The Lazy Approach to Evangelism: A Simple Guide for Conversing with Nonbelievers

BGCT Center for Church Health

Tyson James, Sound Faith Consulting, LLC

Printed in the United States of America.

GC2 Press® Leadership Team:

Associate Executive Director, BGCT: Craig Christina

Treasurer/CFO, BGCT: Ward Hayes

Director, Center for Church Health, BGCT: Phil Miller

Publisher, GC2 Press®: Bob Billups

Publishing Specialist, GC2 Press®: Stan Granberry

Production, Design, and Printing: Randall House

Ordering Information: www.GC2Press.org

First Edition: June 2023

ISBN-978-1-948618-97-7

Contents

Introduction

You Are the Salt of the Earth...

Sit Down and Shut up?

Seeing the perplexed look on my face, the pastor reiterated his remark that nearly made me choke on my food. "I think apologetics is an interesting topic," he said, "but I don't think it has a place behind the pulpit, and certainly not for a Sunday morning service." Given that I'd be speaking to his youth later that evening, I didn't want to argue with the pastor, and thankfully, my sermon was not on apologetics.

As I was called to the stage that night, the youth pastor asked me to give a short introduction, and out of respect for the pastor, I briefly mentioned my role as an apologist, informing the students that if they had questions, they could ask me after the service. Concluding the service, a young man and his mother immediately began marching toward me, arms crossed and obviously annoyed. Wasting no time, the young man pointed at his mother and said, "tell her *you* said we could ask you questions, right?!" I instantly began replaying the sermon in my mind, wondering if I had said something wrong or inappropriate. Startled by the approach, I responded, "Yes, of course. Is everything all right?" Reluctantly, the mother looked at me and said, "Well, as long as you're okay with it, I guess I'll let you two talk," and walked off.

With concern, I asked, "What was that about?" and what he said next shattered my heart: "Well, I'm an atheist. I don't want to attend church, but my mom forces me to, so I come. But I've always had questions. When I began asking these questions to those in the youth group, they couldn't give me an answer, so I was told to ask the youth pastor, and he went to the senior pastor." He paused to look at his feet in embarrassment. "But now it's gotten to the point where they said I'm no longer allowed to 'bother' people in the church with my questions. They made the rule that if I come to church, I must sit down, shut up, and stop asking questions." With hope in his eyes, he looked up at me and said, "But you don't come here, so the rule doesn't apply to you. And you said we could ask you questions, right? So, if it's okay with you, can I ask you some questions?"

I fought back tears as we talked for over an hour. Eventually, the person with the keys to the church asked us to leave, and as I walked to my car, the young man continued with his questions—great questions at that. I realized that while I had provided him with sufficient answers, more time was needed. I informed him that I was having breakfast with the senior pastor in the morning and, if he'd like, I'd ask if we could continue the conversation over the phone or through email. Excited at the opportunity, he ended by expressing gratitude for giving him my time, and we parted ways.

Wasting no time over breakfast, I remarked to the pastor, "You said apologetics has no place behind the pulpit, but you know you have an atheist in your youth group, right?" Fiddling with his napkin, he chuckled nervously and said, "Yea, that's 'Thomas' (real name omitted). We're praying for him." With slight indignation in my voice, I responded, "You know it's going to take more than that, right? He's an *incredibly* bright young man. Only a junior in high school in this small town, and I can assure you that if you lose this kid, he'll easily take half that youth group with him." I continued, "Look, I know your stance on apologetics. Out of respect for you, I didn't give him my card, but here it is with my cell and email. If you're okay with it, would you please give it to him so we can continue the conversation?" That was almost ten years ago. I doubt this young man ever received it because I never heard from him again, nor was I ever invited back.

You Are the Salt of the Earth...

Stories like these are not isolated incidences. Every time I hear these, I'm reminded of Christ's point in Matthew 5:13.

> *You are the salt of the earth. But if the salt loses its saltiness [its function and purpose], how can it be made salty again? It is no longer good for anything, except to be thrown out and trampled underfoot.*

Because of the vast technological gap between the time this was written and now, the meaning of this passage is often misunderstood or overlooked. So, to grasp the point of Christ's analogy, we begin by understanding the use of salt in ancient times.

Back then, people didn't have refrigerators where meat could be stored for long periods. Instead, salt was used as a preservative to prolong the life of meat and keep it from spoiling. Hence, the salt in the analogy represents the church, and the meat represents the world and culture we live in. Note, Scripture is *not* teaching that the church must provide "flavor" or "fashion" to the world as if we were some decoration to it, but rather, we are called to preserve and keep it from spoiling. But ask yourself, is the meat going bad? Undoubtedly, yes. Now consider the point Christ is making with the illustration.

Suppose you lived in these ancient times and purchased a bag of salt from the local market. As commonly practiced, you add salt to various meats in hope of prolonging its shelf life. Over time, however, you notice that no matter how much salt you add, the meat continues to spoil and perish just as it normally would as if it had no salt to begin with. If this continues to happen, then we can no longer ask what is wrong with the meat, but instead, we must step back and ask ourselves, "what's wrong with the salt?"

Some may retort, "But Eric, surely the world is sinful. We should expect it to go bad!" While this is undoubtedly true, it completely misses the point and emphasis of salt in the analogy (i.e., its function and purpose). Per the words of Jesus, we are given the sobering reminder that if the meat goes bad, the salt is to blame. Hence, *"you are the salt of the*

Earth," and if we lose this purpose and function, then according to Jesus, we are "*no longer good for anything, except to be thrown out and trampled underfoot.*" Is the church being walked on today?

To be clear, the goal of this book is not to point fingers or pass the blame to the prior generations. Such a task would be pointless and unfruitful. Instead, my aim is to take an honest look at the culture, the church, and provide you with the relevant tools to identify and address the issues that confront us today, and more pertinently, as they relate to evangelizing those who reject belief in God and Christianity as a whole.

THE OUTLINE OF THIS BOOK

In Part 1, we will address the question, "**WHY Apologetics?**" by examining the nature, function, and biblical mandate of apologetics as it relates to evangelism. Unfortunately, there is much confusion regarding this discipline within the modern-day church, such as the assumption that apologetics is nothing more than "arguing" with atheists. While it may encompass this, it is far from the core objective. In discipling and mentoring other apologists, I have often discouraged them from engaging in debates with nonbelievers. Apologetics is far more than that, and while *all* believers are called to be equipped in apologetics (more on this in the next chapter), not all are called to debate. In line with this, we will address common objections against the biblical mandate of apologetics.

In Part 2, we unpack the question, "**WHO Am I Talking to?**" by understanding what it means to be a "nonbeliever" and examine the tools needed to define and identify the three types of nonbelievers you may encounter. Part 3 addresses the question, "**WHAT Is The Goal?**" in two separate but overlapping tasks. Part A of this section examines the three dominant strongholds in our culture, and we'll learn to identify these strongholds in three C's: *church*, *culture*, and *conversation*. In Part B, you will be given the tools and tactics for responding to these strongholds accordingly.

In Part 4, we answer the question, "**HOW Can We Reach Them?**" This provides a cumulative case for the existence of God that can be used when witnessing to nonbelievers to demonstrate the truth of *what we* *believe* and *why we believe it*. Finally, we end with Part 5 by answering the question, "**WHERE Do We Point Them To?**" which can be seen as an answer to the question, "why Christianity?" Here, we will survey the historical evidence for the truth of the resurrection, showing that if the resurrection occurred, then Christianity must be true, and every other worldview must be false by default.

All of this is for one goal and one purpose: to be the salt of the earth and reach the lost for Christ. As Proverbs 16:21 states, "The wise of heart is called discerning and sweetness of speech increases persuasiveness" (ESV). So, brothers and sisters, let us not just preach the good news but learn to defend it! Not only is this a biblical mandate, but given our day and age, it's vital and necessary—just as it was when Jude wrote these words to the church two thousand years ago:

> *Beloved, while I was very diligent to write to you concerning our common salvation, I found it necessary to write to you exhorting you to contend earnestly for the faith which was once for all delivered to the saints* (Jude 1:3, NKJV).

It is my hope and prayer that this book will be a resource that provides you with the relevant tools to do this.

PART 1

WHY Apologetics? The Biblical Basis and Application

Chapter 1

The Role of Apologetics: Evangelism and Spiritual Warfare

The Meat is Spoiling

A recent Barna study showed that "the percentage of teens who identify as atheist is double that of the general population"[1] and that nearly three out of every four students (up to 70%) will walk away from the faith during their first year of college.[2] As stated in the introduction, although we, the church, are the salt of the earth, there is no denying "the meat" is going bad.

In his book, *The God Delusion*, renowned atheist and scientist Richard Dawkins states the following:

> The God of the Old Testament is arguably the most unpleasant character in all fiction: jealous and proud of it; a petty, unjust, unforgiving control-freak; a vindictive, bloodthirsty ethnic cleanser; a misogynistic, homophobic, racist, infanticidal, genocidal, filicidal, pestilential, megalomaniacal, sadomasochistic, capriciously malevolent bully.[3]

How does this make you feel? But more importantly, how would you respond? Because Dawkins is undeniably one of the most influential atheist popularizers of our time, chances are, your children, grandchildren, and loved ones will be influenced by his work in one way or another.

However, the arguments in his book are incredibly terrible and don't hold up to academic scrutiny. In an article entitled, "Why I Think the New Atheists are a Bloody Disaster," atheist philosopher of science Michael Ruse remarks, "Richard Dawkins in *The God Delusion* would fail any introductory philosophy or religion course. Proudly he criticizes that whereof he knows nothing."[4] Elsewhere, Ruse states that Dawkins' arguments are so bad, it makes him feel "embarrassed to be an atheist."[5]

This sentiment is shared by many in the academic community, and various books have been written in response to Dawkins, such as *The Dawkins Delusion* by former atheist turned Christian theologian Alister McGrath, and, responding to the accusations in Dawkin's quote above, *Is God a Moral Monster? Making Sense Of The Old Testament God*, by philosopher and theologian Paul Copan. Nevertheless, if Dawkins' book has been thoroughly criticized by scholars and rejected by his atheist colleagues, why does it continue to have such an influence? The answer is simple but disheartening.

A Heartbreaking Epiphany

Due to the Covid lockdowns in 2020, I had the opportunity to speak in various countries around the world via zoom. On one occasion, I was invited by Zuriel, the founder of a new online Christian group in the Philippines, to speak on apologetics in evangelism. This group was birthed in response to the rise in atheism in his country and among Filipinos, and he was amazed at how quickly this apologetics group grew. At the time of the interview, it was up to about 2,000 members online, but nothing compared to the atheist group that had 20,000 followers (ten times as many!).

He explained that despite this new atheist movement in the Philippines, the older pastors and church leaders remained uninterested in learning or incorporating apologetics into their services. Hence, they were the first and (at the time) only group of Filipino Christians who were actively trying to engage the culture by learning apologetics. After expressing appreciation for the interview, he asked if I'd be willing to debate one of the founders of the Filipino atheist group online. I happily obliged.

As with all my debates, I prepared by listening to my opponent's debates online, and I was stunned by how weak his arguments were. I thought, "Wow. If *this* is the best their atheists offer, then the Filipino Churches have nothing to worry about!" But then, like a ton of bricks, an epiphany of the opposite thought dawned on me. If this was their "atheist best" and yet, offered no serious challenge to Christianity, then perhaps the rise of atheism in their country was not due to an intellectually rigorous defense of atheism, but due to the lack of substantial, intellectually rigorous responses from the churches. In other words, the atheists weren't "winning" because they had good defenders but were "winning" because Christianity had no defenders at all.

I use this story as a parallel to the state we find ourselves in now. Because if a world-renown atheist like Richard Dawkins has such a loud voice in our culture, then perhaps it isn't because he is bringing some deafening argument to the table. No, maybe he isn't loud at all but only *appears* loud because the church's voice is comparably silent. Hence, we can no longer ask, "what's wrong with the meat?" but must now step back and ask, "what's wrong with the salt?" This is the need for apologetics in evangelism.

APOLOGETICS IN EVANGELISM

What is Apologetics?

In 1 Peter 3:15, we find the clearest mandate and explanation for the biblical task of apologetics:

> *But in your hearts honor Christ the Lord as holy, always being prepared to make a* ***defense*** *to anyone who asks you for a reason for the hope that is in you; yet do it with gentleness and respect* (ESV).

Two observations can be made here for the discipline of apologetics as it relates to evangelism.

First, the Greek word used for "defense" here (other translations say, "an answer") is "apologia" (ἀπολογία), which translates to the English word "defense." Meaning that biblically speaking, apologetics is *giving a defense for what we believe* and, more pertinently, *why* we believe it. Hence, Scripture is commanding (not suggesting) that we be able to "give a defense" to anyone who asks us for "*a reason* for the hope that is in us." Second, this is a mandate given to *all believers*. Contrary to popular belief, apologetics is not some "young thing for young people," as if Scripture places an age limit on this task. Put bluntly, any Christian that is *not* engaging in the discipline and task of apologetics is in rebellious disobedience to the word of God. As we'll see, apologetics is biblically and pragmatically unavoidable.

Two Questions Everyone Must Answer

When teaching on the subject, I've found that the quickest way to explain the biblical discipline and task of apologetics is to present two simple questions and ask if I may respond as a skeptic. They are:

1. Why are you a Christian?
2. Why should someone else be a Christian?

When a person begins to answer these questions, they immediately engage in apologetics. How so? Because the moment we attempt to *explain*, *articulate*, or *defend* the faith, then whether we realize it or not, we are stepping into the role of an apologist and incorporating this task into evangelism. At this point, the only question becomes whether one is engaging in "good," adequate, biblically based apologetics or inadequate, unbiblical, "bad" apologetics.

While I have received various responses to these questions by fellow believers, one reoccurring theme seems to be this: their answer to the first question doesn't apply to (nor is it sufficient for) answering the second. To illustrate, consider two conversations I once had: one with a seminary student and one with a pastor.

The Seminary Student

When the seminary student asked what apologetics was and how it was helpful in evangelism, I began by asking these two questions and explained that I would respond to his answers as a skeptical atheist. Excited at the opportunity, he agreed, and the role-playing conversation went as follows:

Student: I'm a Christian because I was once lost in my sin, but God loved me so much that he sent his only begotten son, Jesus, to die on the cross.

"Atheist" Eric: Well, I don't believe in God, and while I can respect the fact that you do—come on. Sin? I don't believe in that either.

Student: But sin is what separates us from God.

"Atheist" Eric: Again, I don't believe in God, much less sin. So, if I don't believe in God, what "sin" is there to save me from? But still, I'm curious. Explain this "sin" concept to me.

Student: Well, sin is when we do wrong against God.

"Atheist" Eric: Again, don't believe in Him.

Student: Okay. Sin is something that's wrong, and when we do it, it brings evil or harm into our lives.

"Atheist" Eric: Wait a minute, that sounds like karma, which is a Hindu thing. I thought you said you were a Christian, not a Hindu. You don't believe in karma, do you?

Student: No. I mean, it's kind of like that... but it's different.

In visible discomfort, he asked if we could start over. I agreed, and the dialogue began anew.

Student: Okay, look, I'm a Christian because my grandmother was dying of cancer, and I prayed to God with my church *every night* that He would heal her. Then one day, the doctors reported that her cancer was gone. How do you explain that if God doesn't exist?

"Atheist" Eric: Well, let me first say that I am genuinely happy for your grandmother. But I find it interesting that your reason for being a Christian is coincidentally the reason that I'm an atheist.

Student: What do you mean?

"Atheist" Eric: I, too, had a grandmother dying of cancer and, like you, prayed with my church every night that God would heal her. But you know what happened? She died anyway. So, either God *does not* exist, and things just happen, or worse, God *does exist,* and He just loved your grandmother more than mine. Either way, while your response may answer my first question, "why are *you* a Christian?" it doesn't apply to the second, "why *should I* be a Christian?"

The Pastor

As I sat backstage waiting for the conference to begin, a pastor (who was the keynote speaker for the evening) approached me and, in a patronizing tone, started the following discussion:

Pastor: I hear you do apologetics? That's great and all, but you know what they say: a man with an experience is *never* at the mercy of a man with an argument.

Eric: What do you mean?

Pastor: Well, I have my testimony, and no one can argue against that! I was addicted to drugs, an alcoholic, prone to violence, in gangs, and going through a divorce, *but God* changed my life, and no one can argue against my experience. So, I don't need apologetics to defend my faith. I have my testimony.

Without even asking, he had provided an answer to the first question, "why are you a Christian?" So, I modified the second question (why should someone else be a Christian?) and segued into the question of evangelism.

Eric: Well, you realize that you're essentially giving me an argument as to why we shouldn't use arguments, right? But setting that aside, may I ask, do you evangelize, and if so, how?

His face lit up with excitement.

Pastor: Oh yes! Once a month, my church visits this apartment complex where we set up a station, interact with the community, cook hotdogs and hamburgers, and play basketball with the kids. Then, I grab the microphone and share my testimony. And I do this *all without apologetics.*

Eric: That's great! But I'd be interested in your thoughts about a hypothetical scenario with your approach. Suppose an Islamic group comes to that same apartment complex for dinner a few hours after your church leaves. Like you, they set up a station, interact with the community, cook hotdogs and hamburgers, and play basketball with the kids. And, like you, one of their Muslim leaders stands up with a microphone to share their testimony. But for the sake of the story, let's suppose that his testimony is *ten times better* than yours. Let's say he was in ten gangs, addicted to ten different types of drugs, had ten bottles of alcohol, was prone to ten different types of violence, and was going through ten different divorces at once. Then, with confidence in his voice, he leans into the mic and proclaims, "BUT THE ONE TRUE GOD, ALLAH, changed my life!" Now, earlier you said that a man with an experience is never at the mercy of a man with an argument. So, based on his experience, which according to you, no one can argue against, would you drop to your knees, convert to Islam, and devote your life to Allah?

With a pious, preacher tone, he replied, "No! Of course not!" to which I kindly smiled and said, "Right. That's kind of my point."

To be clear, I'm not necessarily saying that personal testimonies are "bad apologetics." Indeed, Scripture tells us that testimonies are to encourage and build each other up. But when it comes to the unbeliever, Scripture also tells us that the preaching of the cross is the *power* to those of us who *believe*, but *foolishness* to those that don't (1 Corinthians 1:18). So, the question is, how do we, as believers, take what the world deems as foolishness and demonstrate its power? I submit to you that this is, in part, the discipline and task of apologetics.

So, if a personal testimony can only answer the first question but not the second, what would be an appropriate response to the two questions above? Simply this: ***because it's true***. Sadly, I've never received this answer from the countless times I've asked Christians these questions. While truth is at the very foundation of our faith, it seems to be lacking in the foundational presentation of our evangelism. To understand the oddity of this, suppose you were to ask, "Eric, why do you believe that water is H2O?" and I responded with the following:

> Well, I've become a much better husband and father since I started believing that water is H2O. And once a week, I meet with a group of other people who believe that water is H2O, and we read these great books about how water is H2O. Sixty-six books, to be exact! Then, we sing these incredibly moving songs about how water is H2O, and I begin to lift my hands with tears rolling down my face. Oh, and recently, this secular rapper came out and publicly announced that he now believes that water is H2O, so you know it must be!

Surely such a response would be odd to you. But is this not the typical response given by believers when asked, "Why are you a Christian?"

Now, imagine if, instead, I said the reason that I believe water is H2O is simply because it's true. This implies that even if I lost my job or, God forbid, lost a loved one, my emotional distress wouldn't invalidate the fact that water is H2O. Why? Because the truth of water being H2O is not based on my testimony or emotional state as a husband or father but is grounded in the reality that the chemical composition of water is, in fact, H2O.

In the same way, the truth of Christianity cannot be taken or presented as something grounded in our emotions, benevolence, or moral integrity. After all, is it not implicitly pretentious to think that the truth of Christianity is *proven* or *disproven* based on our own lives, as if God *needed us* for Christianity to be true? Put differently, if we lost our spouses, children, jobs, or reputation, could Christianity still be true? Thankfully, yes! Why? Because if God exists and rose Jesus from the dead, then

Christianity is true, and *nothing* could ever change this fact. So, suffice it to say that while our personal testimonies and emotions hold value for encouraging other believers, Christianity is neither established by nor dependent on them, and these do virtually nothing for the nonbeliever.

Additionally, consider this dangerous mentality's impact on our youth. Growing up, I remember returning from youth camp "on fire for God," but two weeks later, this "fire" would dwindle. Why? Because, for my generation, being saved and "on fire for God" had become equated with our emotional highs and experiences. Hence, when the emotions faded, then in our minds, so did our salvation. Sadly, this mentality remains prevalent today. But suppose we taught our young people to base their salvation on the truth of Christianity. Not on an emotional high or experience, but on the reality of God's existence and the truth of the resurrection. And call me crazy, *but what if we exemplified this in our lives first*? Do you think this would impact how we evangelize and reach the lost? Indeed, it would, and I've witnessed it firsthand.

APOLOGETICS IN SPIRITUAL WARFARE

> *The weapons we fight with are not the weapons of the world. On the contrary, they have divine power to demolish strongholds. We demolish arguments and every pretension that sets itself up against the knowledge of God, and we take captive every thought to make it obedient to Christ* (2 Corinthians 10:4-5).

According to this passage, the biblical method for engaging in spiritual warfare encompasses the task of *demolishing strongholds*. Growing up, I was told that strongholds were issues of addiction, demon possession, and so forth. While strongholds may encompass these things, we can look to the next verse and allow the Bible to define it for us.

In verse five, a **stronghold** is defined as "*arguments and every pretension that sets itself up against the knowledge of God*." Other translations use words like *theories*, *reasonings*, and *speculations.* Therefore, we can see that biblically speaking, strongholds are, at their core, false *ideologies*, *philosophies*, *thoughts*, *beliefs,* and *arguments* which *go against* and *hinder people* from coming to the saving knowledge of God. For this reason, the Bible commands that we *demolish, destroy*, and *pull* them down. As J. Gresham Machen states:

> False ideas are the greatest obstacles to the reception of the gospel. We may preach with all the fervor of a reformer and yet succeed only in winning a straggler here and there, if we permit the whole collective thought of the nation or the world to be controlled by ideas which, by the resistless force of logic, prevent Christianity from being regarded as anything more than a harmless delusion.[6]

Hence, spiritual warfare encompasses knowing how to *identify and respond to* (i.e., destroy) the strongholds that hinder people from coming to the saving knowledge of God—and this is *precisely* the discipline and task of apologetics. Biblically speaking, this is spiritual warfare, and apologetics is needed. Henceforth, if we wish to be effective in evangelism, discipleship, and spiritual warfare, then according to Scripture, *we must* engage in the discipline and task of apologetics (1 Peter 3:15; 2 Corinthians 10:4-5).

Strongholds: Obstacles in the Church and Evangelism

Note that the notion of a stronghold is not exclusive to nonbelievers. As we have just seen, strongholds encompass any false ideology or belief that undermines the truth and knowledge of God. This means that, whether we realize it or not, Christians can fall prey to strongholds within their theological and doctrinal beliefs. To be clear, this isn't necessarily about heresy (a view that would disqualify one from being saved). Nevertheless, a "non-heretical" belief does not equate to "non-harmful"—especially when representing Christianity or the Gospel in evangelism. False beliefs have consequences, and theology is no exception.

Christianity: A Relationship, a Religion, or Both?

By way of example, consider the typical atheist retort against Christianity that "it is a religion, and religion is responsible for most wars throughout history!" In response, some Christians declare, "But Christianity is not a religion; it's a relationship!" Checkmate? No. Far from it. Again, although false beliefs may seem innocent at the surface, they nonetheless damage our evangelistic efforts. Using this cliché response from a believer, allow me to explain.

First, such a response only devolves the conversation into a debate on whether Christianity is a religion. But what does this accomplish? If it can be proven that Christianity is "not a religion, but a relationship," does this exempt Christianity from criticism? No. Biblically speaking, we are still called to defend it, not try and *exempt* ourselves from defending it.

Second, the purported objection that "religion is the cause of most wars throughout history" is simply false. According to the Encyclopedia of Wars, only 6.8% of all wars throughout history were religiously motivated, and when we factor out Islam, the percentage is cut to roughly 3%.[7] This is not "most wars throughout history" by any stretch of the imagination. Yet, rather than address the falsehood in the claim, the cliché response focuses on an utterly irrelevant point—"Christianity is a relationship, not a religion."

Third, this cliché response is also false. Note how the statement erroneously assumes that Christianity must *either* be a religion *or* a relationship, not both. But is Christianity a religion? Yes. Is that a bad thing? No, why would it be? "But religion is man-made!" some might say. Well, sure, the man-made religions are man-made, but the non-man-made religions are not man-made (i.e., the Christian Judeo Religion).

Putting this point differently, one could technically say the Bible was "man-made." After all, God didn't take some ink and papyri and begin writing things down. Human hands wrote it. "But it was inspired by God!" some might say. Ah, then we can qualify that something can be "God-made" even if human hands have touched it. Could we then not equally say that the religion of Christianity was also "God-made," even though humans were used to write it down and carry it out? Of course.

Moreover, consider James 1:26-27:

> *If anyone thinks he is religious and does not bridle his tongue but deceives his heart, this person's religion is worthless. Religion that is pure and undefiled before God the Father is this: to visit orphans and widows in their affliction, and to keep oneself unstained from the world* (ESV).

Scripture teaches that true religion is pure and undefiled before God, meaning that the Bible distinguishes between "good religion" and "bad religion." Hence, we should agree with the atheist that useless, bad religion must be purged from our societies, but let's not throw out the baby Jesus with the bathwater. Per Scripture, true, pure, and undefiled religion must stay, and mind you, there is only one.

So, is it correct to say that Christianity is a religion? Yes. And is it accurate to say that Christianity is a relationship? Absolutely. But is it right to argue that Christianity is either a religion *or* a relationship? No, because arguing that "Christianity is a relationship, not a religion!" is like arguing that my wife and I are "in a relationship, not a marriage!" Being in a marriage encompasses being in a relationship and being in a relationship with God encompasses being in a religion—and more appropriately, the religion God has approved of by raising Jesus from the dead.

Again, I use this example only to show how 1) even a trivial falsehood can lead to unnecessary disputes, further creating unnecessary obstacles in evangelism, and 2) how a foundational, biblically based apologetic can avoid these. Now, consider the application.

The Relationship Between Theology and Religion

The prominent issue with the cliché above stems from a common misunderstanding of the word "religion" and, more pertinently, its relation to theology (which has also been shunned by some Christians today). Simply put, **theology** encompasses one's *beliefs* about God, whereas **religion** encompasses one's *actions* toward God. Why does this matter? Because in understanding this distinction, we can easily make the connection that one's *beliefs about God* (their theology) will inform one's *actions toward God* (their religion).

For example, if a Christian believes God answers prayer, then their degree of time spent in prayer will be directly correlated to this belief. Hence, a person with adequate knowledge *about* prayer (their theology) will devote sufficient time (their religious devotion) *to* prayer. By contrast, the person who vaguely understands prayer will rarely rely on it as a viable discipline, and this will be reflected in their minimal-to-no-time spent in prayer. So, how much do you pray? Similarly, a person with an adequate grasp, knowledge, and understanding of God (their theology) will reflect this in their devotion and commitment to him (their religion). And here is where apologetics comes into the picture for spiritual maturity and evangelism.

Consider that the more I've learned about my wife, the more I've desired to love her. Similarly, the more I've learned about God through apologetics (a biblical mandate to all believers), the more I've desired to love and make Him known. Hence, the less one knows, the less one is willing to do, whereas the more one knows, the more one willingly *wants* to do. Now consider the inverse, negative implications of this principle.

If one has inadequate, false beliefs about God ("bad theology"), then it will inevitably lead to inadequate, misguided actions toward God ("bad religion"). Take the horrendous attacks on 9/11 carried out by Islamic terrorists. The reason these men committed these atrocious crimes was because of their religion, and the reason their religion encouraged these acts was because of their theology. Thus, if one's theology encompasses the belief that God wants you to kill nonbelievers/Americans, then one's religion will encompass the practice of committing suicide to do so (e.g., flying planes into buildings). Therefore, if we want to get rid of "bad religion," we must first get rid of "bad theology."

In the same vein, why doesn't the atheist pray to God? Because he doesn't believe in prayer. But why doesn't he believe in prayer? Because he doesn't believe in God. Note that although the atheist doesn't *believe in* God, he still holds *beliefs about* God, and such views (though negative) encompass his theology which, in turn, informs his "religion" (or lack thereof). Therefore, if we want a person to engage in the appropriate practices of a "true religion" (Christianity), then we must start by addressing the false theological beliefs (i.e., strongholds) that bind them. And if we wish to succeed at this task, then we (the church) cannot exempt ourselves from this assessment, but must lead by example.

Strongholds in Our Theology: Innocent or Detrimental?

While not all false theological beliefs lead to abhorrent religious practices, they can cause our sermons, prayers, and evangelistic efforts to be misguided in various ways. Put differently, misguided theological beliefs inevitably lead to misguided practices within the church. Consider two occasions where I witnessed this principle firsthand.

Facing Up When We Pray

Before the youth service, I met with the leaders for prayer and was introduced to the young lady leading it. She was their upcoming leader in training, which was evident by the zealous passion in her voice as she prayed. Concluding her prayer, she noticed that I and some of the leaders had bowed our heads during the prayer, and this clearly bothered her. "I don't think we should bow our heads during prayer because God is in heaven," she said, "and if God's in heaven, then we should face up when we pray, not down."

While I could appreciate her desire to convey this "newly found revelation" about prayer, I couldn't help but probe her theology with a question. "And what about the people in China?" I asked. "What do you mean?" "Well," I said, "if God is located at our North and China is on the opposite end of the globe, then aiming *their* faces down directly points to our North. Is it ok for them to bow their heads in prayer?" She looked stunned. "But now I'm curious. What if God is closer to China than He is to America? Shouldn't we bow our heads down? And why assume that God is located at the North or South, as opposed to East or West?"

Obviously, I wasn't trying to figure out which direction to face during prayer. I was making the subtle point that her "newly found revelation" implied that God is confined to a single, physical location. Yet, if according to Scripture, God is both spaceless and omnipresent, then He cannot be localized to a single point in space. Granted, this belief could be seen as relatively innocent, and if you feel the need to pray for my character, please do. Nevertheless, given that this relatively innocent belief was false, it led to a fabricated, uncanny practice (not to mention some borderline blasphemous implications!).

"It's All the Holy Spirit"

On another occasion, a young man had just played his first worship service as the guitarist, so I encouraged him by stating he did an excellent job for his first time on stage. But with a humble smile, he replied, "Oh no, it wasn't me; it was all the Holy Spirit!" Attempting to salvage my compliment, I nudged him on the shoulder and said, "Sure, he used you. But come on, you put in the practice, right? You can take some credit too." "No," he replied. "It was all the Holy Spirit. Give him credit!" At this point, I could no longer help myself. "Well, I did notice that you missed a note or two during the bridge on the second song, and your tempo was a bit fast during the worship. Are you implying that the Holy Spirit doesn't know how to play these songs correctly? Or is that perhaps, given it was your first time on stage, you may have just goofed a time or two?"

Again, please pray for me if you feel led. But in all sincerity, what potential lifestyle could come about from such a mindset? If the Holy Spirit is responsible for *all that we do*, then why pray? And if the Holy Spirit is responsible for all that we are, then why take responsibility for the level of sin or spiritual maturity we have as disciples of Christ? In other words, if it's "all God and not me," then what role do I play in evangelism, spiritual formation, and discipleship? If this young man is correct, I play no role at all because, at the end of the day, "It's all the Holy Spirit." Give him both the credit and the blame.

Strongholds: Stumbling Blocks in Our Evangelism

Misconceptions about God's location or the Holy Spirit's role in our lives may lead to looking silly during prayer or while taking a compliment. But when it comes to evangelism, eternity is at stake. For example, it's not uncommon for a skeptic to reject the God you are presenting to them. Nevertheless, we *must* ensure that the God they're rejecting is an accurate, biblical representation of God, and not some god that we've falsely or inadequately presented. Because, if I may put the point bluntly, *we will fail in evangelism if we cause others to reject God simply because we have presented to them a God that even Scripture rejects*. Theology matters, and it matters deeply.

I've witnessed firsthand that when an erroneous presentation of God is given, the skeptic will not be denying the God of the Bible but will be denying a mischaracterized representation of God that stems from our strongholds. So, with love and integrity, let's learn to remove strongholds for the nonbeliever, not create them. For this reason, we turn to one of apologetics' most vital roles in the believer's life—fulfilling the greatest commandment by loving God with our minds.

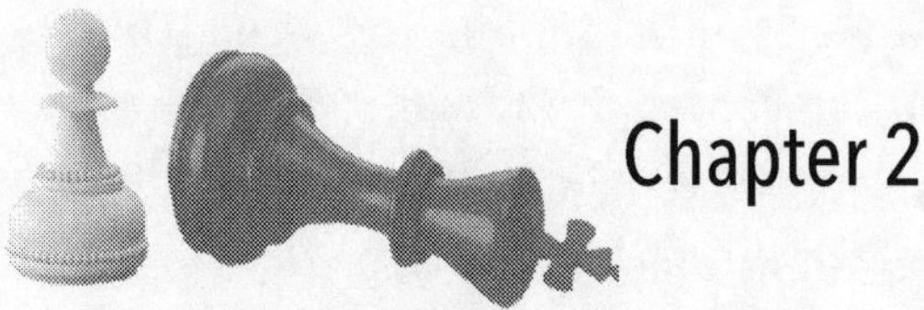

Chapter 2

Apologetics and The Greatest Commandment: Loving God With Our Minds

A Mature Faith

A youth pastor once told me we shouldn't go "too deep" in our sermons because if we do, the people may drown. With a smile, I replied, "Well, pastor, that's why we teach them how to swim!"

In defense of this "not too deep" mentality, some have argued that Matthew 18:3 calls us to have "child-like" faith and not a "deep, theological faith." However, there's a difference between a "child-like" faith and a "child-*ish*" faith. As Paul writes, "Brothers, do not be children in your thinking. Be infants in evil, but in your thinking be mature" (1 Corinthians 14:20, ESV). A child-like faith is a complete trust and confidence in God as our heavenly father, whereas a child-*ish* faith (per 1 Corinthians 14:20) is an immature, *intellectually lazy*, incompetent one. So, how can we fulfill the former while avoiding the latter? By fulfilling the greatest commandment.

Loving God With Our Heart, Strength, and Mind

In Mark 12:28-30, Jesus is asked which of all the commandments is the greatest, and in response, he states, "Love the Lord your God with all <u>your heart</u> and <u>with all your soul</u> and <u>with all your mind</u> and <u>with all</u>

your strength." This provides three aspects of our lives for serving and loving God—*heart, strength*, and *mind* (the soul representing the person as a whole). The **heart** is indicative of our emotions, the **strength** indicates our service, and the **mind** references our intellect. Now consider each of these in light of the modern-day, 21st-Century American church.

I can honestly say that we've done a fair job of loving God with our hearts. We are emotionally invested in who He is; we lift our hands in worship, cry tears at the altar, and it's beautiful. Additionally, we've done a fair job of loving God with our strength. That is, our service for God; we volunteer at church, feed the homeless, and help the less fortunate in our communities. All of these are commendable acts in fulfilling the greatest commandment.

But then there's loving God with the mind, which in Greek is an emphasis on our intellect; our faculty of thought, rationality, and understanding. Sadly, the modern-day, 21st-Century American church has truly dropped the ball in this area. By comparison, take the early church fathers as an example and consider how seriously they took this commandment.

The Early Church

Beginning at A.D.325, we see the early church fathers gathered at the Council of Nicea to flesh out and *defend* the deity of Christ (giving rise to a more precise articulation of the Trinity in later councils). Their greatest concern encompassed the conviction to present and defend the gospel as not only biblical but logically consistent, philosophically coherent, and most importantly, *true*. Keep in mind that at this time, Christianity was still a relatively new religion, and the council of Nicea surfaced, in part, to address the heretical teachings that arose against the divinity of Christ. Thus, seeing the need to present and defend the gospel, the early church actively gathered and engaged in apologetics.

Commenting on this, Melinda Penner remarks, "The person of Christ was the catalyst for the Trinitarian debate... needing more precise expression, which the early church was fully equipped to do with their theological and philosophical skills." [8] Given what we know from church history, we can imagine a paraphrase of these later councils going something like this:

> *How can we adequately articulate the monotheistic nature and doctrine of the Trinity? By explaining this: we worship one God in three persons–one divine substance. And how can we explain the metaphysical relation of the divine substance to the three members? By defending the notion that there is one "what" and three "who's": One God, three persons. Ah, but what is a person? And how should we explain the incarnation of Christ? By specifying that Christ possessed a dual nature. And what is the essence of a nature, and what are the metaphysical implications given the necessary attributes of the divine nature?*

Could you answer these questions? Do you know of any Christians today equipped to adequately address these daunting but foundationally essential questions? Better yet, have you ever met a Christian that has asked, much less answered, these questions for themselves?

If the answer is no, then you're beginning to see the stark difference between the salt of today and the salt of the early church. But what are we lacking? As Melinda notes, "The formulation of the doctrine of the Trinity is a history of the refinement of terms and philosophical categories. Doctrinal development requires rigorous intellectual skills and sound philosophic categories to accurately apply God's revelation... so the tools of reason and philosophy were employed to work out the doctrine of the Trinity in a rigorous and accurate manner."[9]

In other words, the early church was so concerned for the truth and accuracy of Christian doctrine that they *devoted their minds and lives to it*! And here's a sobering point to consider. Around this time, the church experienced the most widespread, gruesome, bloodiest persecution in history. Christians were literally running for their lives: fed to lions, boiled alive, burned at the stake, stoned to death, crucified upside down, tortured, and beheaded. Yet, despite this persecution, their greatest concern remained the conviction to ensure that what they believed and preached was logically consistent, philosophically coherent, biblically accurate, and true.

Now consider us—the modern-day 21st-Century American church and ask, what is our greatest concern?

> *Are the church pews comfortable enough? Do the youth have enough pizza for the lock-in? Is there enough coffee in the lobby for visitors? Will the worship team sing the songs I like? Is our church "cool enough" for millennials?*

Don't get me wrong; all these questions have their place. But in all sincerity, what is our greatest concern in the church today? Because we're not being persecuted, fed to lions, boiled alive, burned at the stake, stoned to death, crucified upside down, tortured, or beheaded for what we believe, and yet, our concerns don't come close to those of the early church. As before, lacking this apologetic discipline not only becomes detrimental to our own lives, but its problems spill into our evangelism.

Our Evangelistic "Pitches"

When we fail to love and honor God with our minds, Christianity becomes just another way to chase life's emotional highs and experiences. As a result, our "evangelistic pitches" today are typically not "become a Christian because it's true," but instead, "become a Christian because it will make you a better person; your life will be much easier and happier!" And this is precisely the problem with modern-day evangelism. As Christian philosopher Dr. J.P. Moreland explains:

> If our allegiance to Christianity is not based on the conviction that it is true and reasonable, then we are treating the faith as a mere means to some self-serving pragmatic end, and that demeans the faith... if we are more concerned with practical application from the Bible than with having good reasons for thinking we have correctly interpreted it, then our bottom line will be that the Bible exists as a tool to make us a success, and we do not exist to place ourselves under what it really says.[10]

Moreover, consider that Christianity could never guarantee a "good and happy" life (look at the early church mentioned above!). As former atheist turned Christian apologist C. S. Lewis once said:

> I didn't go to religion to make me happy. I always knew a bottle of Port would do that. If you want a religion to make you feel really comfortable, I certainly don't recommend Christianity.[11]

Bringing this back to the greatest commandment, I want to be clear: I'm not saying the role of the mind must take precedence over the role of our emotions or service (the heart and strength). Instead, I am saying our emotions and service cannot be elevated *at the neglect of* our intellect and reason (the mind). Fulfilling the greatest commandment is a *holistic endeavor* concerning the believer's heart, strength, and mind. Put differently, deep emotions and courteous service could never be a substitute for intellectual understanding. Not only will apologetics help us accomplish the latter, but as we will see throughout this book, it significantly strengthens our evangelism.

APOLOGETICS: THE RELATIONSHIP BETWEEN FAITH AND KNOWLEDGE

But Isn't It All About Faith?

Unfortunately, "faith" is one of the most misapplied, misunderstood words used today by atheists and Christians. For example, after a heated dialogue with an atheist, some Christians will say, "Look, at the end of the day, it's all about faith!" and in patronizing agreement, the atheist cheerfully retorts, "Well, I don't need faith, I have science!" But what does that even mean? Have both parties applied the word "faith" accurately and biblically? Not by a long shot.

Sadly, not only has the church failed to correct such nonsensical remarks from a secular society, but it has swallowed it hook, line, and sinker. We have allowed the world to redefine the meaning of a biblical term, and in response, we simply give it a threshold, allowing its value to be placed over and above the teaching of Scripture. As Craig and Moreland observe:

> *Our churches are unfortunately overly populated with people whose minds, as Christians, are going to waste… they may be spiritually regenerate, but their minds have not been converted; they still think like nonbelievers.*[12]

So, biblically speaking, what is faith? Simply put, the Greek word for "faith" is *pistis*, which means having *trust* or *confidence* in something. Faith is not (as some have erroneously assumed) a way of *knowing* something, but rather, it is *a response to something that is known*. Faith is not what is left when you have no reasons to believe you're right. Instead, it is an action taken in response to something you *know* to be true. Faith is knowledge-based; it's grounded in knowledge, and thus, it's an action taken in response to knowledge—not opposed to it. Consider the application.

"Trust In" Requires a *"Know That"*

If faith is grounded in knowledge, then it follows that to have "*trust in*" (faith), I must first "*know that*" (possess knowledge about the thing in question). To illustrate, before I can *trust in* the chair, I must first *know that* it's made of durable material. And before I can *trust in* its ability to hold me, I must first *know that* it has four stable legs. The more knowledge I obtain, the more faith (trust or confidence) I will have in what I *know* to be true. Hence, faith is *trust* or *confidence* that is based on *knowledge*. For this reason, I can accurately say that my *knowledge of* God is the reason for which I have *trust*, *confidence*, and *faith* in Him. After all, how can I have trust or confidence in someone I know nothing about? Now consider the application for discipleship.

How do we grow in faith? By growing in our knowledge of the thing we are seeking to trust. Therefore, the more I grow in my knowledge of God, the more confidence (i.e., faith) I have in who he is. The more I learn about God as a healer, the more faith I have in healing. The more I know about God as a redeemer, the more trust I have that He's redeemed me. And the more knowledge I have of God as a Savior, the more confidence I will have in my salvation and His willing ability to save the atheist to whom I am witnessing. Faith is grounded in knowledge, and apologetics aims at growing both.

Objection: Hebrews 11:1

At this point, a common retort is given by citing Hebrews 11:1, "Now faith is the assurance of things hoped for, the conviction of things not seen" (ESV). Some allege this verse contradicts everything I've just said. But *trust* me, I have faith (confidence) it does not. To begin with, consider Hebrews 11:6, which states that "*without faith it is impossible to please God*" and compare this with Hosea 4:6, "*my people are destroyed [perish] from lack of knowledge. Because you have rejected knowledge, I also reject you as my priests.*"

Note that the latter verse doesn't state that my people perish for lack of church, worship, or faith, but *knowledge*. Now, if faith is grounded in knowledge, and without faith, it is impossible to please God, then knowledge becomes a necessary prerequisite for both serving and pleasing God. Put differently, without knowledge, we cannot please God (given that faith is required for it), and when we reject it, we are destroyed and rejected from serving him. For this reason, Hebrews 11:1 cannot mean blind faith devoid of knowledge.

To illustrate, suppose I come home from work and find my house empty. I text my wife asking where she is, and she informs me that she took the kids to the store. In this situation, I have no *visible* evidence that she's at the store; I merely have her word. But do I believe her? Absolutely, because in all my years of marriage, I've *known* my wife to be faithful. Hence, my "*conviction of things not seen*" is grounded in "*the assurance*" of her faithfulness over the years. Meaning that my faith in her is not blind but is grounded in what I *have seen*, providing the evidence for what I currently do not.

Similarly, I didn't marry my wife based on what I *didn't know* about her but based on what *I did*. I had sufficient evidence to *trust* she'd be a woman worth marrying. Although I didn't know every detail of who she was (I'm still learning), I had obtained enough knowledge to drop on one knee and ask for her hand in marriage. Now apply this perspective for witnessing to nonbelievers. Although God has already "dropped on one knee" to ask for our hands in marriage (indeed, we are the bride of Christ), the nonbeliever may need a more refined knowledge of who God is to say, "I do"—and this is precisely why we're commanded to incorporate apologetics into our evangelism.

Objection: But I Rely on the Holy Spirit, Not Apologetics!

A final dismissal toward apologetics (or, more pertinently, an excuse for why one has neglected it) is this: "I rely on the Holy Spirit, not apologetics!"

Some years ago, I was invited as an evangelist to be in a line-up of guest speakers for an international group of pastors and leaders. I was the first speaker that morning, and as I glanced at the schedule, I noticed I was the only apologist on the list but thought nothing of it. As usual, I preached on the biblical mandate for apologetics and demonstrated how this discipline is incorporated into evangelism. After I was done, I received applause, thanked the audience, and took my seat in the front row.

As I listened to the other speakers, it became apparent that I would be the only advocate for apologetics in evangelism. Not because the other speakers failed to reference the word "apologetics" in their presentations, but because they kept referencing and offering rebuttals to mine! One speaker pointed directly at me from the stage and said, "I'm sorry, Eric, but you're wrong. Christianity *is* an experience, and my testimony is the experience God gave me. All that other stuff isn't necessary."

Another speaker, after presenting his evangelistic approach (which was printed on a 4x6 notecard and handed out to everyone), pointed at me and said, "So, you can do what Eric told you to do, or you can follow my approach (now pointing at his 4x6 notecard), which was given to me by the Holy Spirit!" Sitting in the front row, all I could do was listen and smile awkwardly. Fortunately, we would later be in separate rooms for Q&A, and ironically, their remarks drew more people to my room. But I digress. Let's briefly unpack the problematic assumptions behind these objections.

First, note how the phrase, "I rely on the Holy Spirit, not apologetics!" erroneously assumes that incorporating apologetics into evangelism means you don't rely on the Holy Spirit. But consider the statement, "I rely on the Holy Spirit, not my ability to preach!" Who would disagree? Without the work of the Holy Spirit, preaching is fruitless, and yet, we still work on our sermons. Why? Because while nothing can be done without the Holy Spirit, we still must study and do our best to show ourselves approved, "accurately handling and skillfully teaching the word of truth" (2 Timothy 2:15 AMP). So, if the Holy Spirit can use preaching to reach the lost, then why can't the same be said of apologetics?

Second, note the case for incorporating apologetics in evangelism is not my preference or opinion, but as I've aimed to demonstrate, is a biblical mandate to *all believers* (1 Peter 3:15; 2 Corinthians 10:4-5; Mark 12:30). Moreover, Scripture is God-breathed or, said another way, "Holy Spirit inspired" (2 Timothy 3:16-17). Therefore, if the Holy Spirit has inspired Scripture, and if Scripture commands us to engage in the discipline of apologetics, then it follows that when we incorporate apologetics into evangelism, *we are literally relying on the Holy Spirit* by following the very commands He's inspired! So, note the irony of the situation.

The evangelist mentioned above said his approach was "given to him by the Holy Spirit" and claimed that my approach was merely "what Eric is telling you to do." Yet, he was pointing to a text handed to us by him on a 4x6 notecard, whereas I pointed to a text handed to us by the Holy Spirit. Hence, when anyone takes issue with this evangelistic approach, I inform them they can take it up with the Holy Spirit. I just read The Book, but I certainly didn't write it.

PART 1: WHY APOLOGETICS–CONCLUSION AND SUMMARY

Apologetics has been defined as *giving a defense for what we believe and why we believe it.* In a culture plagued with strongholds, it becomes a necessary component of evangelism and spiritual warfare. Additionally, apologetics can help shape a biblical theology, allowing us to grow in our knowledge of God, which, in turn, increases our faith in God. It's a biblical commandment for all believers and is, in part, a fulfillment of the greatest commandment. Moreover, we are followers of Christ first and foremost because Christianity *is true*, and apologetics is how we present and defend its truth in evangelism. This does not mean we neglect the Holy Spirit but rely on the Holy Spirit's inspired words for effective evangelism and spiritual growth. This is the discipline and task of apologetics, and biblically speaking, *this* is why we need it.

PART 2

WHO Am I Talk To? Atheists, Agnostics, and Skeptics

Chapter 3

Defining Atheism, Agnosticism, and Skepticism

We begin our apologetics endeavor by understanding the nonbelieving audience we are trying to reach. Namely, atheists, agnostics, and skeptics. After defining each of these positions, we'll learn how to identify them in conversation, using probing questions to gain further information on the person's perspective. To be clear, this isn't to debate nonbelievers. Contrary to popular belief, that is *not* the focus of apologetics, nor is it the intent of this book. Instead, our aim (especially for this chapter) is to gain a better understanding of the person with whom we are witnessing. Although we'll cover some technical terminology, having this foundation will be essential going forward.

Biblical Basis: Two Principles for Evangelism

> *... I have become all things to all people so that by all possible means I might save some...* (1 Corinthians 9:20-23).

In this passage, Paul lays out a fundamental (though widely neglected) theme for evangelism: *becoming all things to all people,* which is exemplified throughout his ministry. When witnessing to those educated under the law, he reasons from the law; when witnessing to Jews, he cites Scripture, and when witnessing to unbelieving Gentiles, he approvingly quotes pagan philosophers and poets (Acts 17:28). In doing so, Paul employs two principles essential for evangelism:

1. Know who you're talking to.
2. Adapt your approach accordingly.

It could be said that in Paul's day, the two main groups he sought to evangelize were Jews and Gentiles. In our day, we could say our two main groups are *theists* and *non-theists*. Here, the word "theist" refers to someone who *believes* in any god or gods. In this sense, being a "theist" is not limited to those within the Christian faith. Strictly speaking, anyone who *believes* in at least one god (i.e., Muslims, Hindus, or Mormons) is a "theist."

Just as being a "theist" doesn't automatically imply that one is a Christian, being a "non-theist" (i.e., a *nonbeliever*) doesn't automatically imply that one is an atheist. For this reason, we begin by defining three types of nonbelievers you may encounter: **atheists**, **agnostics**, and **skeptics**. Although each view rejects the existence of God in one way or another, understanding their distinctions becomes necessary for accomplishing our first task (know who you're talking to).

DEFINITIONS AND DISTINCTIONS

There are essentially three positions a person can take when answering the question, "Does God exist?" which are **theism**, **atheism**, and **agnosticism**. At this point, skepticism has been omitted. This is because skepticism is not necessarily a position concerning the existence of God but, more pertinently, is a philosophical method of assessing the truth or falsity of a view (more on this later). Although many nonbelievers will carry the label of a "skeptic," it's not a genuine answer to the question, "Does God exist?" Setting this view aside, let's focus on the standard definition for the three positions just listed:

Theism: the belief that a God (or gods) exists.

Atheism: the belief that a God (or gods) does not exist.

Agnosticism: Neither believes nor disbelieves that a God (or gods) exists.

Note that each position revolves around one's *belief* concerning the existence of God (this will be important later). Additionally, note that while the theist and atheist disagree, the agnostic will disagree with both. Put differently, although the agnostic would not say, "I believe that God *does* exist" (theism), he would equally not say, "I believe that God *does not* exist" (atheism). Hence, he holds no belief one way or the other. To grasp these distinctions, consider the following illustration.

Suppose a news reporter asks three random people, "do you believe the home team will win the upcoming Superbowl?" At least three answers can be given:

Person A: I believe the home team will win.

Person B: I believe the home team will lose.

Person C: I don't know, I don't watch football.

Given that the *theist* affirms the belief that God exists, he is analogous to Person A making the positive claim that the home team will win. Given that the *atheist* affirms the belief that God *does not exist*, he is analogous to Person B making the *negative claim* that the home team will lose. But given that the agnostic makes *no claim* either way, he would be analogous to person C, who simply says, "I don't know." He holds no position one way or the other and, thus, is genuinely agnostic on the issue (and may not even care).

Applying the Burden of Proof

Not only is it essential to know which of these positions a nonbeliever holds to, but more pertinently, *why* they hold the position in the first place. This can be accomplished by *applying* **the burden of proof**. In philosophy, this is the notion that for any claim a person makes, there will be an accompanying burden to provide adequate justification (i.e., reasons) for the truth of their belief. This concept is foundational for identifying strongholds, and we must learn how to implement it appropriately. To illustrate, consider the following dialogue:

John: I can jump ten feet high like a superhero.

Robert: Oh yeah? Prove it!

John: No, prove to me I can't!

In this scenario, John claims he can jump like a superhero, and in response, Robert applies the burden of proof to John's claim. This is an *appropriate* application of the burden of proof. By contrast, John's reply, "prove to me I can't," is not, and commits the fallacy of ***inappropriately shifting the burden of proof***. Why? Because it's not Robert's job to prove John is wrong, but rather, it's John's job to prove he is right. Hence, the governing rule for the burden of proof is simple: if you make the claim, you bear the burden.

The Burden of Proof Applied to Theism, Atheism, and Agnosticism

Now apply this concept to the three positions above. If someone were to ask you, a *theist*, what you believe and why you believe it, it's your job to bear the burden of proof and provide an answer. Not only is this a basic rule in philosophy but is precisely what we're commanded to do in 1 Peter 3:15. Similarly, given that the atheist *believes* the claim "God does not exist," he too must shoulder a burden of proof by providing adequate reasons for why he takes this claim to be true. But what about the agnostic?

As defined thus far, no burden of proof applies. Why? Because the agnostic holds no belief one way or the other and therefore, makes no claim on the issue. However, we can now make a further distinction between two types of agnostics: the "**ordinary**" agnostic and "**ornery**" agnostic (also known as **soft agnosticism** vs. **hard agnosticism**).[13]

Soft agnosticism: I don't know if God exists.

Hard agnosticism: I don't know if God exists, and you don't either!

Note that the *ordinary*, **soft agnostic** professes ignorance on the question and simply says, "I don't know." In this case, no burden of proof applies. By contrast, the *ornery*, **hard agnostic** takes it a step further and claims it *cannot be known* if God exists. Given that this assertion is a truth claim, the burden of proof certainly applies. But why would someone make such a claim? Here is where understanding the skeptic comes into play.

SKEPTICISM: UNDERSTANDING THE MINDSET AND METHOD

In this context, **skepticism** is far more than being *skeptical* about a belief and, as previously mentioned, becomes a method of assessing the truth or falsity of a view. While there are various forms and facets of skepticism, we can begin by briefly distinguishing between *global skepticism* and *local skepticism*.

> **Global Skepticism**: There can be no knowledge about anything whatsoever.
>
> **Local Skepticism**: There may be knowledge in some areas (e.g., scientific claims) but not in others (e.g., "religious, spiritual" claims).

Why is this important? Because some nonbelievers assume that knowledge is only possible in some disciplines, such as science and medicine, but claim that knowledge is impossible for "abstract" disciplines, such as theology or religion. To put the point rather bluntly, their "skept-o-meter" is turned down when it comes to areas they agree with (e.g., science and medicine) but conveniently turned up when it comes to areas they reject (e.g., God's existence and theology). Nevertheless, we can simplify our understanding of skepticism by unpacking two key features: **the mindset** and **the method**.

The Mindset: *Knowledge requires certainty. Without certainty, knowledge is impossible.*

The *mindset* of skepticism typically revolves around the notion of certainty and knowledge.[14] According to this view, if one cannot possess *absolute certainty* about a belief in question, then knowing the truth of that belief becomes impossible. For example, if the skeptic can merely raise *the possibility of doubt* about the existence of God, then in their mind, one could never claim to *know* that God exists.

The Method: *Asking the question, "how do you know" repeatedly.*

The most common way a skeptic employs this mindset (that certainty is a necessary requirement for knowledge) is by repeatedly asking a variation of the question, "how do you know?"[15] This is known as an **iterative skeptic**, and he will employ this method *ad nauseum* for the remainder of the conversation. Although calling him an iterative skeptic is unnecessary (he may not be familiar with the title), we must learn to recognize this when it happens.

The Stronghold of Skepticism in Evangelism

With these two key features in mind, we can now see why skepticism was not considered as an answer to the question, "Does God exist?" So why mention it? For at least three reasons. First, most nonbelievers carry the label of self-professed skeptics, and understanding the mindset will help you understand the reason behind their method (asking "how do you know" repeatedly). Second, given that skepticism doesn't answer the question, "Does God exist?," a skeptic could either be an atheist or an agnostic (e.g., the ornery, hard agnostic). Hence, the label doesn't imply nor is it exclusive to one nonbelieving position over the other.

Third and most importantly, whether you realize it or not, we have just encountered our first stronghold for witnessing to nonbelievers. Did you catch it? Recall that a stronghold is any belief or system of beliefs that hinder people from coming to the saving knowledge of God. However, not all strongholds are views that *explicitly* go against the knowledge of God. So, if you couldn't identify the implicit stronghold, allow me to make it explicit.

Suppose you are witnessing to someone who, at face value, seems open to a gospel presentation. As you share your faith, the conversation goes as follows:

Christian: God loves you and sent His Son to die for your sins.

Skeptic: Wow, that's amazing, and you seem so certain about it. [the mindset] Can you please explain how you know this? [the method]

Christian: Absolutely. It says so right here in John 3:16.

Skeptic: Ah, you're right. I remember hearing about this in Sunday school. But what reasons do you have for trusting the Bible? [the method] Couldn't it be wrong? [the mindset]

Christian: Well, the Bible is God's Word, and historians have numerous manuscript copies demonstrating the text's preservation.

Skeptic: But aren't these historians biased because they're Christians? How can you trust what they tell you? [the mindset and method]

Notice how these questions revolve around the mindset and method of skepticism. To be fair, not all skeptics are trying to "play a game" with these questions, so it's essential that we not try and psychoanalyze or attribute ill motives to the person. They may be seeking genuine answers, and by all means, provide the answers if you can. But here's the catch.

Even if we grant that his questions are a genuine way of seeking answers, he may also genuinely believe that knowledge requires certainty. Thus, if he can merely raise *the possibility of doubt* to your answers, then in his mind, believing what you say becomes impossible. Unless you can provide him with 100% absolute certainty, then for him, coming to a salvific knowledge of God is unreasonable. Therefore, even if his questions about God or salvation are genuine, his skeptical-induced doubt becomes a genuine, overriding obstacle. Hence, it's a stronghold, and one that can be difficult to overcome. In a later chapter, we'll examine how to maneuver a productive conversation with such a person.

At this point, we've laid the foundation for applying Paul's first principle in evangelism (know who you're talking to). Now, we learn how to apply this in conversations and segue into the second principle: adapt your approach accordingly.

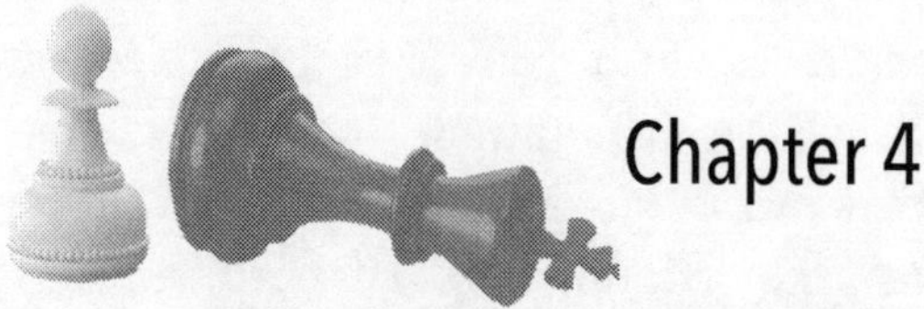

Chapter 4

Identifying the Position in Conversation

Our first step in witnessing to nonbelievers is knowing how to identify their position in conversation, which encompasses learning how to ask the right questions. As before, this is not to jump into a debate, bombarding them with arguments, Scripture, or presenting a case for Christianity. Instead, it's to gather information and allow them to share their perspective with you. In doing so, the conversations are less likely to be heated and more likely to be productive. Although some nonbelievers may be hostile toward you or your beliefs, we'll learn how to avoid altercations, maintain control of the conversation, and keep calm, cool, and collected the entire time.

Asking the Right Questions

Recall the two questions from chapter one I used when teaching apologetics: 1) why are you a Christian, and 2) why should someone else be a Christian? Note how the first question is a call for the other person to bear the burden of proof, and the second is a call for its truth and applicability to me. When modified, this approach can be used to start evangelistic conversations with any given faith or position. To illustrate, consider how I applied this approach with a young lady of the Islamic faith.

"Why Are You a _________?"

After officiating a wedding, I sat with some strangers at the dinner table and introduced myself. As we began conversing, I noticed the young lady beside me had refused all the meat options (including the bacon-wrapped shrimp!). When I asked why she explained that it was due to her faith as a Muslim. For the sake of anonymity, we'll call her Jane. The conversation with Jane proceeded as follows:

Eric: Oh, interesting. Have you always been a member of the Islamic faith? (A variation of the first question, "Why are you a ______?")

Jane: Honestly, no. But my father was a Muslim that passed away a few years ago, and I decided to carry the faith in honor of him.

Observation: Not only did I have an answer to the first question (Why are you a _____?), but have gained information to guide the sensitivity of my approach.

Eric: I'm sorry to hear that about your father, and I can certainly respect your way of honoring him. If I may ask, would you consider your Islamic faith to be true? (Alluding to the first question)

Jane: I think it's true for me, and it's helped me become a better person.

Eric: I see. Given this experience, do you think everyone should become a Muslim? (A variation of the second question)

Jane: No, not necessarily. I think everyone's religion is true for them, even if it's not true for me.

Observation: Through my questions, I have uncovered a stronghold known as **postmodernism**: a view that takes "truth" purely as something pragmatic and relative to the individual (more on this in chapter 6). Because of this, I will direct the remainder of my questions around the notion of truth. Doing so allows me to implement Paul's second principle: *adapt your approach accordingly*.

Eric: As a Christian, I can certainly respect other people's beliefs. But wouldn't it be the case that if Islam is true, then Christianity is false?

Jane: Oh, I would never say you are wrong for being a Christian!

Eric: That's very kind of you. But at the end of the day, not all religions can be equally true, right?

Jane: Well, I've never thought of it that way, and I suppose you're right. But tell me about you. Were you raised in a Christian home?

Observation: Her last question revolved around my upbringing in a religion instead of the ***truth*** of a religion. Hence, I'll respond in a way that brings the focus back to the notion of truth.

Eric: Yes, I was raised in a Christian home, but that's not why I'm a Christian. I'm a Christian today because I learned it was true after examining the evidence for myself.

Jane: Really? But how could anyone know which religion is true?

Eric: By examining the evidence. Because let's face it, if there is a God, and more pertinently, Heaven and hell, then is truth not the most important question to consider when choosing a religion?

Jane: Hmm, you make a good point. But I wouldn't know where to start.

Unfortunately, more guests arrived and brought our conversation to a halt. Nevertheless, note that each question was strategic in my limited time with her. Once I knew her position, I was able to adapt my approach accordingly. I'd ask her a "why" question, and after each response, I *appropriately and respectfully* applied the burden of proof to her answers. I didn't pretend to know her answers, but used the information she provided to ask the next question.

In other words, knowing their position sets the stage for asking the first "why" question, and their proceeding answers will inform you which questions to ask next. In this stage of the conversation, our only goal is to gather information. We are NOT looking for a debate. With this in mind, let's apply this approach to a conversation with a nonbeliever: identifying their position, applying the burden of proof, and then adapting our approach accordingly.

APPLYING THE BURDEN OF PROOF IN CONVERSATION

Given that the term "nonbeliever" doesn't automatically imply the person is an atheist, I have found it helpful to simply ask the person for the position they identify with. After they have answered, you can cordially respond with the initial "why" question. This puts the burden of proof on their shoulders. Although the ordinary, soft agnostic will not bear a burden of proof, he can still provide reasons for rejecting belief in God. Hence, "why are you an agnostic" is an appropriate question to ask.

For the sake of simplicity, we'll focus on applying this approach to the atheist position. Just know that much of what we cover could easily be modified for the agnostic position, as well. Nevertheless, our first "why" question must be formulated in a way relevant to the position with which they identify. In this case, we focus on the atheist.

Applying the Burden of Proof to the Atheist Position

Given that the standard definition of atheism is the belief that God *does not* exist, we can begin by asking, "And what reasons do you have for believing that God does not exist?" Note how the question employs the standard definition of atheism and applies the burden of proof. Hence, this "why" question is appropriately structured to fit the standard definition of atheism: the belief that God does not exist.

All things being equal, the person will share their reasons for believing that God does not exist, which will serve as a guide for assessing the strongholds within their worldview. Again, our goal is simply to use the appropriate questions and gather information, *not to debate or respond to their objections*. While their answers may bother you, remember that it's not about you but them. Allowing the other person to speak their mind demonstrates your ability to listen, showing a genuine concern for what they have to say. With time and practice, this becomes easier.

Dealing With Hostile, Aggressive, or Dodging Responses

Unfortunately, ninety-nine times out of ten (error intended), the conversation does not play out in this fashion. In my experience, many atheists immediately respond by attacking Christianity, attempting to put you in the defensive position for the entire conversation while neglecting to defend their atheism. Many atheists assume that because their position is a "negative claim," they bear no burden of proof. Thus, their method of attacking Christianity is, in their mind, the only approach to take in "defense" of their atheism.

Moreover, it has become increasingly popular for nonbelievers to redefine the word "atheism" in such a way that equivocates it with the agnostic position. This is typically an attempt to avoid the burden of proof and often involves *inappropriately shifting the burden of proof* onto the believer. Such illegitimate responses lead to unproductive conversations at best or heated debates at worst.

For this reason, let's briefly review some of the most common illegitimate responses you may encounter to learn how to identify them and respond accordingly. In no particular order, these types of responses typically fall under the following categories:

1. Attacking Christianity.
2. Claiming there is "no evidence."
3. Redefining the word "atheism."

As before, I'll use examples from past conversations to demonstrate how to navigate our approach while maintaining civility and control of the conversation. However, I do not want you to view what I present as some "script" to be followed. My aim is simply to provide the tools for carrying out this approach, and my prayer is that the Holy Spirit will guide you in using them effectively.

Navigating Illegitimate Responses: Adapt Your Approach Accordingly

1. Attacking Christianity

As I stood up for worship Sunday morning, I noticed the young lady sitting in front of me, aggressively writing in her journal. I knew she was part of a halfway home that the church partnered with, allowing the recovery group members to accumulate community service hours by attending church, taking notes, and writing a paper about their experience. In a moment of curiosity, I glanced at her notes, and to my surprise, I read the following:

> *I want to stand up and yell, "hail Satan!" I bet that would get their attention! These people are so fake and weak-minded. Their "faith" has made them delusional fanatics! If there is a God, I wish He would just kill me now because I can't take any more of this. They get on my nerves!*

I smiled in amusement, tapped her shoulder, and said, "I notice you wrote 'hail Satan.' Are you an atheist?" She slammed the journal shut in embarrassment. "I like your notes," I said. "I think they're funny, and I agree with some of it. Do you mind if we spoke after service?" She agreed. For the sake of anonymity, we'll call her Jan. After the service, our conversation went as follows:

Eric: So, you're an atheist, right? Surely you don't believe in Satan, do you?

Jan: No. I was just trying to be funny. But I do think many people here are blind to the truth. Personally, I can't believe something unless there's evidence for it.

Observation: Given the information she provided, I will strategically use her own choice of words to formulate my first "why" question.

Eric: I can agree that *some* people here may be blind to the truth. But I like what you said. You don't believe anything unless there's evidence for it. So, if you're an atheist, may I ask, what *evidence* do you have that God does not exist?

Jan: The Bible is full of contradictions.

Eric: Well, I disagree. But for the sake of conversation, let's just suppose you're right. How would this prove that God does not exist?

Observation: Consider the strategy behind my response. Jan is not defending her atheism but attacking Christianity. Yet, attacking the truth of Christianity *does not* prove the truth of atheism. Remember, when an atheist attacks Christianity in response to the question, "Why are you an atheist?" they are *inappropriately shifting the burden of proof.*

Unfortunately, many Christians fail to recognize this and immediately begin defending Christianity. Not only does this become a debate, but more pertinently, it allows the person to shift the burden of proof onto you. *Don't take the bait.* Stick to the approach. Again, at this point of the conversation, our goal is to gather information and allow the person to shoulder the burden of proof, not to defend Christianity.

For this reason, I didn't respond to her attack but refocused the conversation back to her position, asking how these alleged "Bible contradictions" proved that God does not exist. The confusion on her face revealed she'd never been asked this question before. It was as if she's never needed to defend this response, likely because most Christians took the bait and began defending the Bible (which, again, allowed her to dodge and shift the burden of proof!). So, to break the awkward silence, I rephrased my question.

Eric: Let me put it this way; if God exists, would He have existed before the Bible was written?

Jan: Sure, but I don't believe in God!

Eric: I understand that but follow me here. If God existed before the Bible was written, then how would a Bible full of alleged "contradictions" make Him disappear or prove that He didn't exist?

Again, note the strategy. I avoided her attempt at shifting the burden of proof onto me, allowed the attack, and refocused the attention on how her response failed to meet the burden of proof for her atheism. At this point, in an all too predictable fashion, she switched to the second illegitimate response.

2. Claiming There is No Evidence

Jan: Ok, well... I'm an atheist because there's no evidence for God's existence!

Eric: And again, I must ask, how does this prove that God does not exist?

Once more, she looked confused. Clearly, she was accustomed to turning the conversation into a debate by attacking Christianity, allowing her to sit back and deny anything the Christian had to offer. But note that thus far, I've not offered her anything. Why? Because that is not the intent at this point of the conversation, and taking this approach avoided a potentially heated exchange. Nevertheless, given that my time with her was limited, I furthered the conversation by explaining why her response failed to justify her atheism.

Eric: For example, I currently have no evidence that there is a flea in this room, but it does not follow from this that, therefore, there is no flea. So, even if I granted that there was "no evidence" for God's existence, how would this prove that atheism is true?

Observation: Throughout this conversation, I have not taken her "shifting the burden of proof bait." I've only pointed out that my "why" question remains unanswered. Hence, I didn't offer responses to her objections but instead, demonstrated that her answers were insufficient to justify her atheism. Had I responded by defending the Bible or providing evidence for God's existence, I would've allowed the conversation to shift from "why are you an atheist" to "why am I a Christian?" Doing so fails to achieve the first principle in evangelism (know who you're talking to), which is vital for achieving the second principle (adapt your approach accordingly).

While it's true that I, as a Christian, bear a burden of proof, I haven't made any claims in the conversation. Why? Because my goal in this stage is to ask questions, *not provide arguments*. Remember, if you cannot identify *what* the person believes and *why* they believe it, you cannot identify their strongholds, much less address them. Hence, it's vitally important that we stick to the first "why" question. I cannot overemphasize that you are neither defending Christianity nor shouldering the burden of proof at this point of the conversation. They are, and we shouldn't confuse the two.

Don't Change the "Why" Question

Thus far, I've demonstrated how the atheist may attempt to shift the burden of proof by attacking Christianity, and I've advised that you not take the bait. If you do, you will be in a defensive position for the remainder of the conversation and are now engaged in a debate. Still, there's another way Christians have fallen into this trap, and I feel it needs to be addressed.

To illustrate, suppose that an atheist answers your first "why" question by stating that the Bible contains "grotesque moral errors, profane verses, and various contradictions." As demonstrated above, we can avoid falling into this trap by reiterating the initial "why" question, showing how their answer fails to justify their position. However, if you respond by changing the "why" question to fit their answer, you have only postponed falling into the trap a few sentences later. Allow me to explain.

By changing the "why" question toward their illegitimate answer, the burden of proof question changes from "why do you believe God does not exist" to "why do you believe the Bible contains grotesque moral errors and profane verses?" In this case, they aren't avoiding the burden of proof, but replacing it with a new one. This is likely worse than the first way of falling into the trap. Why? Because in this second way, the atheist attacks Christianity and you merely ask them to elaborate. As a result, you are now forced to respond to their grocery list of out-of-context Bible verses or leave them unanswered (perhaps because you cannot).

Nevertheless, some Christians feel they can take on any "Bible challenge" and *intentionally* change the initial "why" question toward the atheist's illegitimate answer. As before, *I strongly advise against it*, but now, for additional reasons. First, your burden is no longer a defense of the question, "Why am I a Christian?" but a defense of the question, "Can I, as a Christian, answer this atheist's Bible challenges?" This becomes nothing more than a trivia game where emotion and pride take over. *Even if* you can answer their "Bible challenges," there's no virtue in showing off your biblical knowledge. At this point, you're no longer defending the faith; you're defending yourself.

Second, this atheist is likely looking for a fight, and I can assure you he has ten verses memorized out of context and ready to cite. His goal will not be to defend atheism but to make you as a Christian look dumb by portraying the Bible in an obtuse way. Don't believe me? Consider Ezekiel 23:20 as an example, which I have intentionally omitted just in case this becomes an audiobook and kids are around. Feel free to look up the verse for yourself (and for the "full effect," see the "God's Word" translation). Commenting on this passage, one atheist blogger writes:

> I guarantee that if you told this to a Christian s/he would deny it's in the Bible…The Bible is not filled with the love of Jesus that so many think. There may be statements on love and caring for others, but most of the Bible is filled with death, slavery, and sex. The Bible is an early book of erotica!

Ironically, this blogger calls himself "The Poised Atheist." Nevertheless, note how the verse is not intended as an *actual objection* toward Christianity but is merely presented for shock value (and they'll likely ask you to read it aloud!). Because let's be honest, what does the "flesh" of hooved mammals and their relation to "doted paramours" (King James Version; again, I'm thinking about the kids here) have to do with whether God exists? Nothing. It's an immature senseless move, but one that you invited by taking this approach. So again, even if you feel you can handle any "Bible Challenges," don't. Stick to our approach. Do not take the bait.

3. Redefining Atheism

Finally, some nonbelievers try dodging the burden of proof by redefining the word "atheist," and this is typically presented in one of three ways: 1) by pointing at the etymology (i.e., the origin of a word), 2) by identifying as an "agnostic atheist," or 3) by asserting the impossibility of proving a negative. At the end of this section, I'll advise that you not waste time arguing over definitions. Nevertheless, given that such responses are growing in popularity, it would be helpful to cover some examples to recognize when it happens.

Example #1: The Etymology of "Atheist"

In this example, the nonbeliever argues that the word "atheist" simply describes one who "lacks" or is "without belief" in God. This view is defended by alluding to the etymology (origin) of the word "atheist," which comes from two Greek words: "A"—"Theos." "A" means without, and "Theos" means God. Hence, it's alleged that an atheist is simply one who is "without belief" in God, as opposed to the standard definition of one who *believes there is no God*. What's the difference? The applicability of the burden of proof.

On the standard definition, an atheist is one who *believes there is no God* and thus, must bear the burden to prove his claim. Yet, in this example, the atheist has redefined the word to remove the truth claim and avoids taking on the burden of proof. To illustrate, suppose you've just asked your first "why" question and, after demonstrating that their responses fail to justify their position, the discussion proceeds as follows:

Atheist: Look, I'm not saying that there is NO God. I'm simply saying I have no good reasons to be convinced that a God exists.

Eric: Oh, so you're an agnostic?

Atheist: No, I'm an atheist. Which means I am "without belief" in God. So, I have nothing to prove because I merely lack a belief that a God exists!

Eric: I see. So, given your position, would you agree with me that there are no good reasons to be convinced that God does NOT exist?

Before addressing the etymological issue, note three things about my strategy. First, after rejecting the standard definition of atheism, the nonbeliever has said he's "not convinced" that a God exists. Essentially, he's attempting to frame the conversation as if it's your job to convince him. However, his being convinced or unconvinced is irrelevant to the truth or falsity of God's existence.

Second, if he claims that his position is not that "there is no God" (atheism) and yet, does not *believe* that there is a God (theism), then by his own admission, he is simply an agnostic. For this reason, I respond with a final question relevant to the agnostic position (adapting my approach to the information I have been given) but intentionally refrain from using the label "agnostic" to avoid arguing definitions.

Third, note that I have used his own choice of words. He claimed he did not believe in God because there were no "good reasons to convince him." If he were a genuine agnostic, his reasoning would apply equally to the atheist position. Hence, my last question is worded in such a way that his answer will reveal his genuine conviction on the issue.

If he says "yes," there are no good reasons to be convinced that *God does not exist* (atheism), then he is genuinely an agnostic because he truly holds no belief one way or the other. However, if he says "no" (i.e., he believes there *are* good reasons to believe that God does not exist), then he is not neutral on the topic and, thus, genuinely not an agnostic. Hence, his re-defining of the word "atheism" is merely an attempt to avoid the burden of proof for his *actual* belief that God does not exist, which is the atheist position.

Responding to The Etymological Enigma

Turning now to the etymological argument being employed here, recall the assertion that the etymology of the word "atheist" only describes one who "lacks" or is "without belief in God." For various reasons, this etymological argument is false. First, the etymology of the word "atheist" ("A"—"Theos") would, at best, only mean "without God" and *not* "without *belief* in God." Second, this re-definition tells us nothing about the person's *belief about* God, which is why the word was historically used in the first place. So, not only is this redefining dodge etymologically incorrect, but it removes the entire purpose for which the label was created.

Third, consider the bizarre implications of such a label taken either way. On the one hand, if the word "atheist" means "without belief in God" (which, again, is not the correct etymology), then it would follow that dogs, babies, and rocks are atheists, given that they too are "without belief" in God. Conversely, if the proper definition of an atheist is one who is "without God," then demons must be "atheists" given that, although they *believe* in God, they are, nevertheless, "without God." Indeed, even the demons *believe* in God but tremble (James 2:19)! Problematically, this would imply that one could identify as an "atheist who believes in God, but is without him," which is absurdly counterintuitive. Either way, redefining the word "atheist" according to its etymology not only becomes an invalid attempt to avoid the burden of proof but demeans the nature of what it historically meant to be an atheist in the first place.

Example #2: "An Agnostic Atheist"

In this example, the nonbeliever chooses to identify as an "agnostic atheist." According to this view, a person has four different options when answering the question, "Does God exist?":

- **Agnostic atheist:** one who believes there is no God but doesn't claim "to *know"* there is no God.
- **Gnostic atheist**: one who *believes* and *"knows"* there is no God.
- **Agnostic theist**: one who believes in God but doesn't claim "to *know"* there is a God.
- **Gnostic theist:** one who *believes* and *"knows"* there is a God.

"Agnostic-Atheist": The Semantic Game

In the previous attempt, the atheist redefined the standard definition of the word "atheist" by pointing to the etymology. In this attempt, the redefinition is now focused on the etymology of an "agnostic." As before, this can be broken down into two Greek words: "a," meaning without, and "gnosis," meaning knowledge. Hence, etymologically speaking, an agnostic is one who is "without knowledge." This is correct. However, when combined into the label "agnostic atheist," it becomes nothing more than a semantic game for avoiding the burden of proof.

By claiming to be an "agnostic atheist," the person is implicitly making two claims: 1) *believing* that God does not exist (atheism), but with "humility," 2) not claiming to *know* that God does not exist (purportedly stemming from the etymology of agnosticism). With this move, the burden of proof emphasis shifts from a "belief claim" to a "knowledge claim." Why? Because this person assumes that by not claiming to *know* "God does not exist," he bears no burden to prove his *belief* God does not exist. As with the previous example, this etymological dodge doesn't work.

First, it must be understood that the burden of proof principle applies to *all truth claims*, regardless of whether one is making a "knowledge" claim. Therefore, shifting the emphasis from "belief" to "knowledge" doesn't remove the burden of proving the truth of the belief itself. While there is a distinction between belief and knowledge, suffice it to say that before one can claim to *know* something, one must first *believe* it. Hence, the burden of proof is primarily a concern of one's beliefs, not "knowledge."

Second, it's for this reason that it would be unfruitful to ask this person a "why" question toward his claim to not "know" that God does not exist. Chances are, this is an attempt to bring skepticism into the conversation, dragging you into a debate on the question of certainty and knowledge (see chapter 3). In a later chapter, we'll deal with skepticism as a stronghold. For now, note that this is a semantic game, and we're not interested in playing.

The Etymological Problem of "Agnostic Atheist" as a Label

Recall that the label "agnostic atheist" has been used to denote one who "*believes* God does not exist but is not *claiming to know* God does not exist." This takes the standard definition of atheism at face value and incorporates the etymology of the word "agnostic" (one who is without knowledge). Although the etymology of the word "agnosticism" has been accurately assessed, it doesn't accomplish what the nonbeliever thinks it accomplishes when combined into the label of an "agnostic atheist."

Given that the etymology of an agnostic is "one who is without knowledge," it would follow that an "agnostic atheist" would be, etymologically speaking, one who "does not believe in God but knows nothing," or even more bizarre, "one who does not *know* he *believes* that God does not exist." What an odd concession to make! Clearly this is not what the nonbeliever is trying to convey, and yet, this is precisely what it would have to mean from an etymological perspective. Thus, this etymological dodge fairs no better in this attempt.

Example #3: You Can't Prove a Negative

As previously alluded to, some atheists assume that because their position is a negative claim, the burden of proof doesn't apply. Hence, the atheist in this example doesn't necessarily redefine words to avoid the burden of proof. Instead, he rejects the *applicability* of the burden of proof for atheism altogether. Because of this mentality, he's more likely to openly make claims against God or Christianity. Consider the following example:

Atheist: God does not exist!

Eric: Prove it.

As before, my response is not to defend the existence of God but to apply the burden of proof to his claim. Why? Because the one who makes the claim bears the burden. Remember, it's not our job to prove their claim is wrong; it's their job to prove their claim is right. But for the sake of this example, suppose I took a different approach:

Atheist: God does not exist!

Eric: Can you prove this?

Atheist: No, of course not.

Although the atheist has made a truth claim, he openly admits he cannot bear the burden of proving it. I've always found this to be an odd concession for the atheist to make, given that most claim only to believe something that can be proven. So, I call this out and respond accordingly.

Eric: But didn't you tell me earlier you can only believe things that can be proven? Yet, you've just admitted you cannot prove the truth of your belief that God does not exist. So, are you telling me that as an atheist, you believe in something that cannot be proven? That sounds like an admission of "faith" to me.

Atheist: No! I do only believe in things that can be proven. But my belief that there is no God is a negative claim, not a positive one.

Eric: Sure, but it is a claim to truth, nonetheless.

Atheist: Yes, but it is impossible to prove a negative. YOU are the one making the positive assertion that God DOES exist, so you must bear the burden of proof, not me.

The atheist has now given his alleged justification for not bearing the burden of proof. Namely, that it's impossible to prove a negative claim. However, not only is this an attempt to shift the burden of proof (be it intentional or not), but it's underlying assumption is demonstrably false.

Negative Claims Are Provable

First, even if we granted that one could never prove "God does not exist," at best, this would only lead to agnosticism, *not* atheism. Second, negative claims *are* provable. For example, the claim that the moon is *not* made of green cheese is a negative truth claim, and such a belief can be proven. The belief that I'm *not* the president of the United States is also a negative claim, and yet, this is trivially easy to prove. After showing how this underlying assumption is false, the atheist may modify his response:

Atheist: Ok, while it's possible to prove *some* negative claims, it's impossible to prove a *universal* negative claim!

In defense of this mentality, some have argued that proving a *universal negative claim* requires that one be both omniscient (all-knowing) and omnipresent (at all places at once). For instance, the statement "no ravens are orange" is a universal negative claim. However, given that human beings are neither omniscient nor omnipresent, this universal negative claim cannot be proven. Hence, it's impossible to prove a *universal negative* (or so says this atheist).

Once again, this is demonstrably false, and counterexamples are easily provided. For example, the claim "there are no triangles with four points" is a universal negative claim that is false by definition, and I don't have to leave my desk to prove it. Similarly, the belief that no water molecules are composed of H3O is a universal negative that is provable. If water is H2O, then any chemical composition above or beneath this threshold cannot be water. Hence, this attempt at avoiding the burden of proof is not only inadequate but embarrassingly and demonstrably false.

ATHEISM, SCHMATHEISM: AVOIDING THE DEFINITIONAL QUIBBLING

Arguing over these definitions can be exhaustingly tedious and time-consuming. My advice: if you're confronted with these responses, lay the definitional labels aside and move the conversation forward. Nevertheless, given that the main obstacle with these responses revolves around the labels, I've found it best to grab a pen and paper, write down and number the three standard definitions, *but* omit their labels. This can be written as follows:

1. I believe God exists.
2. I believe God does not exist.
3. I don't hold a belief one way or the other.

From here, present it to the person and ask which view best represents their perspective.

To illustrate, consider the following conversation where I utilized this approach with a nonbeliever, and at the end, we will unpack the strategy behind it.

Atheist: I already told you; I simply lack belief in God, and I'm not claiming to *know* He doesn't exist!

Eric: Okay, so let's cross out the first and second options. Does this mean you don't hold a belief one way or the other? (At this point, I cross out the first two and circle the third option).

Atheist: Sure.

Eric: All right, great! This helps me better understand your perspective, and I appreciate that. Now, would it be fair to say that, like me, you haven't found any valid arguments in favor of the view that "God *does not* exist?" (pointing my pen at the second option)?[16]

Atheist: No, I'm not saying that. I'm saying I can only believe things that are rationally supported with strong evidence and good arguments. And I've not found arguments in favor of God's existence convincing.

Eric: Right. That's why we crossed out the first option (tapping my pen on the first view), and given what you initially said, we crossed out the second option as well. But now you seem to imply that you *do* think there are good reasons to believe God does not exist. Is that correct?

Atheist: Yes, because I think religion is a leading cause of suffering in this world, and most people are only Christians because they were born in America. You'd be a Muslim if you were born in the Middle East!

Eric: I see. So, would you say those arguments are convincing reasons to believe God does not exist?

Atheist: Yeah, I suppose I would.

Eric: So (circling the second option), it seems you would most closely identify with this second option. Is that correct?

Atheist: I suppose so, but I'm not claiming to *know* that God does not exist!

Eric: Right. At this point, I'm simply interested in what you *believe* so I can better understand your position. Historically, this second option has carried the label of an atheist. But we don't have to use these labels. We can just say the position you have expressed thus far is simply this: you believe God does not exist. Is that fair to say?

Atheist: Yeah, that's fair.

Eric: Okay, great! Now, I love what you said earlier, "you can only believe things that are rationally supported with strong evidence and good arguments." Me too! But may I ask, what rationally supported, strong evidence, and good arguments do you have for your belief that God does not exist?

Unpacking the Strategy

His opening comment brings the knowledge question into the discussion, but I avoid the bait and stick to the approach by asking a question about his beliefs, not "knowledge." This sidesteps the debate over skepticism and certainty. Additionally, I've made an intentional effort to point at what I have written down, giving him a visual cue that I'm unwilling to deviate from the goal of assessing what he believes (i.e., his position on the question, "Does God exist?").

My second question was now a burden of proof "why" question concerning the agnostic position, which he initially expressed via the process of elimination (hence, I crossed out the first two options and circled the third). In response, he brings up the notion of being "unconvinced," which is also not relevant to our discussion. I avoid that trap as well. To be clear, it would be inappropriate to assume these "traps" are intentional on his part. He may be accustomed to speaking this way and has never thought through his rhetoric or had it challenged.

Nevertheless, while his response failed to answer my question directly, it provided new information to formulate the next one. Note, I don't immediately call him an atheist or claim that he initially lied to me. Instead, I reverted to my initial task (identifying his position) by asking a question relevant to the view he's now hinting at—atheism. He responds in the affirmative but lodges attacks against Christianity. Again, I avoid the bait, stick to the method, and confirm that he's an atheist.

Once confirmed, I asked my final question, which became the most powerful question in the conversation. Why? Because I applied his rhetoric against the position he's just affirmed—atheism:

> *Given that you can only believe things that are rationally supported with strong evidence and good arguments, may I ask, what rationally supported strong evidence and good arguments do you have for the belief that God does not exist?*

Note how this potent question wasn't achieved because of my "skill" or "intelligence." Instead, it was achieved by listening carefully, waiting patiently, and asking the relevant questions.

You don't have to be the smartest person in the room to use what I've shown you. Such an approach requires minimal effort, and anyone can do it. This isn't sabotage, but strategy. I didn't fight off his attacks; I didn't argue with his responses. Instead, I took the information he provided and turned it into a question. Stick to the strategy, remember the goal, and maneuver the conversation accordingly. If you do this, you're well on your way to having more fruitful, productive discussions with nonbelievers, making you a better listener, questioner, and, most importantly, a better witness for Christ.

Part 2: *WHO AM I TALKING TO*–CONCLUSION AND SUMMARY

In 1 Corinthians 9:20-23, Paul implicitly provides two fundamental principles for evangelism: 1) know who you're talking to and 2) adapt your approach accordingly. These chapters focused primarily on the first principle of identifying a person's position, and after gaining the relevant information, we learned to adapt our approach accordingly. Additionally, we learned there are three positions one could take regarding the existence of God: theism, atheism, and agnosticism. Skepticism was not an answer to this question but was instead, a mindset and method that can be employed by either the atheist or agnostic. Next, we learned the burden of proof was the notion that for any truth claim a person makes, there will be an accompanying burden to provide adequate justifications for their belief.

In this chapter, we covered three types of illegitimate responses that attempt to shift (or avoid) the burden of proof: 1) attacking Christianity, 2) claiming there is no evidence, and 3) redefining atheism. From here, we ended with a strategy for avoiding tedious debates by writing down the standard definitions, omitting the labels, and feeling for their position. We saw how listening attentively not only provided us with valuable information, but for using their rhetoric to formulate the next question against their position. This inevitably gives the question more force while maintaining a cordial conversation with a respectful attitude.

In all this, I emphasized that our goal for this portion of the conversation is not to defend Christianity but to gather information and identify their position. Doing so allowed us to accomplish the first task in evangelism (know who you're talking to) in order to achieve the second (adapt your approach accordingly). Taking this approach keeps you calm, cool, collected, and gives you control of the conversation, allowing you to maneuver away from potentially heated debates and unfruitful altercations. These chapters have served as a foundation for the remainder of this book, and we'll continue to utilize these principles throughout.

PART 3A

What is Our Goal? Identifying Strongholds

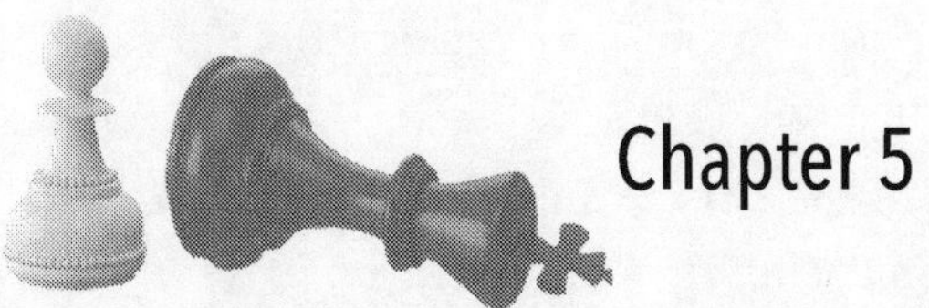

Chapter 5

Understanding the Times

Biblical Basis:

> *From Issachar, men who understood the times and knew what Israel should do...*
>
> –1 Chronicles 12:32

In 1 Chronicles 12, we read about groups of men who came from all over to aid king David in battle, and the text goes out of its way to depict them in intimidating detail. They are described as *courageous men, brave warriors, mighty, ready for battle,* and their faces were *like the faces of lions, swift as gazelles on the mountains.* Concerning their military skills: *experienced soldiers of undivided loyalty, famous in their clan, armed with bows* and *could use the right hand or left to sling stones and shoot arrows,* and *men trained for war, who could handle shield and spear, soldiers prepared for battle with every type of weapon.*

Most groups came by the thousands. Some 3,000, others 20,000, some 50,000, and the largest group was "120,000 men, armed with all kinds of weapons of war for the battle" (AMP). Their numbers and abilities were such a force to be reckoned with that the Bible compares them to "a great army, like the army of God" (AMP).

However, amidst these is an odd group that stands out like a sore thumb and is the smallest reported. From Issachar, a mere 200 men who are described, not with great weapons or ambidextrous talent, but as men who *understood the times* in order to "know what Israel ought to do" (ESV). There is no reference to physical strength and, implicit from the passage, they were not armed with bow or spear, but with *knowledge* and *understanding*. Could it be that fewer numbers and efforts are needed with greater knowledge and understanding? Perhaps the old saying, "knowledge is power," rings true after all.

Now consider this in light of the church's role in evangelism. Much like David's great army, while our churches may be prominent in number and filled with incredible talent, without an understanding of the times, we will lack the knowledge of "what Israel ought to do." Hence, before we can know "what the church ought to do," we must begin by "understanding the times" of the culture we live in.

Plausibility Structures Within Culture

Every culture has what is known as a **plausibility structure**—a background set of ideas or beliefs that people within a culture use to judge what they are and are not willing to listen to, accept, or entertain as *possibly* true. Consequently, if a culture's plausibility structure is permeated with strongholds contrary to the Christian worldview, it will inevitably devalue Christianity as an intellectually viable option.

To put this point differently, it's been said that the heart cannot embrace what the mind regards as nonsense. Meaning that a person cannot believe something if they feel it goes contrary to logic or reason. This is not unique to nonbelievers but is something everyone experiences. To illustrate, I'm not a Buddhist for several reasons, but I'll briefly mention two.

First, a core doctrine within Buddhism is *anatta*, which is the belief that "the self" (i.e., me, the person) does not exist. Ironically, however, for me to believe this doctrine, I, my-self, must believe that there is *no* self. But if that's the case, then who's the one believing that there is no self if not me, the self, itself? Second, another core doctrine within Buddhism is the notion of *nirodha*, which is the Buddhist solution to the problem of suffering. According to this doctrine, to eliminate suffering in life, one must first rid themselves of all desires. Once again, the irony here is that to rid myself of all desires, I must first be driven by the *desire* to rid myself of all desires, which is, itself, a desire that I mustn't rid myself of.

So essentially, I don't reject Buddhism because I don't want it to be true. Rather, I reject Buddhism because I find it oddly irrational and illogical. Hence, Buddhism is simply not within my plausibility structure, but note that for others, neither is Christianity. Given our culture's current structure, Christianity is not only seen as false, but irrational, illogical, and plain silly to believe. Thus, if we wish to reach this culture, then we must "understand the times" and learn to change its structure. As Moreland observes:

> If a culture reaches the point where Christian claims are not even part of its plausibility structure, fewer and fewer people will be able to entertain the possibility that they might be true. Whatever stragglers do come to faith in such a context would do so on the basis of felt needs alone, and the genuineness of such conversions would be questionable to say the least. This is why apologetics is so crucial to evangelism.[17]

For this reason, a primary objective of apologetics in evangelism and spiritual warfare is identifying and responding to the strongholds within the culture. I've often said the biggest threat to Christianity is not Richard Dawkins, atheism, or "science," but intellectually lazy Christians that refuse to recognize and rationally respond to the dominant strongholds within the culture. Therefore, if we wish to change the plausibility structure, then we must address its strongholds, and if we wish to address the strongholds, then we must gain the knowledge and train our eyes to see them.

KNOWLEDGE AND "HAVING THE EYES TO SEE"

To illustrate this point, I'm far from a mechanic, and my knowledge about cars is minimal, whereas my father-in-law once owned his own shop as a mechanic. If you were to open the hood of a car and ask what we see, I could likely identify the location of the engine, the belt, and some bolts, but admittedly, everything else is a "spinning thing" here and a "rubber tube" over there. By contrast, if you had asked my father-in-law what he saw, he would probably have said, "Here is the block where the combustion takes place. These are the pistons that compress the mixture of air and fuel, which move the tires by way of the driveshaft and transmission. Then you have the cylinder head over here, valves for air regulation there, a camshaft, crankshaft, and underneath it all, you have the oil pan." (And yes, I had to google this.)

Granted, when we opened the car's hood, we both saw an engine. But note that his eyes were able to see far more than mine, which was not due to a lack of sight, but a lack of knowledge. Our eyes worked the same, but his knowledge provided the foundation for "having the eyes to see" what mine could not. By understanding the function, not only is he able to identify its parts but, more importantly, identify potential problems.

Pushing the analogy further, it's for this reason that a ticking noise coming from the engine may sound trivial to me, and indeed, it may be for the time being. Pragmatically speaking, if the car continues to function, getting me from point A to point B, what's the harm of ignoring the sound? But for him, it's different. While the noise may initially sound trivial, he knows that if left unaddressed, a simple, quick fix only leads to bigger, more expensive problems in the future.

Evangelism: Cars or People?

I offer this analogy for two reasons. First, I want to emphasize the simple fact that the more one knows, the more one can see. The same principle applies to evangelism and spiritual warfare for identifying strongholds. Second, consider the consequential differences between ignorance and negligence of cars versus ignorance and negligence of people. The great thing about mechanics is that, despite our ignorance or negligence, if our car breaks down, we can always take it to the nearest mechanic and ask them to fix it. But unlike a car, you cannot take your friend, co-worker, or loved one to the nearest apologist and say, "open up the hood and fix them, please; they're an atheist!"

Put differently, our ignorance or negligence of a car may come at a cost, but for most minor issues, we can likely afford it. So, rather than fix the problems when they arise, we find ways to cope. For example, I once had a car that constantly overheated. My solution? I carried around five jugs of water in my trunk. When my car overheated, I simply pulled over, poured the water, and went on with my day. That is until my frugal solution to a relatively minor situation became a bigger, far more expensive problem. But contrast this with a person: a loved one, a son, daughter, close friend, or family member. Can we afford to be ignorant or negligent of the strongholds? I'm afraid not.

The Ticking Sound

According to the Barna Group research, the percentage of people that hold to a biblical worldview statistically declines in each generation.[18] Only 6% of Millennials (my generation) are said to have a biblical worldview, compared to only 4% of Gen Z (the younger generation). In fact, the percentage of Gen Z's that identify as atheists today is *double* that of U.S. adults,[19] and the number of young people leaving the church or faith today is about 64% (nearly 2 out of every 3).[20] But what happened? Did we ignore the ticking sound?

What's more is that for most churches, the opted solution seems to be, consequentially speaking, no different than coping with a car's mechanical issues. If the youth attendance is waning, we "turn up the radio" by bringing in a Christian rapper for a lock-in to get the kids excited. But does this address the problem, or are we merely pouring water on a "hot engine" in the form of pizza, fun, and games? Please, don't misunderstand me. There's *nothing* wrong with hosting such events. But at what point do these become the water jugs in the trunks of our ecclesiastical cars in hopes of postponing an inevitable breakdown?

In the words of apologist Dr. Frank Turek, "what we win them with, we win them to."[21] Additionally, it must also be understood that what we win them with, we can lose them to, and I can assure you that in terms of concerts, music, and entertainment, the church cannot compete with what the world has to offer. Nor should it try. Nevertheless, nothing has been postponed because, according to the statistics, the inevitable "breakdown" is already here. And trust me, these are far more than impersonal statistics.

The Breakdown

I've honestly lost count of all the emails, phone calls, and messages I've received from parents asking if I'd be willing to meet with their child, relative, or co-worker because they've recently come out as atheists. Though honored at the request, I'm only one person with a growing family of my own and, more pertinently, God has placed them in their life, not mine. To be clear, I have no problem sitting with someone over lunch to help them wrestle with their doubts, and I've taken up these offers *numerous* times. But at some point, we must ask ourselves, are we dealing with cars or people?

Along the same lines, after teaching apologetics at various churches, I'm often approached by parents or grandparents asking which of my apologetic teachings they should buy for their relatives because "they're atheists." I've always found this mindset problematic for a few reasons, but the most obvious is this: why are we expecting someone else to learn what we're not willing to learn ourselves? As one study reported, "young Christians lack biblical knowledge on some matters, but not significantly more so than older Christians."[22] Hence, apologetics is not some "young thing for young people" but is a universal, biblical mandate to all believers, regardless of age.

In his book, *Love God With All Your Mind*, Moreland offers three "very important and painful questions" we must ask ourselves. The last of which is the most painful:

> How is it possible for a person to be an active member of an evangelical church for twenty or thirty years and still know next to nothing about the history and theology of the Christian religion, the methods and tools required for serious Bible study, and the skills and information necessary to preach and defend Christianity in a post-Christian, neopagan culture?[23]

Beloved, we can no longer ignore the ticking sound, nor can we afford to merely pour water on the problem. Instead, we *must* learn to respond to the strongholds within our culture, and to do this effectively, we *must* train our eyes to see them.

THE THREE DOMINANT STRONGHOLDS IN OUR CULTURE

With this in mind, three dominant strongholds have shaped the plausibility structure of our culture today. In no particular order, they are *postmodernism*, *scientism*, and *naturalism*. Put succinctly, **postmodernism** is the view that truth is relative and subjective to the individual, **scientism** is the view that science is either the best or *only* way to gain knowledge about reality, and **naturalism** is the view that the physical world is all that exists, nothing more, nothing less. In philosophical language, these are known as **worldviews**.

What Is a Worldview?

It's common to hear the term "worldview" defined as a set of glasses through which a person sees the world. A typical example is that if I have on a pair of red-shaded glasses, then the clouds in the sky will look red to me. Hence, it is my "view of the world." Though helpful, the illustration is mistaken. Because see, if a worldview is merely a set of glasses through which we see the world, then our "view of the world" is never *seeing the world as it is*, but instead, seeing it through the lenses we have chosen.

To elaborate on this problem, consider what is known as the **correspondence theory of truth**, which has been the standard definition of truth throughout history. According to the correspondence view, *truth is that which corresponds to reality*. Hence, the statement "grass is green" is true *if and only if* the grass is, in fact, green. But note how this assessment requires that we view the world as it is and not through "shaded lenses." Otherwise, something will always stand between us and an accurate view of reality (e.g., red-shaded glasses).

Additionally, Christianity itself is a worldview. Yet, it would be ill-advised to say we are "trapped" behind the lenses of Christianity. Why? Because if Christianity is true, then we are not seeing the world through an arbitrary set of "shaded glasses" but are seeing the world clearly *as it is* in light of *the truth*. What, then, is a worldview?

Simply put, a **worldview** can be defined as the sum of what one believes about life's biggest questions: *What is truth, and how can we know it? What exists and is real? What is the nature of man? What is the meaning or purpose of life (if any)?* And so forth. Each of the worldviews listed above (postmodernism, scientism, and naturalism) have answers to these questions, and knowing these answers will provide us with a deeper understanding of them.

For the sake of simplicity, we'll learn how to identify these worldviews (or, in biblical terms, strongholds) by unpacking their answers to the first two sets of questions. In philosophy, these fall under the categories of *epistemology* and *ontology*. Put succinctly, **epistemology** is the study of knowledge, beliefs, and what can be known, whereas **ontology** is the study of ultimate reality and what does or does not exist. Even simpler, epistemology pertains to beliefs, whereas ontology pertains to existence.

Beginning with the next chapter, we'll accomplish this task by asking two questions:

1. What can be *known* in this worldview (the epistemology)?
2. What can *exist* in this worldview (the ontology)?

Answering these provides an *epistemic* and *ontological* backdrop for each stronghold and inevitably exposes how they oppose Christianity in one form or another. From here, we'll develop our "eyes to see" further by learning how to identify the presence and influence of these strongholds in three C's: *church*, *culture*, and *conversation*.

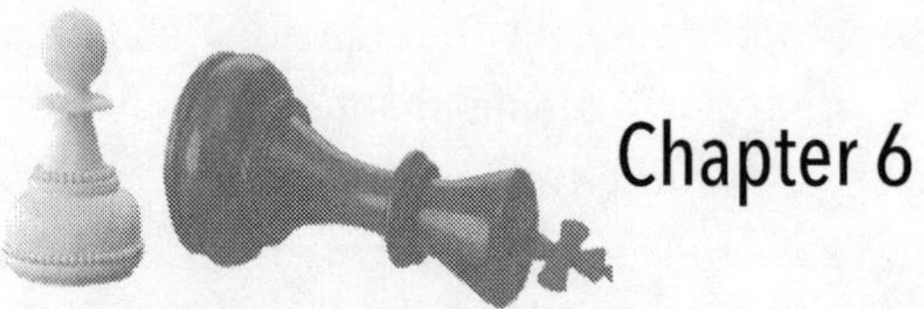

Chapter 6

Identifying Postmodernism

The Epistemology

For our purposes, **postmodernism** can be defined as the view that takes truth as something relative to every culture or individual (sometimes referred to as **relativism** or **subjectivism**).[24] By way of analogy, suppose a dog is sitting next to a tree with two people observing from opposite ends. One person will say there is a dog to the *right* of the tree, whereas the other person will say there is a dog to the *left* of the tree. But given that we have two different answers, which perspective is correct? Well, the answer is that they're both right.

Indeed, there is a dog to the left of the tree *and* a dog to the right, because these "truths" are grounded in the individual subject (hence, **subjectivism**). Although there is only one dog, there are "two truths," each *relative* to the person (hence, **relativism**). In the same way, says the postmodernist, no one is ever "right" or "wrong" because, as demonstrated in the illustration, *all truth* is relative and dependent on each person's perspective.

To further grasp this position, consider the difference between *objective truth* and *subjective truth*. **Objective truth** is independent of human thought or opinion, whereas **subjective truth** is grounded in and *relative to* the person. For example, the statement "Christianity is true" has been presented as *objectively true*, meaning its truth is not grounded in my state of mind, emotions, or personal preferences. By contrast, the statement, "Taco Bell is the best food around, manna sent from Heaven," is a subjective truth grounded in me, the subject.

Within the postmodern worldview, there is no objective, absolute truth, and for some, even if there was, one could never know it (e.g., skepticism). Much like the glasses analogy from the previous chapter, everyone is trapped behind a relative set of lenses through which they see the world. No one possesses the absolute truth and thus, any claims to objective truth are rejected because only subjective truth can exist.

The Ontology

Now consider how a worldview's answer to the ontological question (what exits) is directly correlated with its answer to the epistemic question (what can be known as true). On this view, if a person does not believe Christianity is true, then for that person, the Christian God does not exist. Hence, concerning the epistemic question, truth is merely subjective or relative to the person, and concerning the ontological question, reality is something determined by the individual.

OPPOSITION TO CHRISTIANITY

As previously mentioned, Christianity is a worldview that professes to be *objectively* true. Yet, given the nature of postmodernism, Christianity will always be rejected as something that, in principle, *could ever be* objectively true in the first place. This is not because they believe it's objectively false. After all, for something to be "objectively false," there must first be an objective truth, and within postmodernism, there is neither. So, at best, Christianity can only be something that is "true for you but not for me."

Additionally, consider that a flourishing relationship with God encompasses following the mandates of Scripture. But suppose a person believes that all truth is relative. In that case, Scripture won't be seen as objectively true with valid mandates but as an outdated, culturally relative list of suggestions. For the postmodernist, the Bible may be an ancient book of allegorical stories—but not the infallible, inherent word of God.

Furthermore, not only does postmodernism oppose Christian doctrine, but it creates obstacles in evangelism for the reception of the gospel. For example, Jesus states in John 14:6, "I am the way and the truth and the life. No one comes to the Father except through me." Yet, a postmodernist may find it difficult or arrogant to believe that Christ is *the only* way to God (assuming they believe there is a God in the first place).

For this reason, proclaiming Christianity to be objectively true within a postmodern culture may be seen as inappropriate, disrespectful, or offensive to those who believe differently. Given that there is no objective truth, we mustn't "force our religious views" onto others. So, if you don't agree with same-sex marriage, that's fine (says the postmodernist), but don't impose your "personal" beliefs onto someone else. That's intolerant! Don't agree with abortion? That's fine, too. But that's "your truth," and we shouldn't hinder someone from living out "their truth." My body, my choice; true for you, but not for me.

IDENTIFYING ITS PRESENCE AND INFLUENCE IN THE CHURCH

Not only has this stronghold permeated our culture, but its influence has crept into the church unnoticed. Such is the case with all three of these dominant strongholds, but without having the "eyes to see" it, their presence becomes unapparent to the average believer. To demonstrate this with postmodernism, consider the implicit mentality behind some of our practices for evangelism and Bible study. While these examples may seem trivial at face value, I can assure you that "the engine's ticking noise" will become a deafening sound soon enough.

1. Postmodernism in Our Evangelism

The Barna Group recently published an article with the headline, *Almost Half of Practicing Christian Millennials Say Evangelism Is Wrong*. This study was conducted among four generational groups: Millennials, Gen X, Boomers, and Elders, surveying their opinions on evangelism. At the outset, it states, "among the major findings in this report is the revelation that Christian Millennials feel especially conflicted about evangelism—and, in fact, almost half believe it is wrong to share their faith."[25] That's right, half! But what I found most bizarre about this revelation was its additional statistics. Consider the following:

Up to 97% of "all practicing Christians believe that part of their faith means being a witness about Jesus and that the best thing that could ever happen to someone is for them to know Jesus."[26] Higher than any other generation, 73% of Millennials said that they felt *gifted* and *equipped* to share their faith with other people. Nevertheless, roughly half felt it was wrong to "share one's personal beliefs with someone of a different faith in hopes that they will one day share the same faith."[27] At this point, something seemed off, and a few questions came to mind:

1. Why do roughly half of Millennials feel it's wrong to share their faith?
2. How was "sharing their faith" defined, and why do they feel *gifted* and *equipped* to share their faith with others?
3. How can an entire generation feel that a person coming to know Jesus is *the best thing that could ever happen to them*, and yet, simultaneously feel it's wrong to "share one's personal beliefs with someone of a different faith in hopes that they will one day share the same faith?"

Concerning the first question, the following reasons were given: "Sharing the gospel today is made harder... by an overall cultural resistance to conversations that highlight people's differences," and that evangelism "is difficult in a world of 'you do you' and 'don't criticize anyone's life choices' and emotivism, the feelings-first priority that our culture makes a way of life."[28] Moreover, "three out of five Christian Millennials believe that people today are more likely than in the past to take offense if they share their faith."[29]

Note how these answers echo the postmodern sentiment described above: an emphasis on feelings, an over-sensitivity for avoiding offense, a hesitation towards criticism, and a refrain from claiming that opposing views are wrong. Can you hear the ticking sound? While this answers the first question, the latter two remain unaddressed. But without implying there was an obligation to ask (much less answer) my questions, let's take what we've learned thus far and attempt to answer the latter two.

Our "Gospel Pitch"

It seems that most people today (especially those in my generation—Millennials) define evangelism as merely "sharing my personal experience and testimony with others." As alluded to in the first chapter, this pitches the gospel as a means of achieving gratification and self-fulfillment, making the person and their felt desires (not the truth of the gospel) the focus and center of attention. To an outsider, this approach may sound like we're saying, "Look how God gave me a happy life and made me a good person. Become a Christian to have a great life and be happy, too!"

Again, note the underlying assumptions being promoted here. Namely, that Christianity can be accepted as something that is pragmatically true *relative to my own* beliefs and personal experiences. Put differently, "*I know Christianity is true because I have such a great life and experience happiness.*" Coincidentally, when we hear of "celebrity Christians" renouncing their faith, virtually without exception, they begin their "de-conversion stories" by stating, "*I'm so much happier now,*" as if the foundation of our faith depended on the level of one's happiness. But why would someone think such a thing? Because that's how the "gospel pitch" was presented to them. Hence, if I convert to Christianity for happiness and find that its doctrines impede this goal, it only makes sense to find a different worldview.

Considering this, it may be that for most Millennials surveyed in this study, being "gifted and equipped to share my faith" meant that "*I know how to share my personal experiences and beliefs with others.*" So, if "sharing my faith" means that I talk about myself, then sure, I know of no Millennial who doesn't feel "gifted and equipped" to do this. If this is the case, we have an answer to the second question. But what about the third? Namely, the stark contrast between believing that a person coming to know Jesus is the *best thing* that could ever happen to them and yet, feeling it's "wrong to share one's personal beliefs with someone of a different faith in hopes that they will one day share the same faith?"

To address this question, note the wording of "sharing one's *personal beliefs*." For these Millennials, if sharing "my faith" means sharing my feelings and experiences through personal testimony, then maybe *it is wrong* to share my faith with others in hopes of their salvation. Why? Because perhaps the person I'm witnessing to has had a different set of life experiences, feelings, and a relative story of their own. Thus, Christianity may be "true for me" because of my experiences, but perhaps it is not "true for you" because of yours.

"Personal Testimonies" and Postmodernism

Concerning all I've said regarding the use of personal testimonies in evangelism, you may disagree with me, and that's entirely your prerogative. Perhaps you've always shared your testimony with great success, and I genuinely rejoice. But if you would humor me just for a moment, may I respectfully offer some questions for consideration?

First, given what we've learned in this chapter and the times we live in, would this *still* be the best approach for a younger generation and, more pertinently, a culture permeated with a postmodern mentality? Second, recall the distinction between a subjective truth (depending on the person) and objective truth (independent of the person). Given the bigger picture, ask yourself this: would Christianity still be true even if I didn't have a personal testimony? If your answer is yes, then why? Whatever the answer, would it not be best to start your evangelistic approach with that?

To be clear, I'm not saying there is *no place* for your testimony (if you wish to share one). I'm simply saying that if the truth of Christianity is not predicated on our existence, emotions, or life experiences, then a personal testimony could never be a *substitute* for defending the truth of Christianity in a postmodern culture.

2. Postmodernism in Our Bible Studies

A second example of postmodernism influencing our church practices can be detected in how we approach the text of Scripture or lead a Bible study. For example, have you ever attended a Bible study that began by reading a passage aloud and was followed by the question, "And what does this verse mean to you, personally?" While there's nothing *inherently* wrong with the question, suppose someone gave an outlandish answer that was anachronistic and antithetical to the text of Scripture. Was the response from the Bible study leader a respectful but clear correction on the matter, or was it affirming, congratulatory praise, no matter how inaccurate or poorly reasoned the point was?[30]

Do we treat *any and every* interpretation of Scripture as equally valid as the next? Does a person with devoted time studying the text's language, idioms, and cultural context have a more accurate insight than someone who has merely read the passage for the first time? Put differently, is there an *objective interpretation* and *meaning* to the text, or is the Bible left open to *anyone's* subjective interpretation? According to historic Christianity, it's always been the former.

"Guided" by the Holy Spirit or Unprepared?

A youth pastor once told me that he rarely prepared for his Bible studies because he wanted "the Holy Spirit to lead the lesson." My initial thought (which I kept to myself) was this; could the Holy Spirit not "lead the lesson" by leading you to study and prepare? Ironically, in hopes of sounding spiritual and pious, he'd only revealed that his "lessons" were predictably unorganized, unprepared, and likely, unbiblical. Coincidentally, when I asked how he began his Bible studies, he said, "I open the Bible to where the Spirit 'leads' me, read the verse out loud, and then ask my students, 'What does this verse mean to you, personally?'"

What's even more detrimental in this approach is the implicit assumption that understanding Scripture (or leading a Bible study) doesn't require doing your best to study and show yourself approved, rightly handling the word of truth (2 Timothy 2:15). Admittedly, such a task is not easy, requiring time, understanding, and even correction. Nevertheless, there can be no excuse for neglecting this command.

Ignorance or Arrogance?

A young man once explained that he intentionally refrained from gaining "too much knowledge" because "knowledge puffs up" and can make one proud. With humility in his voice, he said, "I know many people who are very smart but sadly, have become prideful and arrogant because of it." So, with humility in my voice, I responded, "Well, I know a lot of people who are very dumb, but sadly, have become prideful and arrogant because of it, as well." Being ignorant and arrogant is no more virtuous than being intelligent and prideful.

To make this point biblically, consider the words of the apostle Peter. Commenting on Paul's wisdom, he writes, "His letters contain some things that are hard to understand" and concludes by adding, "which ignorant and unstable people distort, as they do the other Scriptures, to their own destruction" (2 Peter 3:16). As the apostle Peter acknowledges, yes, Scripture can sometimes be hard to understand (especially when one does not fulfill the command of 2 Timothy 2:15). Nevertheless, he warns that without a proper understanding of Scripture, the "ignorant and unstable" person will twist and "distort them to their own destruction." As Puritan minister Cotton Mather observed, "Ignorance is the Mother not of Devotion but of HERESY."[31]

IDENTIFYING ITS PRESENCE AND INFLUENCE IN CULTURE

By nature, a worldview will shape a society's thoughts, values, and morals. Although its strongholds may not directly determine these behaviors, it's a fair way of detecting its presence. For this reason, at least two things are worth observing within a culture: the authority figures and the emphasis of its media.

Authority Figures

For every culture, intellectual authority is held by those who purportedly possess the relevant knowledge for a given subject and, as a result, have the right to be believed and demand compliance. Hence, identifying those deemed as authority figures will naturally point us to that culture's values and beliefs (i.e., its plausibility structure). To do this, we can take note of the positions held by those who are sought after for guidance through their professed wisdom and insight. To be clear, this isn't inherently a bad thing.

For instance, Christians take the apostles as noteworthy authority figures with the relevant insight to write Scripture as canon. Thus, we take Paul's letters as objective truth, wisdom for Christian living, and spiritual guidance. Additionally, if a person has a legitimate calling from God, we hold pastors and evangelists (to name a few) as authority figures who can offer wisdom and guidance—assuming the final authority of Scripture backs it. But contrast this with a postmodern worldview.

Given that truth is relative to the individual, there will not be a single, *sole* authoritative figure for a given subject. Why? Because every person's views or opinions are as equally valid as the next. As a result, a postmodernist will typically consult a variety of people because, in their mind, gaining multiple perspectives will aid them in coming to their "own truth," as opposed to absolute, objective truth (because, of course, there is none).

The Postmodern Emphasis in Media

The media's emphasis within a culture includes music, movies, and the news. And as Andrew Fletcher famously said, "Let me write the songs of a nation, and I care not who makes its laws."[32] For popular culture, one can recognize the influence of a worldview by observing the lyrics in a song or movie, such as "live out your truth" or "create your own reality." These phrases convey the idea that there is no objective truth; thus, one is free to create reality and live by whatever one *believes* to be true. The underlying message being that truth and reality revolve around the individual's preferences, feelings, or experiences. Hence, observing what is prioritized or sung about most within a culture will often indicate the presence or influence of a stronghold.

A Postmodern Influence on Our Worship?

If analyzing music within a culture is a fair way of detecting the presence or influence of a stronghold, then Christianity cannot be exempt from this test. As a thought experiment, consider the songs that are typically sung for your Sunday morning worship and count how many times the words "I" or "me" appear and contrast this with how many times the words "you" or "God" appear. Additionally, count how many times the conjunction of these words is used (e.g., "I" and "God"), but without the verse referencing what the individual feels or the "benefits" she receives from being a Christian.

Now ask yourself, is this song about God or me? Put differently, how often is the focus of a verse solely on God, and how often is the focus of a verse centered around me, the individual? Recall that with the influence of postmodernism, an individual's feelings, emotions, and experiences become the central emphasis of how they evaluate truth and reality.

From what I've found, songs that overuse the words "I" or "me" tend to be about what the person feels or the "benefits" they receive from being a Christian, making the focus of worship centered around the person, not God. Moreover, songs that focus heavily on feelings, emotions, or experiences imply that our worship correlates with the measure of ourselves and not the measure of God and His character. Consequently, if my worship revolves around me, the worshipper, then I only worship God because I feel good, not because He is good. Similarly, if my worship is solely about me and what God has done in my life, then I worship God because of who *I am*, not because of who *He is*.

To be clear, there's nothing *inherently* wrong with bringing our emotional experiences into worship. However, the problem arises when our worship becomes *directly dependent on our emotions or experiences*, which constantly fluctuate and change. By contrast, biblical worship always depends on God and His character, which changes not. Therefore, if we wish to avoid the influence, we *must* ensure the focus of our worship is centered around God, not us.

IDENTIFYING ITS PRESENCE AND INFLUENCE IN CONVERSATION

Recognizing the presence and influence of postmodernism in a conversation becomes most notable when it comes to the topic of morality. Within postmodernism, when a particular perspective or belief is held amongst an entire society, it's often called **cultural relativism**. When applied to morality, it's known as **moral relativism**. Like truth, morality is no longer something that's *objectively* right or wrong but is instead relative to an individual's perspective, convictions, or feelings. When this occurs, two key features naturally arise.

1. Morality Is Replaced With Politics

First, if there is no objective sense of right or wrong, then there can be no objective sense of moral or immoral. Consequently, the moral language of being "right and wrong" is replaced with the political language of being "politically correct or incorrect."

2. Tolerance Is Redefined

The second feature that arises with postmodernism is the redefining of the notion of tolerance.[33] Historically speaking, tolerance is the idea that while I disagree with an individual's beliefs or behaviors, I continue treating them with dignity, respect, and fight for their right to voice their views in public. This is known as the **classical sense of tolerance**. By contrast, the **modern version of tolerance** has become the idea that the very act of disagreement itself is "intolerant," hateful, or bigoted. Note the distinction.

In the classical sense, tolerance implies that while I love and respect the person, I still disagree with their beliefs or behaviors. After all, if I approve of their perspective, I am not "tolerating" their view but agreeing with it! On the other hand, if tolerance means I shouldn't judge another person's opinion as "wrong" (as in the modern sense), then the person who professes disagreement must be a hateful bigot. For such a culture, voicing judgment, dissent, or claiming that an opposing view is false makes one "intolerant."

Recognizing These Features in Conversations

To recognize these features in conversation, pay careful attention to how the person expresses their position. For instance, you may hear someone say, "I'll never have an abortion myself, but I could never tell a person that they're *wrong* for choosing what *they feel* is best for their life." Note the pragmatic mindset. On this view, the question of abortion is no longer about the moral status and life of the unborn, but instead, about the desires and needs of the individual. Much like truth, morality is something that each person must decide for themselves *subjectively*, as opposed to something that is objectively right or wrong, *independent of* one's personal preference or opinion.

Similarly, it's often said, "If you don't like same-sex marriage, then don't have one, but don't tell someone else that they don't have the right to be happy!" Once again, moral positions are reduced to one's preferences or political opinions. We'll deal with responses to these features in a later chapter, but for now, understand the importance of paying careful attention to how a person implicitly expresses their position. This will not only help us understand their perspective but, more pertinently, will help us identify the stronghold.

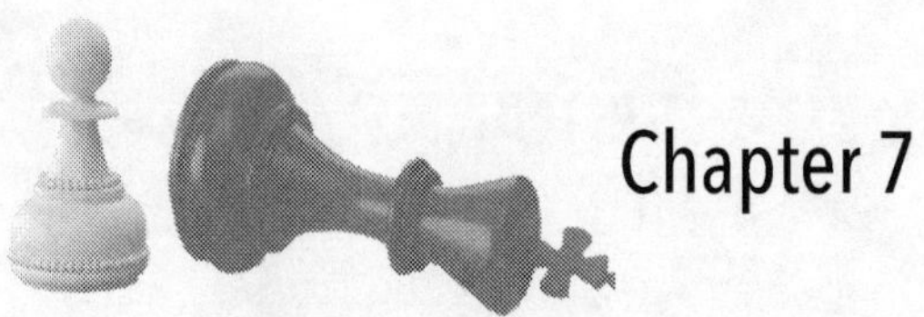

Chapter 7

Identifying Scientism

The Epistemology

At its core, scientism is an epistemic position concerning what can be known about reality. According to this worldview, science and science alone is "the very paradigm of truth and rationality."[34] It's the hard sciences that "provide the only genuine knowledge of reality" and is "vastly superior to what we can know from any other discipline" (e.g., philosophy or theology).[35] Therefore, something can be known *if and only if* it can be tested through the hard sciences. Put differently, only that which can be discovered scientifically is *objectively* true. Hence, although objective truth is affirmed in this view, it's limited to the realm of scientific investigation. If something cannot be investigated or tested scientifically, then it either cannot be known or cannot be true.

The Ontology

Given its epistemology (knowledge is limited and only discoverable by science), that which exists (its ontology) is limited to what can be verified through scientific investigation. So, on this view, given that God cannot be tested "scientifically," then ontologically speaking, His existence either cannot be known (agnosticism), or He simply does not exist, to begin with (atheism).

To be clear, the stronghold of scientism is far more than an appreciation for science. Instead, it's a philosophical claim that treats science as the ultimate authority for truth and knowledge. Hence, we are not talking about science but scientism, and we shouldn't confuse one's passion for science with the stronghold of scientism.

OPPOSITION TO CHRISTIANITY

When scientism is left unaddressed within a culture, it naturally creates epistemic and ontological barriers to accepting the truth of Christianity.

The Epistemic Barrier: "Science vs. Faith"

A culture permeated with scientism tends to assume a **false dichotomy** (juxtaposing two positions as if they are mutually exclusive) between science and "faith." For example, a nonbeliever may say, "I have science, not faith!" The assumption being that science and faith are competing epistemologies for knowledge. But as we saw in chapter two, faith is not a way of knowing something but is a response to something already known. Nevertheless, if "faith" claims are non-scientific affirmations, then given scientism, such claims could never amount to reliable knowledge about reality. Instead, they are outdated, superstitious, personal beliefs that cannot be objectively proven.

Moreover, this epistemic barrier further assumes a necessary separation between "the secular and the sacred," making science a matter of the "head" and religion a matter of the "heart."[36] Hence, if you want your feelings tickled and your heart warmed, then go to a pastor, but if you want facts, reason, and logic, go to a scientist. For such a culture, it's one or the other, but certainly not both.

The Ontological Barrier for Evangelism, a Stumbling Block for Salvation

To grasp the ontological barriers this creates for evangelism and salvation, consider the Christian doctrines of the afterlife. Given scientism, Christianity's belief about the afterlife, even if true, cannot *be known* to be true, because these claims cannot be investigated scientifically. After all, one cannot take a testing lab to Heaven and come back with a "scientific" conclusion. Nevertheless, given that the truth of Christianity hinges on the truth of the resurrection (which entails an afterlife), such a stronghold inevitably leads to a deep-seated skepticism towards Christianity (agnosticism), or worse, a rejection of it altogether (atheism).

For this reason, the presence and influence of scientism within a culture will always be correlated with resistance to Christianity. If the church doesn't learn how to respond to this stronghold, then not only will we encounter daunting barriers in evangelism, but daunting stumbling blocks for salvation.

IDENTIFYING ITS PRESENCE AND INFLUENCE IN THE CHURCH

The rise of scientism in our culture has caused two types of extremes in our churches today, both of which are unbiblical and harmful.

The First Extreme: Fideism

In this first extreme, the church reacts by taking faith as an epistemology and, more pertinently, one that is opposed to reason or rationality. This is known as **fideism**—the belief that faith is *separate from* and *incompatible with* reason. This can be identified when a believer, confronted with scientism, becomes defensive and punts to faith as an alternative to science. Feeling stuck in a corner, she may say, "Look, at the end of the day, it's all about faith!" And rather than provide an adequate response, the Christian plays right into the hand of this stronghold. Allow me to explain the implicit influence and problem.

First, this response concedes that science and reason are opposed to faith, which is precisely the mentality of this stronghold. When forced to pick one, the Christian chooses "faith over science," granting that the two are somehow incompatible. But suppose someone were to ask, "Who do you love: your spouse or your children?" Surely the response wouldn't be to pick one over the other but deny the "either-or" mentality. Concerning the scientism dichotomy, the same principle should apply.

Second, this response furthers the idea that science and reason are a product of the intellect, which belongs to "the head," whereas one's theological convictions are a product of "faith," which belongs to "the heart." Hence, the pseudo-separation of "the secular and sacred." As evidence of this mindset in the church, when a person answers the call to become a pastor or an evangelist, we say they are "doing the work of God." But if they become teachers, scientists, or doctors, we say they've chosen a "secular" vocation—as if there's no ministerial work of God in these areas. I've yet to find a proof text for such a belief.

Finally, like scientism, fideism takes faith as an epistemology (a way of knowing) that is opposed to reason or rationality. Not only is this false, but unbiblical. God said to Isaiah, "come now, let us reason together" (Isaiah 1:18, ESV). But when fideism is represented in the church, we force nonbelievers to choose one over the other. Not only will they choose "science and reason" over faith, but (perhaps inadvertently), we further harden their heart toward the reception of the Gospel. Why? Because fideism is simply not within the plausibility structure of the nonbeliever, and it shouldn't be within the plausibility structure of the believer, either.

The Second Extreme: Naturalizing the Supernatural

In this extreme, rather than reject science and spiritualize the natural (as in the first extreme), the temptation becomes explaining *everything* through science and naturalizing the spiritual. To illustrate, I once heard a minister claim that the miracles in the gospels can be taken as credible because we now have "scientific explanations" for them. As an example, he claimed that the miracle of Peter walking on water could be explained through the science of epigenetics. Allegedly, when Jesus told Peter to walk on water, the tone of his voice "activated" some gene in Peter's legs, causing his body to float over the water. Now, I have no quarrel speculating about the *possibility* of God using natural means to accomplish what we perceive as miracles, but his motive behind the attempt is what was problematic.

First, his desire to provide natural, scientific explanations for these miracles was grounded in the anxiety to appease the cultural influence of scientism. Suffice it to say, he wasn't refuting the stronghold, but falling prey to it. Second, although such speculations are possible, they're just that—*speculations*. One cannot go back in time, test the genetic activity in Peter's legs, and verify that, yes, *this* scientific explanation demonstrates how the miracle occurred. Again, while it's a *possibility*, there's no way to confirm it was an *actuality*. After all, it's equally *possible* that God could've secretly inflated Peter's shoes with floatation devices, but *possibilities* do not equal *actualities*.

Finally, even if this *could* be scientifically verified, conspicuous by its absence is an explanation for how Jesus was able to walk on water. Because if Jesus didn't need this "epigenetic gene activation," then why use this for Peter? Could we not say that both occurrences were, oh, I don't know, a miracle? While it's God's prerogative to use secondary, natural means to bring about a miraculous event, it's equally His prerogative to be God and intervene in supernatural, miraculous ways.[37]

While more can be said here, my point is simply this: *not every natural thing can be spiritualized, and not every spiritual thing can be naturalized*, and the influential pressure of scientism should not drive the church to one extreme or the other. If it does, then Christianity becomes undesirably irrelevant at best (the first extreme) or pathetically contrived at worst (the second extreme).

IDENTIFYING ITS PRESENCE AND INFLUENCE IN CULTURE

I once saw a meme that read, "Scientists have discovered that people will believe anything when you claim scientists have discovered it." This was by far the clearest explanation of the presence and influence of scientism in our culture. Nevertheless, as with postmodernism, we can learn to identify this stronghold by observing its authority figures and the emphasis of its media.

Authority Figures

As Moreland observes, "Scientism accords the right to define reality and speak with knowledge and authority to scientists and scientists alone. Sadly, this posture is pervasive throughout our culture."[38] Note, I'm not saying that within such a culture, only scientists are consulted for scientific matters. That's a given. Instead, I'm saying that for such a culture, scientific authority *alone* must be consulted to know the truth on any given subject whatsoever. Theological and religious matters included.

To illustrate, consider that questions regarding the afterlife, prayer, or miracles are typically reserved for clergy. However, when a journalist or talk-show host is seeking answers to these questions, they're more likely to shine the spotlight on a scientist rather than a pastor. This isn't to say that religious leaders are ignored altogether (that would be intolerant!). But if given the platform, these leaders will be portrayed merely as "authority figures" for conveying their religion's beliefs on these matters, but never as *actual* authority figures who could *prove* their religious beliefs are true. Truth is reserved for the realm of science, not "religion." Now consider how this subtle mentality is emphasized in the media.

The Emphasis of Scientism in the Media

Suppose the History Channel is doing a documentary on the existence of an afterlife. At the outset, the journalist begins by interviewing a pastor, and of course, they've chosen the worst one to represent Christianity. His theology is off, he doesn't exegete a single text, and his eschatological (i.e., end times) view is not the one you hold. Nevertheless, they end by asking about Heaven, and he gives a decent explanation of how one is saved through Christ alone. Despite everything else, you feel a modicum of comfort knowing that the gospel was broadcasted to millions. However, the scene changes to an interview with a different leader from a non-Christian religion. Then shortly after, a Muslim leader, a Buddhist monk, a Hindu priest, and so forth.

After interviewing about ten leaders from various religions, the camera fades to a prestigious-looking scientist wearing a white lab coat. Behind him is a hanging model of a skeleton, some test tubes, a few microscopes, and some bubbling blue liquid in the background, so you know he's legit. They interview one or two scientists, three at most, each experts in their own fields. When it's all said and done, you reflect on the documentary and wonder if there was an intentional bias. Here's what you noticed.

First, the questions were phrased differently for both groups. When interviewing the religious leaders, they were asked about their "*personal beliefs*," but when interviewing the scientists, they were asked about their "scientific *knowledge*." Although the religious leaders were free to share their *beliefs*, genuine *knowledge* was only afforded to the scientists.

Second, you wonder why multiple religious leaders were interviewed compared to only three scientists. This was a way of paying pseudo-homage to these religions, treating their beliefs, *not* as equally true or valid (that would be postmodernism) but as equally speculative, personal opinions. These were conducted more as an inquiry into what a particular religion has historically believed about the afterlife, but not what is *objectively* true or correct to believe about the afterlife.

By contrast, the reason for only interviewing a handful of scientists was to gain a variety of scientific explanations, all of which were presented as equally objectively true and authoritative. Contrary to what was said by the religious leaders, the neuroscientist explained away all NDEs (near-death experiences where a person dies and claims to leave their body) as nothing more than neural malfunctions caused by oxygen deprivation in the brain. Next, the chemist explained how certain drugs used for surgery can cause chemically induced hallucinations, implying the person didn't leave their body but was just heavily drugged. And finally, the evolutionist (acting more like a psychologist) explains how through evolution, human beings have manufactured superstitious beliefs about the afterlife to cope with the fear of death. Hence, the "spiritual" is reduced to the natural.

Therefore, we have on the one hand, the "priests of religion" who are the authorities of their personal beliefs, but on the other, the "priests of science" who are the final authorities on knowledge. Who do you think will be believed and seen as the real authority figures here?

Scientism in Pop-Culture

When it comes to pop culture, the same sentiment applies, but often with less ambiguity. In movies and tv shows, Christians are often portrayed as anti-science, naive, close-minded individuals who are always trying to force their "religious beliefs" on the other characters. By contrast, the protagonist is portrayed as a charming, witty, intelligent individual who knows that religion is nothing more than a superstitious fairy tale for weak-minded individuals. I challenge you to think of one popular level production that depicts a religious character as an intellectual or, at the very least, a character that *accurately* presents Christian theology. I certainly cannot.

IDENTIFYING ITS PRESENCE AND INFLUENCE IN CONVERSATION

As we'll see, scientism and naturalism (our next stronghold) often go hand-in-hand when influencing a person or culture. For this reason, we'll utilize this section in the next chapter for identifying both strongholds in conversation.

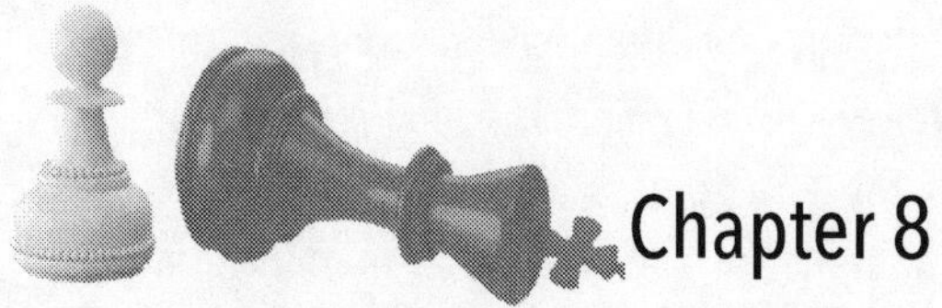

Chapter 8

Identifying Naturalism

The Epistemology and the Ontology

At its core, naturalism is an ontological position (dealing with what is real and exists), but one that has epistemic implications (concerning what can be known and is true). Essentially, it is a view that rejects any supernatural, immaterial explanations, concluding that the physical, material world is all that exists—nothing more, nothing less. Hence, for the naturalist, the physical world is all that exists (the ontology), and thus, knowledge is limited to that which can be discovered about the physical (the epistemology). To elaborate on these features, consider my prelude to this stronghold.

My Exposure to Naturalism

During my freshman year of college, I intentionally took a class in philosophy from an atheist professor whom all my peers warned me to avoid. We'll call him Professor P. This professor was known for being condescendingly hostile toward Christianity, and I was told that if I took his course, I might lose my faith. While much can be said about my time in his class, one day stands as the pivotal shift in my life and ministry, and on this day, I was introduced to the forceful weight of naturalism.

As class began, Professor P reached into his pocket, pulled out a small anti-depressant pill, and held it to the light for us to see. After gazing at the pill pinched between his fingers, he began his lecture:

> Religion wants us to believe in some "immaterial soul," and because of this, we can have hope in an afterlife, seeing our friends and family that have gone before us. And according to Christianity, my thoughts, emotions, and sensations–allegedly immaterial as well–all reside within my "non-physical soul." But here's the problem. If I took this anti-depressant pill, *which is physical*, it has the power to change my thoughts, emotions, and sensations. But how can this be? How can something tiny and physical affect the immaterial?
>
> Because see, every time a neurologist scans the brain, all he sees are neurons firing, and every time a scientist examines the body under a microscope, all he finds are the basic elements of carbon, hydrogen, and oxygen. But no scientist has ever found *anything* even remotely close to something like a soul. How do we explain this? I'll tell you how, and the answer is simple. There is no soul. There is no Heaven, there is no hell, there is no God, and there is no afterlife. We are nothing more than a physical brain and body. A meat machine of physics and chemistry, and we must learn to live with this fact, get on with our lives, and stop believing in these fanciful fairy tales... Class dismissed.

As a freshman in college, I'd never met someone who didn't believe in the soul (I thought everyone did!), and I'd never heard an argument against it. But something even more troubling crossed my mind because I knew the existence of the soul was no small matter for Christianity.

To paraphrase the words of Paul in 1 Corinthians 15:13-18, if Christ has not been raised from the dead, then Christianity is false. Hence, the truth of Christianity literally hinges on the truth of the resurrection. But now consider this; if there is no soul, then there can be no resurrection, and once again, if there is no resurrection, then Christianity cannot be true.[39] So, for the first time in my life, I heard an argument that, if true, would prove that Christianity was false! How would you respond?

Unfortunately, it's beyond the scope of this book to provide an in-depth response to his remarks (I'm kidding, sort of) but rest assured we'll address these points in a later chapter. For now, some observations from Professor P's argument can be made for identifying three key "*isms*" associated with (if not inherent to) naturalism as a worldview. Namely, **empiricism**, **reductionism**, and **physicalism**.

Three Key "Isms" of Naturalism

Empiricism. According to naturalism, if all that exists within reality is physical (the ontology), then the only things that can be tested or discovered are purely physical entities. This leads to an epistemology known as **empiricism**—the view that *knowledge is restricted and limited to the five senses*[40] (i.e., empirical science, e.g., scientism).

Reductionism. From this, it follows that on naturalism, everything *can* and *must* be explained through natural processes. This leads to what is known as **reductionism**—the attempt to explain some entity X (in this case, the soul) by reducing it to some entity Y (the brain and body). This can be identified by spotting the "*nothing but*" or "*nothing more than*" language. For instance, if I said that marriage is *nothing but* signing a piece of paper for the government, then I've reduced the essence of marriage to *nothing more than* a legal document. Within naturalism, everything (prayers, miracles, souls, etc.) is reduced and explained away as *nothing more than* physics and chemistry.

Physicalism. As a result of the first two, most naturalists hold to what is known as physicalism (sometimes referred to as **materialism**—the view that all things are composed of matter), which is essentially the naturalist ontology applied to human beings. According to **physicalism**, human beings are reducible to *nothing more than* physical properties and parts; no soul is needed to explain anything.

Now consider how each of these "isms" is present in Professor P's argument. In defense of his conclusion that there is no soul, he alludes to *looking* at brains and *examining* bodies. This is empiricism (the idea that knowledge is discovered solely through the five senses). Next, we can immediately spot reductionism in the "nothing more than" language, reducing human beings to *nothing more than* a physical brain and body, leading to what we now know as physicalism (the idea that human beings are purely physical objects).

So, in summation, suffice it to say that on naturalism, empiricism (that knowledge is limited to the five senses) can be seen as its epistemology, physicalism (that human beings are purely physical objects) stems from its ontology, and reductionism (reducing some entity X to some entity Y) is how everything will be explained away in terms of chemistry and physics (i.e., natural processes).

OPPOSITION TO CHRISTIANITY

To reiterate, if there is no resurrection, Christianity cannot be true (1 Corinthians 15:13-18). By the same token, if there is no soul, then there can be no resurrection and, thus, Christianity is false. In this way, naturalism directly opposes Christianity, inevitably creating barriers for *considering the possibility that Christianity might be true*. Furthermore, if one believes the natural world is all that exists, then a God who is, by definition, supernatural (literally, beyond nature) cannot exist. Therefore, naturalism doesn't merely lead to skepticism regarding Christianity, but if true, would be an outright refutation of it.

IDENTIFYING ITS PRESENCE AND INFLUENCE IN THE CHURCH

Given what we've discussed, you may think that such a stronghold could never infiltrate the church because detecting its presence would be obvious, right? Sadly, this is not the case. Not only has naturalism influenced our beliefs within the church, but its presence has gone largely unnoticed. When teaching at various churches on the subject, I've learned to demonstrate this influence by asking a few questions. This requires audience participation, and I'd like for you, the reader, to participate as well.

God, Brains, and Thinking

First, I ask the congregation to point to which part of their body thinks. Virtually everyone points to their head, signifying that the brain thinks (was this your response as well?). I confirm this by asking if the brain is necessary for thinking, and most respond by nodding their head yes. Then, my next question is this—does God have a brain? At this point, most people either refrain from answering or gaze in confusion as if the thought has never crossed their minds. What's worse is that some respond by saying "yes," God has a brain!

After glancing at the church's sign to confirm I'm not in a Mormon church (Mormons believe that God has a *physical* body), I explain that the answer is no, God does not have a brain. As Scripture teaches, "God is spirit, and those who worship him must worship in spirit and in truth" (John 4:24, ESV). But does God think? Undoubtedly, yes, and Scripture states His thoughts are more than the grains of sand (Psalms 139:17-18). But now it seems we have a conundrum on our hands.

If the brain is what thinks and is necessary for it, then how is it that God has no brain and yet thinks just fine? Moreover, are we not made in His image, and if so, why do we believe it's the brain that thinks? Put differently, why do churches find themselves in this conundrum after being presented with these questions? Because, quite frankly, this never should've been a conundrum to begin with.

Throughout the history of Christianity, the church has always held to the doctrine of a soul that grounds one's faculty of mind, both of which are immaterial, non-physical entities. So, if I may come clean, my first question (What part of your body thinks?) was a trick question. Because see, if we are made in God's image—immaterial souls with minds—then there is *no part of your body* that "thinks." Nevertheless, because we've allowed the worldview of naturalism (via reductionism) to infiltrate our thinking, this stronghold has gone largely unnoticed. Allow me to explain the problem.

Naturalism and the Separation of "The Secular and The Sacred"

As with scientism, when the church withdraws from the public sphere of ideas, it allows for the false dichotomy of "the secular and the sacred." As a result, these strongholds drive our culture, lead our academic institutions, and make the church irrelevant and unnecessary.

To illustrate, we now know that when a person thinks there is neurological activity in the brain. Because of this, we're told by a naturalized culture that it's the brain that thinks. Perceiving this to be a point of neutrality, the church happily concedes the matter and reserves "spiritual" discussions about the soul for Sunday school. Granted, we are immaterial souls made in the image of an immaterial God, but sure, let's agree it's the brain that thinks, *not the immaterial mind*. No harm, no foul. But surely, this isn't a point of neutrality, but naturalism!

Nevertheless, because we've failed to develop the eyes to see it, we unquestionably follow these ideas, assuming they're innocent and unrelated to "spiritual matters." Hence, we engage in their language—talking about "brains that think"—then arrive at church on Sunday morning, lift our hands, and worship a God that has no brain and thinks just fine. But woe is the day we take our theology seriously and allow these contradictory beliefs to meet. Instead, we set these beliefs aside and enable the culture to inform us on the "secular" while we handle the "sacred."

Lacking Holistic, Worldview Thinking

Note how a "secular and sacred" separation makes Christian doctrine a subset of beliefs only relevant on Sundays, whereas the rest of the week encompasses "secular" beliefs relevant to our vocations. As Moreland observes,

> "…there has emerged a secular/sacred separation in our understanding of the Christian life with the result that Christian teaching and practice are privatized and placed in a separate compartment from the public or so-called secular activities of life."[41]

So, in essence, the central problem isn't that the church doesn't think about these issues, but that it hasn't trained its members *to think holistically* about these issues as they relate to worldview. Put differently, it is not that we've failed to think, but that we've failed to *think about our thinking*; not that we've failed to form beliefs, but have failed to learn how to form *beliefs about our beliefs*. We lack holistic, worldview thinking. Hence, there was no implicit conundrum in my questions above, just an implicit conundrum in how we un-holistically think about these issues.

IDENTIFYING ITS PRESENCE AND INFLUENCE IN CULTURE

Authority Figures

As with scientism, epistemic authority is currently given to figures within any field of study that utilizes empirical methods of investigation. Accordingly, only those who have the knowledge and skills necessary for studying the physical world (i.e., scientists) are the ones that have the right to declare what exists (ontology) and what can be objectively known about reality (epistemology).

For instance, suppose a Christian reports feeling a profound sense of God's presence when they pray. If interviewed, the journalist may ask about their personal experiences or beliefs about prayer. However, the scientific naturalist will explain how a region in the brain elicits these feelings of euphoria and deep connection, but that's all they are: deep, artificial feelings caused by neuronal activity. Hence, the person is not feeling God (says the reductionist) but feeling the placebo effect of prayer via chemical reactions. Nothing more, nothing less.

So, while a journalist may ask a believer about the pragmatic effects of prayer, he'll ultimately turn to a scientist to learn the "objective truths" about prayer. Not because this adds to what the Christian has said about prayer, but because they believe the Christian is wrong and there's no God to pray to in the first place. Hence, although the act of prayer is affirmed, its effects are reduced to natural, therapeutic practices that stimulate chemicals in the brain.

Additionally, some atheists claim "scientists have discovered" how these effects can be reproduced in the lab, proving once and for all there is no God. While writing this paragraph, I did a quick online search for "presence of God during prayer in the brain," and here is what I found.

The Emphasis of Naturalism in the Media

The top search result was from *Medical News Today* with an article entitled "What Religion Does to Your Brain." The first sentence of the first paragraph read, "Whether or not a divine power truly does exist might be a matter of opinion, but the neurophysiological effects of religious belief are scientific facts that can be accurately measured."[42] Additionally, there's now a "neuroscience of theological belief" known as "neurotheology," which purportedly "made some surprising discoveries that are bound to change how we think about spirituality." Consider the following excerpts:

- Research has suggested that damage to a certain brain region can make you feel as though someone's in the room when nobody's there.
- If a divine experience proves to be biologically predetermined, does having the right scientific information enable us to create the illusion of a god?
- Pieces of the puzzle are coming together to form a scientific picture of divinity that is shaping up to be quite different from those we find in the holy books.
- Participants were "feeling the spirit," those who reported the most intense spiritual feelings displayed increased activity in the bilateral nucleus accumbens, as well as the frontal attentional and ventromedial prefrontal cortical loci.
- Out-of-body experiences are in your body.
- Dr. Michael Persinger...designed what came to be known as the "God Helmet"... a device that is able to simulate religious experiences by stimulating an individual's temporoparietal lobes using magnetic fields.

At any rate, we can sum up the entire article with the following statement: scientists have discovered that when you pray, stuff happens in the brain. What a remarkable discovery. And this can be recreated by stimulating those same regions in the brain? Incredible. But what follows from this? Nothing important nor profound.

To illustrate, suppose I'm asked to think about the beach while a neuroscientist identifies the brain patterns correlated with my experience. Next, they place a "Beach Helmet" on and stimulate these regions, which, in turn, recreate the euphoric feelings of being at the beach. Would it follow from this that, therefore, beaches do not exist? Of course not. Yet, when it comes to theological matters, this somehow disproves the existence of God and the reality of prayer? My eyes strain from rolling. But I digress.

Suffice it to say that only about 5% of the article contained *actual* empirical science. The rest was poorly reasoned, unchecked philosophical speculation based on a prior commitment to naturalism. Oxford professor and philosopher of science, Dr. John Lennox, sums up my sentiment best:

> What this all goes to show is that nonsense remains nonsense, even when talked by world-famous scientists. What serves to obscure the illogicality of such statements is the fact that they are made by scientists; and the general public, not surprisingly, assumes that they are statements of science and takes them on authority. That is why it is important to point out that they are not statements of science, and any statement, whether made by a scientist or not, should be open to logical analysis. Immense prestige and authority does not compensate for faulty logic.[43]

Naturalism in Pop-Culture

In popular culture, naturalism can be identified by its emphasis on physicalism and reductionism. For example, when it comes to issues of morality, ethics is reduced to the neurological effects of pleasure and pain. Thus, abortion becomes *nothing more than* removing a clump of cells from the body. When it comes to love, it is *nothing but* chemical reactions in the brain, making intercourse *nothing more than* two consenting adults of any gender exchanging bodily fluids. When it comes to persons, there is no soul, only brains and bodies devoid of free will, acting in a way that's causally determined by the laws of chemistry and physics. And when it comes to our self-worth (given that human beings are reducible to our elemental parts), one article stated that the average person is worth "just $1."[44] It's no wonder we see a shift in our culture concerning the sanctity of marriage, love, the life of the unborn, moral responsibility, self-respect, and a rise in anxiety and depression.

IDENTIFYING ITS PRESENCE AND INFLUENCE IN CONVERSATION

Scientific-Naturalism (Scientism and Naturalism Combined)

As previously mentioned, scientism and naturalism typically go hand-in-hand as strongholds. Taken together, they're referred to as the single worldview known as **scientific naturalism**. Scientism representing the epistemic question, and what's known as **philosophical naturalism** (the view that only the physical realm exists) representing the ontological question.

As we'll see in chapter 17, presenting evidence and arguments is fundamental for witnessing to nonbelievers. However, many will dismiss much (if not all) of the relevant evidence needed for answering the question "Does God exist?" when holding to this worldview. For this reason, gathering their perspective on evidence will be important, and this can be accomplished during the "why" portion of the conversation (see chapter 4).

The most basic way to identify this stronghold is to ask the person for the type of evidence they're looking for and, more pertinently, what evidence would convince them God exists. Why this approach? Because according to scientific naturalism, all existing entities and events are part of the physical, natural world. Thus, for the scientific naturalist, all claims *must be subject to scientific, empirical investigation*.

Although this perspective is common among nonbelievers, do not assume this, but learn to identify the stronghold by paying careful attention to the kind of evidence they request. For example, a nonbeliever may ask:

- What *scientific evidence* do you have for God?
- Can you *demonstrate* this evidence?
- How can you *test* this evidence?

Given that all these claims revolve around the notion of "evidence," it becomes essential to ask what the person means by "evidence." Most of the time, the revealing answer will be "empirical evidence" or "scientific evidence," and some may go as far as to say, "The only evidence that is available to us: science!"

What we've learned in the previous sections of this chapter has provided explicit (or implicit) ways for identifying this stronghold. Rather than repeat these here, I encourage you to go back and study or discuss these sections with your family or small group to see if you can further develop methods for identifying these on your own. As we move into providing responses to these strongholds in the coming chapters, we'll simultaneously further our approach for identifying them as well.

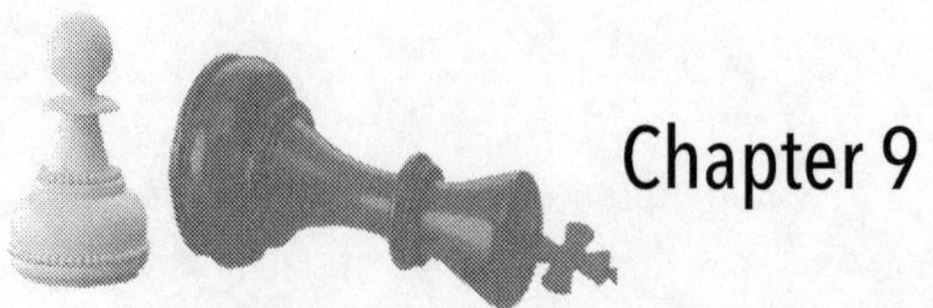

Chapter 9

Creating Opportunities for Evangelism

Given what we've learned about the culture and identifying its strongholds, consider how "having the eyes to see" them can create evangelistic opportunities in everyday conversations. Starting such conversations can feel awkward and unnatural for most people, waiting for the opportunity to forcefully and "artificially redirect the discussion to our testimony or something of the sort."[45] But this need not be the case. As Moreland observes, "A life of study and intellectual growth enhances one's effectiveness in personal evangelism in many ways."

For instance, I've often said that every person I meet wants to talk about God and apologetics. I say this jokingly, but the principle conveys how any occasion becomes an opportunity for gospel conversations. Why? Because, quite frankly, there is no separation between the "the secular and sacred." All truth is God's truth, and all that exists is, in one way or another, grounded in His nature. All things point back to Him, and incorporating this principle simply takes a developed mind (Mark 12:30), an understanding of the times (1 Chronicles 12:32), and having eyes to see the connections (all of which has been covered in previous chapters). Summarizing this sentiment, Moreland states:

> If a person has developed a Christian mind, she can relax because she has an understanding of and a Christian view about a number of "secular" topics. In such a situation, it would be hard to have a normal conversation without Christianity coming up naturally and in a way relevant to the topic of discus-

> sion. Moreover, a well-developed mind can see connections between what a friend is saying and other issues of which the friend may not be aware... If a person sees the connections, she can simply ask well-placed questions that naturally lead to a discussion of broader worldview issues, including God and our relationship to Him. In such a case, the pressure is off because a person has the intellectual categories necessary to make natural connections between Christianity and a host of regular conversation topics. There is no need to try to find a crack in the discussion to insert a gospel presentation utterly unrelated to the flow of conversation. What a joyful fruit of the intellectual life this is![46]

In the early stages of writing this book, I began explaining this concept to my brother-in-law who, for 30 years, has been involved in law enforcement, working in pro-active units, investigations, and extensive amounts of tactical training. Before I could finish the thought, he stopped me and said, "Oh, yea. I know exactly what you're talking about. We do this all the time!"

In his line of work, this is known as **situational awareness**. When entering a building, he explained how paying attention to the environment and its people is natural. He identifies the exits, entrances, and potential escape routes. He looks for factors that don't fit the environment, such as body language, attire inappropriate for the weather, and the shape of bulges underneath clothing that extend past the body.

Given this description, you may think he's the type of person that sees everything as a threat, riddled with anxiety, fidgeting his hands in fear, and constantly on his feet. But I can assure you he is one of the most calm, collected, soft-spoken people I know. Because, see, when you understand the environment and remain vigilant, threats are minimized, and opportunities for assertiveness can be created if needed. With respect to apologetics in evangelism, the same principle applies.

APOLOGETIC AWARENESS IN CASUAL CONVERSATIONS

Given my exposure to naturalism in college, my main area of study has been **the philosophy of mind**, which deals with questions of the soul, free will, and the nature of consciousness. Because of this, I typically cringe when I hear others (especially Christians) use the words "mind" and "brain" synonymously. Have you ever heard someone say, "the thought is in my brain" or, when referring to someone intelligent, say, "that person's brain contains a lot of information!" Those who know me personally know this is a pet peeve of mine.

When Christians utter these statements, I remind them that we are immaterial souls that possess immaterial minds and that our thoughts are in the mind, *not* the brain. But the response from fellow believers is typically, "meh, same thing." Is it, though? Granted, we may know what the person means by these statements, and maybe I'm just being nitpicky with semantics. Am I, though? Perhaps. Or, perhaps it's that the influence of naturalism is so prevalent in our culture that it's even reflected in the way we think and speak as believers.

I share this as a preface for demonstrating how possessing the relevant knowledge in these areas has led to evangelistic opportunities and, given what we've learned thus far, I want to show how you can do this as well. Surprisingly, the first time this happened for me, it was unintentional.

Example #1: Pick My Brain?

In a previous job, a coworker once asked if they could "pick my brain," and I jokingly replied, "why would you want to do a thing like that?" Confused by my failed humor, they explained that they had a few questions about a situation and wanted my input. "Oh, in that case," I said, "I'll do you one better. I'll let you pick my mind, given that my brain only contains matter and fluid."

What began as a joking response to a non-spiritual question quickly became an evangelistic opportunity. Within minutes, the conversation revolved around the existence of the soul, how we know it's real, and ended with me sharing about the nature of God and how we relate to

Him. I discovered that my apologetic awareness became a powerful tool for starting evangelistic conversations, and moving forward, I became intentional with this approach.

Example #2: Rights, Values, and Robot "Persons"

Later that year, I was casually chatting with coworkers when the conversation turned into a discussion about the latest sci-fi show on television. The plot revolved around the creation of artificial intelligence and how the government was creating robots that were indistinguishable from human beings. One coworker remarked that if such a thing happened, then "due to the science," we'd have to grant human rights to these "sentient" machines because they'd be "no different than us." In response, I asked for his thoughts on what makes something a "person" and what it is about being human that grants us objective rights or value in the first place. From here, the discussion inevitably became an evangelistic conversation.

Note, I wasn't forcing the discussion to go in this direction. How not? Because I used what my coworker said and asked a few questions about his views. But consider the strategy behind my questions. Given the Christian worldview, we are human beings with souls (grounding our personhood) that bear the image of God (grounding our intrinsic value). Additionally, objective moral values, if they exist, must be grounded in an eternal, personal being that transcends our existence—namely, God (an argument that we'll unpack in Chapter 20). Hence, the question of God and salvation was at the heart of the discussion.

Taking this approach kept the conversation cordial, non-combative, and after providing his views on the subject, he naturally asked about mine. Thus, what began as a casual discussion about a tv show became an evangelistic opportunity in an everyday conversation.

Unpacking the Examples

In these examples, we can see the assumptions of scientism and naturalism embedded within the discussion. Nevertheless, even if a point was made in jest (as in the first example), it opened the conversation to philosophical, spiritual reflections that led to a more serious though relaxed discussion. Granted, it was relaxing and enjoyable for me because I've familiarized myself with these issues and was able to implement a sense of "apologetic situational awareness" into the discussion. This allowed me to maneuver the conversation into an area I was comfortable with naturally and casually, turning these everyday conversations into evangelistic opportunities. I can assure you that the information in this book, if you study and take it seriously, can and will help you do the same.

To demonstrate, I'd like to propose a final example for you to use what we've discussed in the previous chapters and apply it to the scenario. Given what you've learned thus far, I'm confident you will have the "eyes to see" and identify the stronghold for yourself.

Example #3: Tolerating All Views?

Jane: But I think we should tolerate all points of view.

Eric: What about those who believe we should *not* tolerate all points of view? Should we tolerate those as well?

Jane: What do you mean?

Eric: Consider the terrorist attacks on 9/11. Those men committed these crimes because of their beliefs. Should we tolerate their point of view?

Jane: Well, no, but if people are not harming one another, we can all agree that everyone is entitled to their own religion, right?

Eric: Sure, but could we also agree that not everyone is entitled to their own truth?

By now, you should be able to recognize the postmodern sentiment in the discussion. But note, I never brought up the word "postmodernism" or explicitly labeled her view as relativism. Nevertheless, because I recognized the stronghold in her comments, I was able to cordially maneuver the conversation forward by formulating questions appropriate to her position (hence, adapt your approach accordingly).

From here, the person may ask what truth is, how we can know which religion is true, or lead to a further discussion of tolerance. Either way, by having the eyes to see the stronghold, an opportunity for evangelism has been created. As you read the coming chapters, think of ways to implement what you learn into everyday conversations. With time and practice, utilizing this skill becomes easier, and you'll find that *any conversation* can be the right opportunity.

PART 3B

What is Our Goal? Responding to the Strongholds

Chapter 10

Maneuvering a Conversation: A Foundation for Tools and Tactics

Thus far, we've learned how to identify who we're talking to (atheist, agnostic, or skeptic), identify the stronghold (in church, culture, and conversation), and are now in a position to further adapt our approach accordingly. That is the purpose of this chapter. To provide you with a foundation of tools and tactics to maneuver a conversation, set up the response, and tear down the stronghold.

TWO BIBLICAL PRINCIPLES FOR OFFERING RESPONSES

Biblical Basis: Colossians 4:5-6

Conduct yourself with wisdom in your interactions with outsiders (non-believers), make the most of each opportunity [treating it as something precious]. Let your speech at all times be gracious and pleasant, seasoned with salt, so that you will know how to answer each one [who questions you] (AMP).

In this passage, we are presented with two important principles for conversing with and responding to the challenges, claims, or positions of the nonbeliever:

1. Make the most use of the time.

2. Know *how* to answer.

Before unpacking these, consider the word of advice that precedes each principle. "*Conduct yourself with wisdom*" (to know how to make the most use of your time) and "*let your conversation always be full of grace, pleasant, and seasoned with salt*" (so that you may know how to answer everyone). In all this, Paul's overarching theme is simple: *keep the-main-thing-the-main-thing*, and sticking to these principles will help us do just that.

1. Make the Most Use of the Time (Theological Triage)

To illustrate this first principle, suppose you had one hour to speak with a nonbeliever before Christ returned. In this time frame, at least four topics could be discussed:

- The age of the earth.
- Creation vs. evolution.
- Biblical inerrancy.
- The existence of God and the resurrection of Jesus.

Now ask yourself, which one of these is essential for salvation? Only the latter: the existence of God and the resurrection of Jesus. To be clear, I'm not saying the other three are not suitable topics for discussion, but that belief in those three is *not essential for salvation*.

If this troubles you, think of this as a sort of "theological triage." In medical practices, if a patient were rushed into the emergency room with a scraped knee, a broken wrist, and a bullet in the chest, which of these should the doctor address first? Clearly, the bullet in the chest. In the medical community, this is known as **triage**: the prioritization of treating wounds or illnesses in order of their severity. When witnessing to nonbelievers, the same principle applies.

Is a fully developed theology important? Absolutely! I argued for this in the first chapter. But again, what is the priority? To see them come to a salvific knowledge of God. Thankfully, entrance into Heaven is *not* predicated on passing a theological exam. Indeed, *every one of us* will inevitably enter the afterlife with *some* false theological beliefs, and I would rather the person go to Heaven with false theological beliefs than go to hell with false theological beliefs.

Therefore, if we wish to "make the most of every opportunity" with nonbelievers, then we *must learn* to keep the-main-thing-the-main-thing. Again, salvation is the priority, and this will undoubtedly require theological triage.

2. Knowing HOW to Answer (Not WHAT to Answer)

In this second principle for conversing with nonbelievers, Paul chooses his words carefully in saying that we ought to know *how* to answer and not *what* to answer. This distinction is vitally important. To illustrate, suppose someone asked, "have you stopped beating your wife, yes or no?" If you answer yes, you've admitted that while you're not *currently* beating your wife, you did at one point. If you answer no, you've admitted that you still are. But is a "yes or no" the only possible response? Clearly not. One could respond by saying that you've never beaten your wife to begin with, or, as one middle school student replied, "Wife? I don't even have a girlfriend!"

However, there is another way of responding that doesn't answer the question directly but instead, questions the question. "Why would you assume that I beat my wife?" (or "Why would you assume I'm married?). In other words, if I disagree with the underlying assumption behind a question, then questioning the question becomes appropriate. In this instance, it's not essential that we know *what* to answer but *how* to answer. As we'll see, not all questions merit direct responses, and questioning a question can help clarify and further the conversation.

Putting a Pebble in Their Shoe: Gardening vs. Harvesting

While it would be ideal that every person we witness to drops to their knees and surrenders their life to Christ, it should be stated upfront that our goal for this portion of the conversation is a modest one. As author and apologist Greg Koukl states, we simply want to "put a stone in their shoe."[47] That is, we want to give the nonbeliever something to think about. A "nugget of truth" that causes their walk to be a little uncomfortable, forcing each step to press against the pebble of truth we've given them.

To grasp this point, Koukl provides a helpful distinction between gardening and harvesting in evangelism. We all want a harvest, but before there can be a harvest, there must first be a gardener. In this way, apologetics is a "gardening" type of ministry, and a good gardener knows how to cultivate the soil, supply adequate water, and sweats on his knees to pull weeds. Such work takes time, patience, and requires the relevant "gardening knowledge" to address the situation.

In evangelism, this is like witnessing to a nonbeliever—listening to their story, answering their questions, and helping them wrestle with their doubt. When this is done effectively, the harvester may later come and "reap where he has not sown." As Jesus explains, "the saying 'One sows and another reaps' is true. I sent you to reap what you have not worked for. Others have done the hard work, and you have reaped the benefits of their labor" (John 4:37-38). While we may not all be harvesters in evangelism, we all have our place in gardening so "the sower and the reaper may be glad together" (John 4:36). Both are working toward the same purpose, and God alone makes it grow (1 Corinthians 3:5-9).

A FOUNDATION FOR TOOLS AND TACTICS

If you go back, you'll discover that Paul's two principles for offering responses have been implemented from the beginning. Recall the young lady who said the Bible was "full of contradictions" in answer to the question, "Why are you an atheist?" Rather than respond to her attacks against Christianity, I focused on the central issue; "And how does this prove God does not exist?" Hence, I 1) made the most use of my time (the first principle) by 2) knowing *how* to answer as opposed to *what* to answer (the second principle). This allowed me to keep the conversation on track, keep the main-thing-the-main-thing, and, more importantly, accomplish our modest goal of putting a pebble in her shoe. I want to show you how to do this as well, and it begins by laying a foundation of tools and tactics for maneuvering the conversation.

The Strategy: Battleship or Chess?

Consider the difference between a game of Battleship and a game of chess. In a Battleship game, your moves are generally random guesses, arbitrarily calling out coordinates in hopes of hitting your opponent's ships. It is, in every sense, a "hit-or-miss" strategy. By contrast, a chess game requires far more strategy, encompassing careful thought, timely execution, and knowing how to maneuver the pieces with precision. Before touching the board, a chess master can identify the pieces and knows the possible routes each can take. As a result, not only can he plan out his moves, but more importantly, can anticipate his opponent's next move. It is a game of intellect that, in every sense, requires having the "eyes to see."

Similarly, our strategy for witnessing to nonbelievers must be more akin to chess than Battleship. That is, we do not want our questions or responses to be given randomly or in the dark, but with precision and accuracy toward the desired end (1 Corinthians 9:24, 26). I'm not implying that we view our conversations with nonbelievers as a game. Instead, I'm stating that the same strategic mentality must apply if we wish to conduct fruitful, time-worthy conversations.

For this reason, we spent the last few chapters familiarizing ourselves with the dominant strongholds of our culture, knowing the "possible routes" each view may take. For instance, we now know that a skeptic will likely turn the conversation to a discussion about knowledge and certainty, a postmodernist may move to the question of truth, a person holding to scientism will appeal to science, and a naturalist will likely take a reductionistic approach toward persons (i.e., physicalism), miracles, or prayer.

However, merely knowing "the moves" that a position *may take* does not tell us the move they *will make* in the conversation. Much like in a game of chess, one begins with an overall strategy until the first move is made and the approach is adapted accordingly. While there is no particular order for these "moves" when conversing with nonbelievers, there is always a first step; gather information.

Two Powerful Questions for Gathering Information:

In his book, *Tactics: A Game Plan for Discussing Your Christian Convictions*, Koukl offers two powerful questions for gathering information:

1. What do you mean by that?
2. How did you come to that conclusion?

Consider how these can be applied to a stronghold in conversation. For example, you may suspect that the person you are speaking with is a postmodernist—evident by their move to shift the conversation to the question of truth. Rather than respond to the stronghold immediately, ensure this is their position by using a variation of one (if not both) of the two questions above (e.g., "What do you mean by truth?"). Moreover, if a person claims that "science is the *only* way to gain knowledge about reality" (scientism), then you can simply ask, "And how did you come to that conclusion?" If a person asserts that we are "*nothing more than* brains and bodies" (naturalism via reductionism), then you can either ask, "What do you mean by that?" or, "How did you come to that conclusion?"

When doing so, Koukl explains:

> Don't be surprised, then, when you ask the question... and you get a blank stare and dead air in return... much of the time, people simply do not know what they mean... Even though people have strong opinions, they rarely reflect on their views. Often they're merely repeating slogans...They're forced to think about what they do mean, so be patient with the pause in the dialogue.[48]

Put differently, learn to allow the conversation to sit in uncomfortable silence when needed. This alone can have a powerful effect, even though all you've done is ask an honest, though strategically placed question.

Gain Clarity: Reword the Position in Your Own Words

From here, if the person has explained their view, it's a good idea to reiterate their position back to them in your own words for clarity. Remember, before we can offer a response to their view, we must first ensure we've understood it. Doing so accomplishes one of two things, if not both. First, it eliminates the common mistake of talking past each other due to a simple misunderstanding and keeps us from mischaracterizing their position. Second, as you'll see, *strategically* rewording a person's position may ironically serve as an implicit response to their claim. You'd be surprised how often this move exposes the absurdity of a view.

As an example, consider the following dialogue I had with a student after speaking at a secular college campus on abortion.

Student: I agree that the unborn are human persons, and I would even say that I disagree with abortion. But if we don't allow legal abortions, women will end up harming themselves when seeking unsafe, illegal abortions.

Eric: Before I respond, let me see if I understand your position. It seems you're saying that if we don't allow women to *kill their innocent, unborn children* legally, they might be harmed when trying to *kill their innocent, unborn children* illegally. Is that correct?

Student: Well, that's a good point. I suppose you're right.

Eric: But I haven't made a point. I've only reworded the position back to you.

Reword a Position With a Counter Example

In addition to rewording a person's position for clarity, we can also offer counterexamples (applying their position to a different scenario) to ensure that we've, at the very least, understood the *principle* of their position. This too can expose the irrationality of a view and serve as an implicit response. Continuing the discussion with the student above, I applied this tool accordingly.

Eric: But let me respond to your view by applying it to a different scenario and tell me if you still think the argument is valid. Suppose I provided statistics that showed how burglars were increasingly injuring themselves by breaking into homes through windows, barb-wired fences, and so forth. Because of this, I argue that if we legalized burglary, these criminals would no longer injure themselves by illegally breaking into homes. Would you agree with this argument?

Student: Well, no, because what they're doing ultimately harms innocent people, and that's not right.

Eric: Exactly. Which is precisely my point against abortion.

Maneuvering the Pieces With Precision

Returning to the analogy once more, note that while a chess master begins with an overall strategy, his proceeding moves are guided by the previous moves of his opponent. In the same way, when we are provided with answers to our questions, we must learn to adapt our approach in accordance with the new information we've been given. Just as no two games of chess are identical, no two conversations with nonbelievers will be the same.

At each point in the discussion, you may ask another question, respond to their answer, or both; offer a response to their answer in the form of a question (as demonstrated above). Although the overall goal remains the same, how we achieve this goal will vary from stronghold to stronghold, and more specifically, from person to person, and even more so, from conversation to conversation.

Two Types of Responses: Refuting vs. Rebutting

One of the most important distinctions to remember when knowing *how* to answer (as opposed to *what* to answer) is the distinction between a *refutation* and a *rebuttal*. In a **refutation**, you aim to prove that the person's conclusion is false. In a **rebuttal**, you're simply showing they haven't proven their conclusion is true (i.e., it fails to meet its burden of proof). To practice this concept, consider the following claim:

Claim: It will rain today because I am wearing brown shoes.

First, we can break down the claim into two parts. The **conclusion**, "it will rain today," and the **justification**, "because I am wearing brown shoes." In a *refutation*, you attack the conclusion, whereas in a *rebuttal*, you attack the justification.

A Refutation: No, it will not rain today because the atmospheric pressure, temperature, weather, and moisture in the air are insufficient to provide rain.

A Rebuttal: No, not necessarily, because you wore brown shoes yesterday, and it didn't rain.

Note how a refutation requires far more work and knowledge of a subject, whereas a rebuttal only requires knowledge of their justification (which is already provided in the claim). Hence, providing a *refutation* of this claim requires that I possess *all the relevant knowledge* concerning atmospheric pressure, temperature, weather, and moisture in the air. However, such knowledge may not be available to me, and thus, providing a refutation becomes virtually impossible. By contrast, given that I already possess the relevant knowledge of their justification, providing a rebuttal is easily available. So, even when refutations are impossible, rebuttals can and will suffice as adequate responses for dismantling the stronghold.

Offering Rebuttals Over Refutations

Again, providing a refutation requires far more work and background knowledge concerning a particular issue, whereas offering a rebuttal comes much easier and with less effort. In evangelism, there are at least two more advantages for preferring rebuttals over refutations.

First, consider that when a person is deeply devoted to a worldview, they're less likely to consider alternatives. But note that with a rebuttal, we can concede for the sake of argument that the other person's claim *may be* true and yet demonstrate how their reasons for believing so are inadequate (e.g., wearing brown shoes without rain). Consequently, offering rebuttals can be far more impactful than refutations.

Second, consider that a person may hold to a view, not because it has sufficient evidence, but because it fits comfortably with their lifestyle—and such beliefs have gone largely unchallenged. Hence, they may not have seriously considered the rationale behind their position, and offering a rebuttal forces them to closely examine the epistemic structure of their worldview.

For these reasons, a critical task of apologetics in evangelism (specifically in tearing down strongholds) is to help the other person recognize the overall inconsistency, flaws, or absurdity of their position. Remember, when offering rebuttals, we're not attacking the conclusion but exposing the weakness of its justification. This is, in every sense, putting a pebble in their shoe.

Chapter 11

The "Lazy Approach"

Now that we've laid a foundation for maneuvering a conversation, I'd like to introduce you to the approach I take when responding to the nonbeliever's beliefs, claims, or position. I call it ***The Lazy Approach***. In actuality, there's nothing *inherently* lazy about it, but I've given it this name to convey a minimalist approach that takes little effort and has a maximum impact. I've used this approach in all my evangelistic encounters, ranging from casual conversations to formal public debates, and we'll employ these tools in our responses going forward. So, building on the previous chapter, allow me to unpack the **tactical tools** for what I have called *The Lazy Approach*.

TACTICAL TOOL #1: USE QUESTIONS TO MAKE A POINT

When a question is used to make a point, it has a far greater impact than when the same point is made in a statement. As Koukl advises, "Never make a statement, at least at first, when a question will do the job."[49] Moreover, questions allow you to maneuver the conversation toward your desired goal. As author and talk show host Hugh Hewitt states:

> The habit of asking questions will inevitably give you advantages in every setting... and being an asker allows you control of situations that statement makers rarely achieve. Once you learn how to guide a conversation, you have also learned to control it.[50]

The Example of Jesus

Unsurprisingly, Jesus utilized this tool brilliantly when responding to a hostile audience. An example of this can be found after the Pharisees publicly approach Him and ask, "What is your opinion? Is it right to pay the imperial tax to Caesar or not?"[51] This was a trap to silence Him. If He said no, He'd be arrested (and possibly executed) for treason against the Roman government.[52] If He said yes, He'd be accused of bowing the knee to Caesar, losing credibility as the Messiah. How did Jesus avoid the trap? By using a question to make a point.

> "Bring me a denarius and let me look at it… Whose image is this and whose inscription?" "Caesar's," they replied. Then Jesus said to them, "Give back to Caesar what is Caesar's and give to God what is God's." When they heard this, they were amazed. So they left him and went away.[53]

Consider the argument Jesus seems to be making with the question. If something bears an image, then 1) it rightfully belongs to that person, and 2) we are living in their kingdom. Hence, He concedes this is Caesar's kingdom because the coin bears his image. But now consider the implicit point being made by the question. If an image points to a kingdom and informs us of the king over it, then the question in the mind of His audience becomes, "and who's image is on us?" Because if we bear God's image, then by the same line of logic, it follows that we live in God's kingdom, and thus, we must give God what rightfully belongs to Him.

So, rather than play their political game, Jesus uses a question that causes them to reach the point He's trying to make. As David Reed observes, "Rather than shower his listeners with information he used questions to draw answers out of them, thereby causing them to think about the subject."[54] Taking this approach with nonbelievers can have the same effect.

TACTICAL TOOL #2: REWORD THE POSITION TO EXPOSE THE PROBLEM

As demonstrated in the last chapter, rewording a person's position can serve as an implicit rebuttal by exposing the problems with a claim. When the student argued that illegal abortions could potentially harm women, I reworded his position in such a way that "removed the fluff," bringing the focus back to the issue of abortion and the life of the unborn. This was combined with the previous tool and presented as a question. "So, you're saying that if we don't allow women to kill their innocent, unborn children legally, then they might be harmed when killing their innocent, unborn children illegally?"

Additionally, we saw how rewording *the principle* of a position and applying it to a counterexample could also serve as an implicit rebuttal. The underlying principle behind the student's argument was that making something legal could reduce the harm for those committing the act. Hence, I asked if the same principle could be applied to burglars for reducing their harm when breaking into homes. He denied the example because, in his words, *the act itself was harmful* to those it was being committed against, which was precisely my argument against abortion. This allowed him to draw the conclusion on his own, and ironically, he made the point for me. Thus, if one denies the principle in one area (burglaries), it should be denied for the other (abortion).

A third way of utilizing this tactic can be done in the "reverse." Recall that one reason for rewording the position was to ensure we had not misunderstood or mischaracterized the other person's position. This principle of charity should work both ways. For instance, suppose you give an argument for God's existence and find that the person's objection doesn't apply (because they've misunderstood or mischaracterized your position). In that case, it's perfectly acceptable to pause and ask the person to reiterate your position back to you. This helps identify where they've misunderstood your argument, and further clarification (or elaboration) can be given to help them grasp your point. As before, this keeps the conversation cordial and ensures that both of you are on the same page.

TACTICAL TOOL #3: EMPHASIZE REBUTTALS

When taking *The Lazy Approach*, there will always be an emphasis on offering rebuttals over refutations. Aside from the advantages stated in the previous chapter, consider why this tactic is emphasized in *The Lazy Approach*.

1. The Pressure Is on Them, Not You

Recall the principle of applying the burden of proof onto a claim and remember that with a rebuttal, you're not trying to show the other person is wrong (i.e., a refutation) but simply showing that the other person hasn't proven they're right. Hence, each rebuttal you provide keeps the "burden of proof ball" in their court until it's met. If it's not met, you're under no rational obligation to take their argument, objection, or claim to be true.

As a result, they're now forced to re-consider their rational allegiance to their position given that it's been demonstrated to be unjustified by your rebuttal (e.g., you wore brown shoes yesterday and it did not rain, so what other reasons do you have for believing it will rain today?). When done effectively, the pressure is off you, and, like the walls of Jericho, the strongholds begin to fall on their own (maybe that was a little dramatic, but you get the idea!).

2. "Laziness": A Matter of Practicality

The second reason for emphasizing rebuttals over refutations within *The Lazy Approach* is simply a matter of practicality. Too often, I've seen Christians try and respond to an alleged argument or objection (typically by trying to offer a refutation) when the claim has not been given good reasons to take it seriously. To illustrate, a young man once told me he left Christianity because the Bible was "corrupted and changed by the church to gain control." Thus, we could never trust the words of Scripture. At this point, believers are usually quick to try and prove this assertion false. But why? If he made the claim, then it's not your job to prove he's wrong, it's his job to prove he's right. You be "lazy" and let them do the work.

Eric: Could you provide a source to prove your claim is true?

Observation: Note how my immediate response is to apply the burden of proof to his claim with a variation of the question, "how did you come to that conclusion?" Of course, he didn't have a source for his claim, which meant I had no reason to take his objection seriously. Nevertheless, I allowed him to proceed for the sake of conversation.

Atheist: But we know this because we've found lost copies that are different from the ones we initially had.

Eric: So, you're saying that our current Bible is untrustworthy because they have recently discovered copies from the original? (Rewording his position)

Atheist: Yes, exactly!

Eric: So, what's the problem?

Atheist: What do you mean?

Eric: Well, if what we previously had was incorrect, and if this is proven because what we found is authentic, then what's the problem? Couldn't you say it wasn't *until now* that we can trust the words of the Bible going forward?

After allowing the point to sink in, I proceeded.

Eric: In other words, *even if* what you're saying is true, you should rejoice with me knowing we can *now* trust the original, authentic claims and teachings of Scripture! But if this is the case, then I'm having trouble seeing why you feel this is a valid argument against the Bible, Christianity, or, more pertinently, a justifiable reason for being an atheist.

Recall that with a rebuttal, we can concede for the sake of argument that a person's claim *might* be true and yet, show how the claim doesn't justify their overall position. Hence, I didn't try and argue that his objection was false (though it was) but instead showed how his claim, *even if true*, doesn't grant him a rational reason for atheism.

TACTICAL TOOL #4: DISCERNMENT–NEITHER REFUTATION NOR REBUTTAL

As discussed, when it comes to offering responses and knowing *how* to answer (as opposed to *what* to answer), *The Lazy Approach* emphasizes prioritizing rebuttals over refutations. However, not all claims, assertions, or purported objections merit either type of response. Why not? Because sometimes, the nonbeliever isn't providing an *actual objection, rebuttal*, or *refutation* to your position but is instead, making a declarative statement, asserting a claim without justification, or passionately expressing their emotions about your views. They've not offered anything to advance the conversation further, and in such instances, neither a refutation nor rebuttal is needed. Allow me to demonstrate.

"Go on..."

Suppose an atheist says he's not a believer because "Christians are hypocrites." Here are a few ways of implementing this tool in a response, ranking from the "laziest," the "less lazy," and "only a modicum amount of more work."

Claim*:* Christians are hypocrites!

1) **The Laziest:** Go on...
2) **The Less Lazy:** Sure, some are. But how does this prove there is no God?
3) **Only a Modicum Amount of More Work:** Sure, and some atheists are hypocrites too. So what?

Or, a witty response suggested by a pastor:

Pastor's "Bonus" Response: Yup, that's true, the church is full of them, but I'm sure we have room for one more!

Setting the "bonus" response aside, note that neither of these responses is an attempt to refute or rebut the claim. Why? Because the assertion, even if true, does nothing to advance his position, refute what you have said, or further the conversation in a meaningful way. Hence, by providing a dispassionate "*go on*," I'm implying that there's nothing for me to respond to because their assertion is not an argument or objection but is just that—an assertion.[55]

"That's Not an Argument"

Consider a different scenario in which this tool can be applied. Suppose the nonbeliever is offering an objection against the existence of God, but by paying careful attention, you notice that what he's saying is not actually an argument or objection. This was the case during one conversation where an atheist claimed his "biggest obstacle to belief in God" was the existence of evil.

Atheist: But how can you believe in God when there is so much evil in the world?

Eric: Are you saying that if evil exists, then God cannot? (Rewording his position for clarification)

Atheist: Yes!

Eric: Explain.

Atheist: Well, it's just that! If there is a loving God, there shouldn't be any evil.

Eric: Why?

Atheist: Because He's all loving.

Eric: Yes.

Atheist: And He wouldn't want there to be any evil.

Eric: Why not?

Atheist: Well, because He's all loving!

Eric: Go on…

At this point, there was an awkward silence (which seems to be a reoccurring theme with *The Lazy Approach*). Evidently, he'd never been challenged to think through his own argument. So, I sat patiently and allowed him to reflect. It became clear to him that he hadn't provided an explicit contradiction between the existence of an all-loving God and evil in the world. Thus, there was nothing for me to respond to.

In other words, whatever the purported objection may be, it must first be unpacked for me to offer a substantive response. Yet, no explicit objection had been provided. Instead, he had merely expressed *what he felt* should not be the case. But this is no different from saying "if grass is green, then the sky shouldn't be blue." This isn't an objection. It's merely a statement that needs elaboration to justify why such things cannot be the case.

At this point, he said, "Well, you know what I'm trying to say." To which I replied, "Well, I think I do. But if you want a response to the objection, I first need to know what the objection actually is. So far, you've only repeated your assertion but have not unpacked the implications that make it an objection."

This wasn't me trying to be pedantic or "cute." After all, he previously said this was his "biggest obstacle to belief in God," and yet, he couldn't make the case for the objection. And why not? Because he's never had to. Chances are, no Christian had ever challenged the validity of his thinking, and in his mind, this was a valid excuse for rejecting belief in God and, more importantly, salvation.

Sadly, it seems the prevalence of such false beliefs is not due to their strength but due to the weak responses that have been offered against them. Hence, the reason for apologetics in evangelism. *This* is tearing down strongholds. At any rate, to advance the discussion (and after my point had been made), I offered some clarification.

Eric: I'm still not sure I'm getting it, but you seem to be implying that if God existed, then there would be no evil in the world. Is that correct?

Atheist: Yes! Exactly.

Eric: I see. Well, let me ask you this, can I take my kids to the doctor, which may include painful shots, and still be considered a loving father?

Atheist: Sure. *But only* because you're doing it for a greater good.

Eric: Precisely. But if I could allow suffering in my children's lives and still be a loving father, then I'm having trouble seeing where your problem lies with the existence of evil in the world and God as an all-loving father. Could this same principle not apply to Him?

Interlude: Emotional Doubt vs. Intellectual Doubt

Before unpacking some key takeaways from this interaction, it's worth noting what's occurring here. Regarding apologetics, philosophers have identified a helpful distinction between an *emotional objection* and an *intellectual objection* (also referred to as **emotional doubt** vs. **intellectual doubt**). A primary difference between the two is this: an **intellectual objection** can be written down or formulated into an argument (i.e., a syllogism—see chapter 15), whereas an **emotional objection** cannot. Such objections are not driven intellectually but emotionally; the person may not *like* or *want* a certain conclusion to be true.

By way of example, consider the renowned atheist philosopher, Thomas Nagel, ranked as one of the top living philosophers of our time. In a bleak moment of truth, Nagel provides an honest, sobering insight of self-reflection. In his book, *The Last Word*, he writes:

> I want atheism to be true and am made uneasy by the fact that some of the most intelligent and well-informed people I know are religious believers. It isn't just that I don't believe in God and, naturally, hope that I'm right in my belief. It's that I hope there is no God! I don't want there to be a God; I don't want the universe to be like that.[56]

While it's beyond the scope of this book to unpack these notions further, suffice it to say that both the intellect and the emotions occur in the mind, a fertile ground in which most, if not all, spiritual warfare is fought (Romans 8:5-7).

Moreover, many nonbelievers may not realize that, at its core, their objections are grounded, not in their intellect but in their emotions. For this reason, exposing the weaknesses, flaws, or irrationality of a view may be the precise "pebble in the shoe" they need to reconsider their position. As Scripture states, we must "not be conformed to the pattern of this world, but be transformed by the renewing of your mind."[57] Hence, apologetics in evangelism encompasses eradicating false ideologies and strongholds that bind the mind, to begin with. Remember, this is gardening work, and the plausibility structure begins to shift when the strongholds begin to fall. When this happens, the soil may become fertile and receptive to the seeds of salvation, and the church must continue to labor until the harvest arrives.

Returning to the Discussion

Returning to the discussion above, there are two key takeaways that I briefly want to mention. First, note that I began by asking clarifying questions to understand his position, which allowed me to end with a rebuttal, but still, in the form of a question. This was an implementation of tactics 1, 3, and 4. Hence, the tools within this approach need not be taken in isolation but can be flexibly combined when needed.

Second, note that I was able to *respectfully* challenge his beliefs in a way he'd not encountered before. Yet, I gave no verbose answers or refutations. Instead, I asked strategically placed questions that addressed the overall structure of his claim. This forced him to rethink his position and arrive at my point for himself. Namely, that an all-loving God can exist even if evil and suffering exist. As Reed explains:

> A person can close his ears to facts he doesn't want to hear, but if a pointed question causes him to form the answer in his own mind, he can't escape the conclusion, because it's a conclusion that he has reached himself.[58]

TACTICAL TOOL #5: IDENTIFY LOGICAL FALLACIES

Our final tool within this approach deals with knowing how to identify logical fallacies within a claim, position, or argument. A **logical fallacy** is an error in logic or reason and, as such, could never justify a claim, position, or argument. Consequently, learning to detect and expose logical fallacies in conversations suffice as implicit rebuttals (and sometimes, implicit refutations). Because this tool can be incredibly effective, the entirety of chapter 16 is devoted to recognizing the most common logical fallacies you may encounter.

For now, let's briefly unpack this tactic by examining the discussion above and noting, not how I *did* respond, but how I *could have* responded. While you may not have "the eyes to see" it just yet, there was at least one logical fallacy within his reasoning known as **circular reasoning** (sometimes called **arguing in a circle**). This occurred when he claimed that an all-loving God didn't exist because there was so much evil in the world, but then implied there was so much evil in the world because an all-loving God didn't exist. Hence, his entire argument was based on the logical fallacy of circular reasoning, and pointing this out would've served as a "quick and easy" rebuttal. This is because, as my good friend Dr. Tim Stratton explains, "Any argument based on a logical fallacy is no argument at all."[59]

Chapter Summary: The "Lazy Approach"

Beginning with the next chapter, we'll learn how to apply this approach to skepticism as a "warm-up." Then, to the three dominant strongholds within our culture: postmodernism, scientism, and naturalism. For now, let's briefly review the five tactical tools for what I have called *The Lazy Approach*.

TACTICAL TOOL #1: USE QUESTIONS TO MAKE A POINT

- Using a question to make a point has a far greater impact than when the same point is made in a statement.
- Never make a statement when a question will do the job.
- Use questions to maneuver the conversation toward your goal, causing the other person to reach the point you're trying to make on their own.

TACTICAL TOOL #2: REWORD THE POSITION TO EXPOSE THE PROBLEM

- Reword a person's position to expose the hidden problems within the claim (this can "remove the fluff" and serve as an implicit rebuttal).
- Reword *the principle* of a position and apply it to a counterexample (this can also serve as an implicit rebuttal). If they deny the principle for one position, it must be denied for the other.
- Ask the other person to reword your argument if you feel they've misunderstood or mischaracterized your position. This helps you identify where they've misunderstood your argument, and further clarification or elaboration can be given.

TACTICAL TOOL #3: EMPHASIZE REBUTTALS

- Emphasize rebuttals over refutations. It's not your job to prove they're wrong, it's their job to prove they're right.
- Keep the ball in their court with a rebuttal (the pressure is on them, not you).
- Concede that their claim might be true and show how it still doesn't justify their position (you be "lazy" and let them do the work).

TACTICAL TOOL #4: DISCERNMENT–NEITHER REFUTATION NOR REBUTTAL

- Discern whether they are giving you an argument or an assertion (assertions do not require refutations or rebuttals).
- You can respond to assertions with a "go on" or "so what" and allow them to unpack the objection. If an objection isn't given, no response is needed.
- Sit in silence when needed and allow them to think through their position.

TACTICAL TOOL #5: IDENTIFY LOGICAL FALLACIES

- A logical fallacy is an error in logic or reason that cannot be used to justify a claim (any argument based on a logical fallacy is no argument at all).
- Expose the logical fallacy for a "quick and easy" rebuttal.

In the examples provided above, my responses were kept as short as possible, forcing the other person to unpack and articulate the hidden assumptions behind their claim. Moreover, questions were used to draw out and expose the weakness of a person's position, allowing them to come to this conclusion on their own. As previously stated, no set order, move, or script must be followed when implementing this approach, and we saw how a combination of these tools could be utilized in a single response or conversation. Each person will be different, each conversation unique, and each stronghold carries its own peculiar weaknesses.

It should go without saying that the purpose of these tactical tools is to tear down ideas, not people. Thus, our aim has been to identify the stronghold, adapt our approach accordingly, and tear, pull down, demolish, and destroy them as Scripture commands. This is the role of apologetics in evangelism (1 Peter 3:15, Jude 1:3); this is spiritual warfare (2 Corinthians 10:4-5).

Chapter 12

Responding to Skepticism

Biblical Basis: Proverbs 21:22

> *A wise man scales the city of the mighty and brings down the stronghold in which they trust* (ESV).

Reviewing Skepticism

In chapter 3, we learned to identify skepticism by two key features: the mindset and the method. The mindset of skepticism revolved around the notion of certainty as a necessary condition for knowledge, whereas the method encompassed asking a variation of the question "how do you know" after every response you provide. Although skepticism is not necessarily a dominant stronghold within our culture, it's a dominant stronghold amongst nonbelievers. Using the tactical tools from *The Lazy Approach*, let's briefly go over various ways in which responses to skepticism can be provided.

RESPONDING TO THE MINDSET

Recall that a stronghold is a belief (or set of beliefs) that hinders people from coming to the knowledge of God. As previously mentioned in chapter 10, at least two beliefs are necessary for salvation: the existence of God and the resurrection of Jesus. As we'll see in Part 5 of this book, a supporting detail in the case for the resurrection is that the risen Jesus appeared to more than five hundred people at once after His death.[60] But suppose you're presenting this to a nonbeliever and the conversation proceeds as follows:

Skeptic: But how can you trust what these five hundred people claimed to see? Isn't it *possible* their senses were deceiving them?

Eric: What do you mean?

Skeptic: Well, haven't your senses ever deceived you? Have you ever driven down a highway and, further down the road, it appeared there was water on the pavement, but as you approached it, realized there was never water there, to begin with?

Eric: Like a mirage? Yes, that's happened.

Skeptic: Right, so we know our senses can deceive us. And isn't it *possible* your senses can be deceiving you now?

Eric: Sure, I suppose it's possible.

Skeptic: Well, that's my point! If we have reasons to doubt our senses, and *if it's possible* our senses could even be deceiving us now, then why should we trust the senses of an uneducated, superstitious multitude written in an ancient book two thousand years ago? Because if that's part of your case for the resurrection, then I have reason to doubt the claim's validity and reject your case for Christianity.

Before proceeding, let's unpack the conversation thus far. First, note that I've let the skeptic do most of the talking. This is a good rule of thumb because it allows us to gather information along the way (the first step for any evangelistic conversation). Second, I now have the growing suspicion that I'm dealing with a skeptic. But remember, we always want to verify their position, not assume it. So, rather than ask if he's a skeptic (he may not be familiar with the terminology), I'll simply apply the definitional characteristics of skepticism in the form of a question to gain clarity. If my suspicions are correct, this allows me to "set up" my final question as a rebuttal.

Using Tactical Tool #2: Reword the Position to Gain Clarity

Eric: Before I respond, let me see if I understand you correctly. Are you implying that if the mere possibility of doubt arises, then the thing in question cannot be known?

Skeptic: Yes, exactly! We cannot claim to know something unless we can demonstrate it with certainty. But the problem is, we can't be certain about anything!

Observation: Now that I've confirmed I'm talking to a skeptic, I'm ready to set up my response. As before, my approach will not be to defend Christianity but to rebut the mindset of his skepticism. To do this, I will incorporate tactical tool #5 and demonstrate how the nature of his skepticism commits the logical fallacy of being **self-defeating**. This fallacy occurs when a position proves itself false by its own standards, and I'll make this point with a question (tactical tool #1).

Reword the Position to Expose the Fallacy with a Question

Eric: If I understand correctly, you're saying that knowledge requires certainty.

Skeptic: Yes.

Eric: And then you said that *nothing* could be known for certain.

Skeptic: Correct.

Eric: But wouldn't it follow from this that, therefore, we cannot claim to know *anything*?

Skeptic: Yes, that's precisely my point!

Eric: Sure. But here's my point. If we cannot claim to know *anything*, then how do you *know* that? Are you claiming *to know* we *cannot know* anything?

[Silence]

Eric: Then you applied this to Scripture, *claiming to know* we could never trust our senses. But something about your example confuses me.

Skeptic: How so?

Eric: Well, you explained we couldn't trust our senses because we "know" our senses have deceived us in the past. In your example, I see a puddle of water down the road but later use my eyes to see it was merely a mirage.

Skeptic: Right.

Eric: But here's where I'm having trouble. Given your example, it would seem that in order to know I cannot rely on my sense of sight, *I must first rely on my sense of sight* to inform me that my sense of sight is unreliable. But wouldn't this mean that I'd have to trust my senses to "know" my senses cannot be trusted, or am I missing something here?

[awkward silence]

Eric: Because if that's the case, I now have reasons to doubt your criteria, your example, and your objection. And given your standards, if I can doubt your claim, then I have reason to reject your argument. Is that correct?

Unpacking the Response

To begin with, let's break down the claim into its conclusion and its justification. His conclusion was that our senses couldn't be trusted (and because of this, we cannot trust that the 500 witnesses in 1 Corinthians 15 saw Jesus), and his justification was that our senses have deceived us in the past (using the example of seeing water on the pavement). Now consider how our tactical tools were used in my response.

First, I attacked his justification (as opposed to his conclusion), and my response came as a rebuttal (tactical tool #3). Second, because I understood (had the "eyes to see") the nature of his position (skepticism), I was able to use strategically placed questions to expose his overall argument as self-defeating. This incorporated tactical tools #5 (identifying the logical fallacy), #2 (rewording his position, first to gain clarity and then to expose the problem), and was presented in the form of a question (#1).

Additionally, note how in this case, utilizing tactical tool #5 not only served as a rebuttal to his argument, but as an implicit *refutation* to his overall position. Why? Because a self-defeating position is not only logically fallacious but *necessarily* false. For this reason, the fallacy is also known as a **self-refutation** (a position that provides an inherent refutation to itself). His standard for not trusting his senses as reliable required that he begins by trusting that his senses were reliable, which is clearly self-refuting. As previously mentioned, utilizing this tool can serve as a "quick and easy" rebuttal, and in this case, it also serves as a refutation. Now consider how the same goal can be accomplished with just one probing question.

Tactical Tool #5: Identifying Self-Defeating Claims

Example #1: *Certainty*

Skeptic: We cannot be absolutely certain about anything.

Eric: Are you absolutely certain about that?

Example #2: *Knowledge*

Skeptic: No one could ever claim to know anything.

Eric: Are you claiming to know that?

Example #3: *A Skeptic Who Is "Spiritual, but Not Religious"*

Skeptic: We cannot know anything about God.

Eric: And how do you *know that* about God?

As before, the strategy is not to argue with the skeptic about certainty or knowledge, but to get at the heart of the stronghold by exposing the fallacy with a question (tactical tools #1 and #5). Learning how to "set up" these questions in conversations becomes natural with time and practice.

RESPONDING TO THE METHOD

Concerning the method, a skeptic may respond by repeatedly asking, "How do you know?" after every answer you provide. This might be combined with the mindset if they ask, "but how can you be certain?" Though innocent on the surface, the repetitive nature of the skeptic turns these questions into nothing more than a verbal game. When this is done, it becomes appropriate (indeed, necessary) to voice our disagreement with the skeptic's criterion of taking certainty as a requirement for knowledge. Once again, responding with an initial question keeps the conversation cordial and non-combative.

Example #1

Skeptic: And how can you be absolutely certain?

Eric: You've repeated this question several times. Are you insinuating that absolute certainty is a requirement for knowledge?

Skeptic: Yes, of course, it is!

Eric: And are you absolutely certain of this?

Skeptic: No, because nothing can be known with absolute certainty.

Eric: Then how can you *know* that your position is valid?

Given that this method is based on the belief that certainty is a requirement for knowledge (which I have exposed by asking a clarifying question), rather than try and refute the position, I concede his view (for the sake of argument) and ask how the skeptic can be certain that certainty is a requirement for knowledge. This is not to agree with the skeptic's position but to reverse the skeptic's view onto his own claim and expose the problem with his method (i.e., it's self-defeating).

<u>**Example #2**</u>

Skeptic: And how do you know?

Eric: You ask this after every response I provide, which seems to imply that you're doubting my case.

Skeptic: I am.

Eric: Well, perhaps I'm missing something here. So, rather than answer the question again, can you provide a justifiable reason for rejecting my case?

Observation: Note my strategy here. Knowing the skeptic's overall position, I'm trying to break down the claim into its conclusion (that my argument can be doubted and rejected) and its justification (because it's possible I'm mistaken). However, he's yet to provide this justification in the conversation. Thus, I "set up my pieces" and use a question to draw it out.

Skeptic: Yes. If it's possible you can be mistaken, then I have sufficient reason to doubt and reject the validity of your case.

Now that he's provided the justification, I can apply the claim to itself and expose his position as self-defeating.

Eric: Well, given that it's *possible* you're mistaken about this, it must follow that I, too, have reason to reject the validity of your position, making the claim, by your own standards, null and void.

<u>**Example #3**</u>

At this point, a skeptic may try and justify why his doubt or rejection of your position is appropriate.

Skeptic: Well, not every expert agrees that your position is valid.

Eric: Sure, but isn't it also the case that not every expert agrees that a consensus of expert agreement is necessary for the validity of a position?

In this instance, the skeptic appeals to expert agreement. However, given that not all experts agree with this criterion, it rebuts his position by its own standards.

Conclusion

As we've seen, exposing the logical fallacies in a position can reveal the flawed inconsistencies or errors within a worldview and demonstrate why it must be inherently false (e.g., self-defeating). Hence, 1) claiming not to have knowledge is a claim to knowledge, 2) one claims to know that knowledge requires certainty while being uncertain, and 3) assuming that the *mere possibility* of being mistaken justifies the rejection of a view while having the possibility of being mistaken about this criterion—all demonstrate how skepticism is self-refuting and, thus, necessarily false. These not only served as rebuttals but implicit refutations, as well.

While there are various ways to utilize *The Lazy Approach* when responding to the skeptic, it's crucial that you not take these examples as a script to be followed. Again, each person is different, each conversation unique, and each stronghold has its own weakness. Thus, my aim here (and going forward) is to show you how to use the tools, set up a response, and tear down the strongholds.

Chapter 13

Responding to Postmodernism

There is one thing a professor can be absolutely certain of: almost every student entering the university believes, or says he believes, that truth is relative.[61]

– Alan Bloom, The Closing of the American Mind

Reviewing Postmodernism

Recall that postmodernism revolves around the notion of truth, taking it as something pragmatic or relative to the individual. While this may not be immediately evident in a conversation, listening carefully to their choice of words may inevitably reveal the sentiment. To illustrate, suppose you're witnessing to a person, and they interrupt by saying, "Look, I'm glad that Christianity is true and helpful for you, but it's just not for me." Note two things about this response.

First, although the person rejects Christianity, they aren't claiming it's false—posing as though they're being respectful to your position. However, we know this is because the notion of being objectively wrong entails an objective right, and within postmodernism, there is neither. Second, this response assumes Christianity is merely a "crutch" or placebo effect one believes for practical purposes. Hence, the person is not viewing Christianity as something that can be *objectively* "true" or "false," but as something that can be "helpful" or "unhelpful." Given the implications, we know we're conversing with a postmodernist.

EXPOSING THE SELF-DEFEATING NATURE OF POSTMODERNISM

As demonstrated in the last chapter, knowing how to identify and expose self-defeating claims when they're the byproduct of a worldview is one of the quickest and easiest ways to tear down the stronghold. The same applies when responding to postmodernism by turning a claim onto itself in the form of a question (combining tactical tools #1 and #5).

"There Is No truth"

Jane: But Christianity couldn't possibly be true.

Eric: Why not?

Jane: Because there is no truth!

Eric: Is that true?

Note that the statement "there is no truth" *is* a claim that's being *presented as true*. Yet, if there is no truth, then her very claim that "there is no truth" cannot possibly be true, to begin with. Therefore, if she believes there is no truth, then by her own standards, she cannot believe what she just told me is true. It is self-refuting and, thus, necessarily false. As before, the same goal can be accomplished with one question:

- It's true for you but not me.
    - Is that statement true for you but not me?
- There are no universal truths.
    - Is that truth universal?
- Truth is relative to the individual
    - Is that true for everyone, or just you, the individual?

Reviewing the Cultural Shifts of Postmodernism

Recall that when postmodernism permeates a culture, at least two shifts occur: 1) morality is replaced with (or reduced to) political disputes, and 2) the notion of tolerance is redefined. This leads to what is known as **moral relativism** and **cultural relativism.**

With cultural relativism, morality becomes dependent on what the culture believes to be "true," and what is "wrong" for one culture or society may not be "wrong" in another. Morality is no longer grounded in something eternal, transcendent, and objective (i.e., God), but is instead, grounded in the state, country, or political perspectives of the community (which may shift in every election). As a result, political parties and leaders are given the power to determine what is "right" or "wrong" for society, and thus, it becomes a fight to change the political landscape, not the moral one. As Dr. Moreland observes:

> It is obvious why so many secularists are addicted to politics today because political power is a surrogate for a Higher Power… the state would come to be a surrogate god for many.[62]

Naturally, this lends to the second shift of redefining the notion of tolerance and labeling anyone who disagrees with the political sway of the culture as bigoted, closeminded, or "intolerant."

RESPONDING TO THE SHIFTS

Once these shifts are identified in conversation, we can begin applying *The Lazy Approach* in various ways. First, we can continue implementing tactical tool #5 by exposing the self-defeating nature of a claim. This is especially helpful when your time with a person is limited.

1. Exposing the Fallacy with Limited Time

I was once invited to be on a secular, liberal radio station to talk about Christianity. To demonstrate their "tolerance and open-mindedness" toward other perspectives, the station occasionally invited someone from the community to talk about their beliefs. With an opportunity to represent Christianity and share the gospel on a secular radio station, I happily obliged. Knowing that my time would be limited, my goal was simple; I wanted to place a pebble of truth in the shoes of those listening.

On the day of the program, I arrived with five arguments for the existence of God on ten pages of notes. However, as I was about to walk into the live studio, the technician stopped me and asked if I'd be willing to take live calls during the broadcast. He explained that the program's purpose was not only to allow others to share their views but allow the community to interact with the guests they invite. With this new information, I knew my time would be even more limited than before. Hence, I'd have to use it strategically and adapt my approach along the way.

After agreeing to take calls, we walked into the studio, and the live broadcast began. By the first commercial break, I was barely on my second point when the host said, "I know there's more you wanted to talk about, but all the phone lines are ringing. Would you be willing to start taking calls?" "I'm not even halfway through my presentation," I said, "but sure, let's take some calls."

One of the first callers was notably upset by my presentation, explaining that while he was fine with me talking about a generic God, he became increasingly uncomfortable that I had begun defending the Christian God, in particular. The on-air, live conversation proceeded as follows:

Caller: Look, I don't care if you want to talk about God. Everyone believes in something. But are you asserting that Christianity is the *only* true religion?

Eric: Well, I'm not just asserting it. I'm providing evidence for it.

Caller: Wow! So, you openly admit this is what you're trying to do? Good! Now, are you willing to admit to the thousands of people who believe in a different god that you think they're wrong?!

Eric: Yes.

Caller: But you can't do that! Who are YOU to tell people they're wrong?!

Given that I was on a live radio program with other callers waiting, I had little time to respond. Nevertheless, because I understood the stronghold from which his objection stemmed (postmodernism), I knew

I could quickly address the issue with *The Lazy Approach*. So, I began with a clarifying question that would set up a final response to his claim.

Eric: Let me see if I understand you correctly. Are you telling me it's inappropriate or immoral to tell another person they're wrong?

Caller: Yes! There are so many religions, and you can't go around telling people they're wrong!

Eric: I see. Then I only have one question. If you believe it's wrong to tell others they're wrong, then can you please explain why you're calling me on *live, public* radio to tell me that I'm wrong?

He had no more questions after that.

Unpacking the Response

Note a few things about this interaction. First, he was essentially doing what he claimed I ought not do—tell people they're wrong. I didn't argue, disagree, or try and refute his objection. Instead, I reworded his position and turned the objection on itself (tactical tool #2). Second, given his postmodernism, I knew his answer to my clarifying question would naturally set the stage for my final question, exposing the self-defeating nature of his claim, allowing him to come to this conclusion on his own. Hence, *understanding* the stronghold provided me with the insight for *knowing* how to quickly address the issue (1 Chronicles 12:32). For this reason, we devoted an entire chapter to developing our eyes for identifying strongholds and learned to adapt our approach accordingly. I cannot overemphasize the importance of this for apologetics in evangelism—especially when our time with a person is limited.

Testing Your Eyes to See

Consider two more callers that shared a similar sentiment and a final example from a different occasion. Before showing you how I responded, use what you've learned to think through how you'd respond if you were in my shoes.

Caller #2: But aren't you a Christian, and didn't Christ say, "thou shalt not judge?" You seem to be judging people when you tell them they're wrong.

Caller #3: How can you say Christianity is true when no one possesses the absolute truth?

Person #4: Christians are so intolerant!

My Responses:

Caller #2: "Judging"

Given that we were on live radio with others listening in, I felt it was necessary first to address the passage he quoted.

Eric: To your first statement, no, not exactly. Jesus explained that we'd be judged by the same measure we judge others—meaning we shouldn't judge hypocritically. So, if anything, He's giving us a standard for *how* to judge, not necessarily saying we *shouldn't judge*.[63]

Caller #2: I don't care how you choose to interpret that. Whether you believe in God or not, you shouldn't judge others!

Eric: Well, if you strongly believe we shouldn't judge others, then may I ask why you're judging me for doing this?

Caller #3: "Absolute Truth"

Caller #3: How can you say Christianity is true when no one possesses the absolute truth?

Eric: Is what you just said an absolute truth that you possess?

Person #4: "Tolerance"

Person #4: Christians are so intolerant!

Eric: Are you insinuating that we should tolerate everyone's beliefs?

Person #4: Yes!

Eric: Then why are you not tolerant of mine?

2. Exposing the Absurd Implications of Postmodernism

A second way of responding to these cultural shifts in conversation is to expose the implicit consequences of consistent yet unlivable behaviors that are logically compatible within a worldview. Put differently, if you can show that consistently living out a worldview leads to irrational, morally reprehensible consequences, then you'll simultaneously show why the worldview must be rejected. In philosophy, this exposes a logical fallacy known as a ***reductio ad absurdum*** (Latin for "reduces to absurdity").

To illustrate, consider how in postmodernism, something can be "true for you but not me." However, when it comes to taking medicine, no postmodernist lives as if the information on the label is "true for you but not them." Yet, if postmodernism is true, then everyone should freely ignore the labels, live out "their truth," and take whichever medication they wish. But this "logical consistency" is absurd. Even a postmodernist knows that medicinal labels convey an *objective truth* and that ignoring these truths can have fatal consequences.

Similarly, if the postmodernists truly believed their worldview, they should have no problem with doctors prescribing rat poison instead of aspirin for a headache—as long as that doctor believed this was "their truth." Coincidentally, such a proposal causes moral indignation, even in a postmodernist! Why? Because when taken to its logical conclusion, postmodernism is not only false but unlivable and dangerously absurd. Hence, I remind them that their indignation shouldn't be directed toward me, but toward the implications of their worldview. If they reject such behaviors, then I further explain that their worldview, which logically permits these behaviors, must be rejected as well (tactical tools #5 and #2).

APPLYING *THE LAZY APPROACH* TO MORAL DISCUSSIONS

Using Questions to Make a Point (Tactical Tool #1)

Consider the assertion, "Don't impose your 'religious' morality onto me," or "All Christians are intolerant, closeminded bigots." Because these can devolve into heated altercations, it's worth surveying some direct but cordial responses. When presented as general assertions, the previous method of responding applies:

- You can't tell other people what to do with their life. It's wrong!
  - Then why are you telling me what to do with my life?
- Stop forcing your morality on everybody else!
  - Is that your moral position, and if so, then why are you forcing it onto me?
- It's wrong to impose your views on other people.
  - Then may I ask why you're imposing that view onto me?

If these assertions become targeted accusations, a little more work is needed to defuse the situation, and here is where our two questions from chapter ten become helpful: 1) What do you mean by that? and 2) How did you come to that conclusion? Consider how these questions can be modified in response to the following accusation:

- "You Christians are intolerant, bigoted, and closeminded!"
  1. What do you mean by "intolerant," "bigoted," or "closeminded?"
  2. What about my position makes me intolerant?

Note how each question forces the person to think carefully about their accusations, requiring that they articulate *precisely* what they mean by these labels. Once they answer, the stage is set to make your point clearly but respectfully.

- Because you think YOU are right and everyone else is wrong!
    - This is true. But don't you think you're right and I'm wrong? Why is it when I think I'm right, I'm intolerant, but when you think you're right, you're just right? What am I missing here?[64]

Now suppose the person brings Christianity into the mix of politics and says, "But aren't you Christians aware of the separation of church and state? You can't legislate morality! Christians need to leave their religious views out of politics. Don't impose your religious views on everyone else!" As a response, Koukl offers the following questions:

> Do you vote? When you vote for someone, are you expecting your candidate to pass laws reflecting your point of view? Wouldn't that essentially be forcing your views on others? How is that different from what you're troubled about here? Is it your view that only nonreligious people should be allowed to vote or participate in politics, or did I misunderstand you? Where specifically in the Constitution are religious people excluded from the political process because of their spiritual convictions? Don't all laws force a morality of some sort? Can you give me an example of legislation that does not have a moral element underlying the law?[65]

Commenting on this, he explains:

> My initial response in a situation like this is not to preach about my view or even disagree with theirs. Rather, I want to draw them out, to invite them to talk more about what they think. This takes a lot of pressure off me because when I ask a question, the ball is back in their court. It also protects me from jumping to conclusions and unwittingly distorting their meaning. The more they talk, the more information I have to work with to maneuver in the conversation.[66]

Turning the Tables on Hot Topic, Controversial Issues

Now consider the manifestation of these shifts when discussing social issues such as abortion and same-sex marriage. Again, note how these are essentially *moral issues* and not mere "political perspectives."

When dealing with these hot topic, controversial issues, learn to set the tone of the discussion with a question. Koukl calls this "**turning the tables**." "If you are placed in a situation in which you suspect your convictions will be labeled intolerant, bigoted, narrow-minded, or judgmental... turn the tables."[67]

For instance, suppose someone approaches you in a condescending tone and asks, "So, as a Christian, what are *your* views on same-sex marriage?" In this situation, Koukl offers the following:

> You know, this is actually a very personal question you're asking. I don't mind answering, but before I do, I want to know if it's safe to offer my views. So let me ask you a question first:
>
> - Do you consider yourself a tolerant person or an intolerant person on issues like this?
> - Is it safe to give my opinion, or are you going to judge me for my point of view?
> - Do you respect diverse points of view, or do you condemn others for having convictions that differ from your own?

In taking this approach, he notes, "If you first set the stage for your conversation in this way, then when you give your point of view, it's going to be difficult for anyone to call you intolerant or judgmental without looking guilty too."[68]

EXPOSING THE INCONSISTENCIES IN A POSITION

Utilizing Tactical Tool #2: Reword the Position to Expose Inconsistencies

A final point to consider is that a person's rhetoric or ambiguous language might make it hard to identify the stronghold within the claim. Recall that rewording a person's position not only helps you understand their argument but can simultaneously "remove the fluff" in their statement to expose the problems with the view. Again, we *must pay careful attention* to how a person expresses their position. In doing so, you may discover that while no individual statement is logically problematic, their overall position (when taken together as a whole) becomes incoherent, self-defeating, absurd, or all the above.

To illustrate, I once debated the topic of abortion on a secular college campus against a female lawyer and feminist who was the executive director of NARAL Pro-Choice Texas (one of the biggest abortion advocacy groups in the nation). In this debate, many things were said, and not necessarily in an orderly, piecemeal fashion. Nevertheless, by paying careful attention to the way she expressed her views, I was able to produce a list of questions to expose the overall incoherence in her claims, noting when they were self-defeating, inconsistent in practice (by the implications of certain behaviors entailed by her view), or outright absurd. Consider the following highlights from this debate:

HIGHLIGHT #1

Heather: I don't think a human embryo is a person in the sense of a living, breathing, walking, sentient human being.

Eric: Well, they are *living*, *breathing*, and *sentient*, but not walking. But by that line of logic, would it not be permissible to kill a disabled person confined to a wheelchair *because* they're not walking?

[Awkward laughter]

Heather: I'm not even going to answer that. That's preposterous.

Eric: Well, I agree it's preposterous, but that's not my argument, that's your argument.

HIGHLIGHT #2

In her opening statement, Heather stated that we have a *moral obligation* to feed and care for the children who are "already here." By this, of course, she meant *only* the children *outside* the womb. Noting this subtle but revealing caveat, I proceeded with a question for clarification and ended with a question to expose this absurd caveat to the audience.

Eric: You stated earlier that we have a moral obligation to feed and care for the children already here, correct?

Heather: Yes.

Eric: Well, where are the unborn if not "here," and why don't we have *a moral obligation* to feed and care for them?

HIGHLIGHT #3

Heather: A six-week-old embryo is not a fully formed human being.

Eric: I never said it was. It's a *whole* human being, just not fully formed. After all, many students here aren't fully formed yet, but we can't kill them, can we?

HIGHLIGHT #4

In Heather's opening, she stated that abortion was about "fairness." "No one should be denied '*healthcare*' because of their zip code or what's in their bank account... *I want children to be healthy*." The point she was *trying* to make was that anti-abortion laws "discriminate" against people based on the laws of their state (hence, their "zip code") or their financial status (hence, their "bank account"). After clarifying that I accurately understood her position, I proceeded with a question to, once again, make an implicit point explicit.

Eric: You said you wouldn't deny someone "healthcare" because of their zip code or bank account and that children needed to be healthy. Well, the unborn may not have a "zip code," but they certainly have a location, and they don't have a bank account. So, why discriminate against the unborn when it comes to their health?

HIGHLIGHT #5

In defense of abortion as "health care," Heather stated that every person should have the necessary resources to have a "healthy pregnancy and healthy birth." Using a variation of the question, "what do you mean by that?" I brought the focus back to abortion to make my point.

Eric: How is an abortion a "healthy pregnancy?"

Heather: Because if someone is not ready or able to be pregnant, they shouldn't be "forced" to be pregnant.

Eric: But that doesn't sound like a healthy pregnancy; that sounds like killing an unborn human person.

HIGHLIGHT #6

In the previous examples, most of my questions were directly correlated with a statement she had just given, making it easier to reword her position and expose the implicit problems with her arguments. But in this last example, a bit more work was needed. Although this question became the most powerful point against her position, it was not an obvious one to ask (at least not at face value). To do this, I had to piece together her statements using the information I gathered and carefully assess their implications. Before presenting this question, consider the following claims she made (either explicitly or implicitly) on separate occasions during the debate:

1. Everyone should have equal rights and opportunities for "healthcare" regardless of race, religion, gender, or sexual orientation (e.g., gay, straight, transgender, etc.).
2. We shouldn't judge, protest, shame, or guilt a woman's decision to have an abortion when they feel it's best for them.
3. For me it's not about deciding for other people whether they can have an abortion. Regardless of your own viewpoints on abortion, if someone does not want to remain pregnant, then that person's decision should be respected.

Putting yourself in my shoes, take a moment and see if you can use this information to formulate a question of your own. Then, consider how I utilized these statements to make a point by presenting the following question.

Rewording the Position Holistically

Eric: So, I have a hypothetical scenario for you. You're saying anti-abortion laws are bad [i.e., they do not provide equal rights for all races, religions, genders, or sexual orientations] and that we should respect a woman's decision to have an abortion, even if we disagree with their reasons, correct?

Heather: (nodding in agreement)

Eric: Okay. Suppose a religious woman approached you, claiming she needed an abortion. As a hypothetical, let's suppose technology was available that could not only tell you the sex of the baby but could even tell you the baby's sexual orientation. So, this woman says, "I just discovered that my baby is going to be born gay, and I don't want a 'gay baby.'" Would you support that decision to abort? Because if you do, then you're implicitly allowing the killing of homosexuals for other people's preferences. But if you don't, then you're going against a woman's choice, which, by your standards, should be respected no matter what.

The room grew so quiet you could hear a pin drop. After an awkward laugh, she responded:

Heather: Well, that technology doesn't exist, so...

The room erupted with laughter, and she continued to shrug off the question. But I wasn't going to let this one go. I wanted an answer.

Eric: Well, it's a hypothetical. And even if it didn't exist, let's say she believed it—let's say she was lied to. Regardless of whether it exists or not, this is *her position*. This is *her choice*. Are you pro-choice in this instance?

Suffice it to say she never answered the question, and to alleviate the tension in the room, the moderator interjected and forced us to move on. Nevertheless, my point was made clear to everyone in the room. Her entire position was holistically incoherent, rationally inconsistent, and at times, absurdly self-defeating when taken to its logical conclusion.

After the debate, many young women informed me they'd arrived that night as either pro-choice or on the fence, but because of *this* debate, left as pro-life advocates. Additionally, during my opening presentation I briefly "snuck" the gospel in, letting the students know there was a God who *still* loved them. A God who offered forgiveness and salvation to all by giving up His son, even if they had given up theirs. As a result, some shared their story with me while others asked for prayer—right there on a secular college campus. Suffice it to say that when strongholds are torn down, the gospel will always flourish.

Chapter Summary and Conclusion

In responding to postmodernism, we used virtually every tool in *The Lazy Approach*. At the outset, we saw how the postmodernist epistemology of truth was self-defeating (tactical tool #5) and learned to expose this in the form of a question (tactical tool #1). This became especially helpful when our time with a person was limited.

Using the same tools, we focused on exposing a *reductio ad absurdum* fallacy by taking the logical consequences of a worldview and applying them to implicitly permissible behaviors. This incorporated tactical tool #2: rewording the principle of a position and applying its implications to a different scenario. We saw that if a person rejected these implicitly permissible behaviors, then they must further reject the worldview that logically allowed for the behaviors to begin with.

Next, we applied *The Lazy Approach* toward moral discussions for dealing with hostile accusations. Although we continued using the previous tools, we emphasized the tactic of using questions to make our point (tactical tool #1). This kept the conversation cordial when dealing with hot topic, controversial issues. When anticipating the potential of a heated exchange, we learned how to set the tone of the discussion with a question.

- What are YOUR views on same-sex marriage as a Christian?
  - Before I answer your question, may I ask if you consider yourself to be a tolerant person, or are you going to judge me for my point of view?

Approaching the situation in this way makes it difficult for someone to label you intolerant or judgmental without looking guilty, too.

Finally, we ended by implementing tactical tool #2 when a person's rhetoric or ambiguous language made it difficult to identify the problem. By paying careful attention to their claims, we saw how employing this tactic *holistically* exposed the entirety of a position to be logically inconsistent, rationally incoherent, or absurdly self-defeating.

Claim 1: We should equally respect people regardless of their sexual orientation.

Claim 2: We should support a woman's decision to have an abortion, even if we disagree with their reason.

Question: Would you support a woman's decision to have an abortion just because she thought her baby was gay?

Nothing about these responses was incredibly difficult to achieve. It simply took listening attentively, gathering information, and using questions to draw out the conclusions.

Chapter 14

Responding to Scientism

The greatest conflict of the 21st century... will be between modern civilization and anti-modernists; between those who believe in the primacy of the individual and those who believe that human beings owe their allegiance and identity to a higher authority... between those who believe in science, reason, and logic and those who believe that truth is revealed through Scripture and religious dogma.[69]

–Robert Reich, former professor at Harvard University

Reviewing Scientism

Recall that scientism is essentially an epistemic position that sees science as the *best* or *only way* to obtain knowledge about reality. If something cannot be tested scientifically, then it either cannot be known or cannot be true. Hence, a nonbeliever may say, "I can only believe what science tells me," or, "if you want me to believe in God, then show me the scientific evidence!" Such sentiments reveal an influence of scientism, implying that the person will only accept "scientific evidence" for any claim you make.

A Preface for Responding

Two things should be kept in mind as we respond to our remaining strongholds. First, each stronghold is unique with its specific problems—meaning that a different combination of tools and tactics may be needed. Second, the weaknesses and fallacies within these worldviews are not always apparent—meaning that a deeper understanding of them may be required to expose their problems. In the last chapter, we saw that refuting a stronghold can be achieved by demonstrating how at its core, it's self-defeating. The same can be said of scientism, but showing why this is the case takes a bit more effort. Utilizing tactical tool #5, we begin our response with this method.

EXPOSING THE FALLACIES OF SCIENTISM

1. Self-Refuting: Scientism Is Philosophy, NOT Science

The first step in exposing the self-refuting nature of scientism is understanding the appropriate category under which it falls. To reiterate, the stronghold of scientism is far more than an appreciation for science and is fundamentally a *philosophical claim* that treats science as the ultimate authority for knowledge. Scientism is an epistemology, and epistemology is a branch of philosophy. Hence, scientism is a *philosophical position*, NOT a scientific one. As a result, most assertions promoting scientism become inherently self-defeating.

"I Can Only Believe What Science Tells Me"

Consider the statement, "I can only believe what science tells me." Ironically, the statement itself is not a scientific claim, but rather, a *philosophical* claim *about* science. Put differently, it's *not* a claim that "science can tell you," because it's an assertion of philosophy, not science. Therefore, given that the statement, "I can only believe what science tells me" is a philosophical claim—and not a scientific one—then by its own standards, no one should believe it!

In other words, scientism is a philosophical position that implies no philosophical position can be known to be true; it's a *non-scientific utterance* that implies one *cannot trust* non-scientific utterances.[70] Therefore, if the statement implies a rejection of philosophical assertions, and yet, is itself, a philosophical assertion, then by its own standards, it must be rejected as well. Hence, if a person believes that scientism is true, then we should inform them they ought to simultaneously believe scientism is false.

As Moreland states in his book, *Scientism and Secularism: Learning to Respond to a Dangerous Ideology*:

> The irony is that strong scientism is a philosophical statement, expressing an epistemological viewpoint about science; it is not a statement of science ... it is not only false and self-refuting, but it is *necessarily* so...Christians, therefore, should not be intellectually intimidated when they hear very smart people with advanced degrees sitting in positions of authority say things that are self-refuting.[71]

2. God and Scientism: A Category Fallacy

When it comes to the question of God's existence, the epistemology of scientism becomes a category fallacy. A **category fallacy** is an error in reasoning that mistakenly conflates categories that do not belong together. Consider the question, "how much does the number two weigh, and how many can you fit in your pocket?" Given that numbers have neither weight nor mass, the question implicitly commits the logical error of being a category fallacy.

In the same way, when witnessing to nonbelievers, I'm frequently asked to provide "scientific evidence for God." My typical response is, "And why would I want to do a silly thing like that?" Because this is often met with a look of confusion, I offer the following explanation:

> God, if He exists, is *by definition* a non-physical entity, whereas science, though a wonderful tool for studying the physical world, is a tool that is *limited to only studying the physical world*. Hence, one cannot demand that a discipline like science, which is limited to the physical, must be used to investigate something non-physical. It is a category fallacy.

By way of analogy, suppose your friend returns from spending hours on the beach with a metal detector and concludes there's no plastic on the beach. Yet, you glance over his shoulder and see the beach is littered with plastic. Defending his conclusion, he explains that after laboring for hours on the beach, his metal detector discovered lots of metal, but never once detected an ounce of plastic. Because of this, he not only claims there's no plastic on the beach, but now believes plastic must not exist! Confused by this, you point out how his metal detector is made predominantly of plastic.[72] Nevertheless, he retorts, "then why didn't it detect any plastic on the beach?" The answer is embarrassingly obvious. The tool he was using was a *metal* detector, *not* a plastic detector.

Similarly, demanding that science be used to "try and find God" in the universe is like demanding that a metal detector be used to try and find plastic on the beach. It's simply the wrong tool for the assessment. Hence, claiming that "if science cannot answer the God question, then He must not exist" is no different than claiming that if a metal detector cannot detect plastic, plastic must not exist. It's neither a valid argument nor objection, but a category fallacy.

SCIENTISM IS FALSE: EXPOSING THE *REDUCTIO AD ABSURDUM*

Not only is scientism self-refuting and, when applied to God, categorically fallacious, but the epistemology is demonstrably false. Recall that those with a strong view of scientism will claim science is the *only way* to gain knowledge about reality. This raises two unique problems for scientism as an epistemology—both of which become a *reductio ad absurdum* against the view (tactical tool #5).

First, *science is subordinate to philosophy*. Philosophy itself provides the very foundation for science, and without it, science would be impossible. Second, many things we know go beyond the realm of science. That is, *the availability of non-scientific knowledge* that cannot be proven by science itself. Exposing these problems in conversation can successfully convey the limits of science as an epistemology and, more appropriately, demonstrate why scientism is false.

1. Science is Subordinate to Philosophy

In their book, *Philosophical Foundations for a Christian Worldview*, Dr. William Lane Craig and Dr. J. P. Moreland present ten philosophical presuppositions of science:[73]

1. the existence of a theory-independent, external world
2. the orderly nature of the external world
3. the knowability of the external world
4. the existence of truth
5. the laws of logic
6. the reliability of our cognitive faculties
7. the adequacy of language to describe the world
8. the existence of values used in science (e.g., "test theories fairly and report test results honestly")
9. the uniformity of nature and induction
10. the existence of numbers

All of these are foundational items of knowledge that cannot be proven (or disproven) by science because, without exception, these truths are grounded philosophically, *not* scientifically. Ergo, before science can "get off the ground," it must rely on these philosophical presuppositions for its foundation. As atheist philosopher of science Daniel Dennett notes, "There is no such thing as philosophy-free science; there is only science whose philosophical baggage is taken on board without examination."[74] Following Dennett's advice, let's briefly examine two of these philosophical presuppositions: the existence of truth and the laws of logic.

Scientism and the Existence of Truth

To grasp this first point, ask yourself (or the person you are witnessing to) the following question, "What scientific experiment could we employ to discover whether or not truth exists?" When I ask this to nonbelievers, they typically respond with a hypothetical scenario of a scientist who makes a hypothesis, conducts empirical investigations, and concludes whether the initial hypothesis was true. Essentially, they're describing *the scientific method*. But note, this was not my question.

I didn't ask if people could conduct experiments to discover whether something *is* true. Instead, I asked what experiment could be done to discover whether truth *exists in the first place*. When a person conducts an experiment, they already presuppose that their results will lead to true or false conclusions. Hence, their experiment doesn't *prove truth exists,* but *assumes it.* Yet, this is the very thing in question. So, not only does this response fail to answer my question, but coincidentally illustrates the very point I'm trying to make; science does not *prove* truth exists but assumes it.

So again, I ask, what scientific experiment could we conduct to discover whether or not truth exists? I mean, seriously. What would that even look like? Would one write the word "truth" on a piece of paper, burn it with a match, spill the ashes in liquid, heat it to 102 degrees Fahrenheit, stir it for 38 seconds, and if it turns blue, then truth exists? No, because at the end of the day, the existence of truth is something science presupposes, not concludes via scientific inquiry.[75]

Therefore, if science is the *only* way to gain knowledge about reality, and yet, the existence of truth is a *philosophical question* that science cannot answer, then it follows that on scientism, *one could never know whether or not truth exists.* However, if truth *does exist* and is *knowable,* then it logically follows that scientism is false.

Scientism and the Laws of Logic

There are three fundamental laws of logic (also referred to as the "laws of thought"):

- **The Law of Identity**: something is what it is and not something else. "A is A" (A=A)
- **The Law of Non-contradiction**: Nothing can be both A and not A simultaneously and in the same way. "A is *not* -A" (A ≠ -A)
- **The Law of Excluded Middle**: A statement is either true or false, not something in between. "A is either true or false" (A = T or F)

Each of these are *non-scientific,* philosophical laws that must be employed by any rational discipline. They cannot be proven or disproven by science (or any other discipline for that matter) because the moment one attempts to do so, they automatically assume them.

To illustrate, take the law of non-contradiction and the law of the excluded middle: something is either true or false and cannot be both. To argue that these laws are not true, one assumes they are false (the law of excluded middle) and that they cannot be both true and false simultaneously (the law of non-contradiction). Hence, to try and prove them false, one must first assume they're true.

Subsequently then, science must presuppose the laws of logic as a foundation, and logic is a branch of philosophy. Thus, *science is and always will be subordinate to philosophy*. This is the foundation for any rational discipline, and no foundation is deeper than the very laws of logic on which it stands. As Moreland explains:

> Just as the structure of a building cannot be more reliable than the foundation on which it rests, so the *conclusions* of science (i.e., the structure) cannot be more certain than the *presuppositions* of science (i.e., its foundation)... In this way, then, scientism ends up loosening the foundations of science itself, jeopardizing the entire edifice.[76]

As a result, scientism becomes an enemy, not just of Christianity but of science. Therefore, if science is the only way to gain knowledge about reality, and yet, it cannot account for these foundational laws of logic, then scientism becomes illogical (and false) by default.

2. The Availability of Non-scientific Knowledge

We limit our examination of this problem to the realm of morality and behavior. Both fall under the discipline, not of science, but of ethics, which is itself a field of philosophy. **Ethics** is the study of morality that "is concerned with our beliefs and judgments regarding right and wrong motives, attitudes, character, and conduct."[77] In philosophy, it's common to use reprehensible **thought experiments** (hypothetical scenarios for reflecting on the merits of a view) to make a point as strongly as possible—especially within the field of ethics. Using this method, let's examine how scientism becomes impotent for providing even the most basic knowledge regarding morality and ethics.

Scientism, Morality, and Ethics: A Thought Experiment

Suppose a young man knew that when his grandmother passed away, he'd receive millions of dollars as an inheritance. However, while his grandmother was quite old, she was also quite healthy. Eager to receive the money, he decides to "speed up the process" by baking the cake for her next birthday and lacing it with poisonous chemicals. Consequently, she consumes the cake and passes away.

Now, it should be obvious to anyone without a scientific degree that what the young man did was morally wrong. However, if scientism is true, we can *only* arrive at and confirm this conclusion by appealing to science. So, suppose we consult the authority figures. The world's leading scientists, each Nobel prize winners in their field, and ask them to examine the situation for a "moral analysis." If scientism is true, *then through scientific investigation alone*, they should be able to come to the same conclusion that any sane person would. Namely, that what the young man did was *morally wrong*. But what will they discover? Let's find out.

First, the world's leading nutritional scientist informs us about the cake's ingredients, calories, and nutritional value. However, analyzing ingredients and calories cannot provide a moral analysis. Next, we bring in a renowned toxicologist to identify the poisons used in the cake. But, unfortunately, knowing about the various poisons in the cake doesn't tell us whether it was morally wrong to use them. After this, we bring in the world's leading chemist who explains the chemical composition of the poisons, how each fused with the cake as it baked, and how the chemicals broke down in the body after digestion. As before, this provides us with no moral answers. Finally, we bring in the leading hematologist, an expert who specializes in blood analysis and diseases. After examining the body, she provides a step-by-step analysis of how the poison entered the bloodstream, affected the main arteries, and eventually led to her death. But, still, knowing the process of *how* the death occurred doesn't tell us whether the death, ethically speaking, *should have* occurred to begin with.

After it's all said and done, we'll have *a complete scientific analysis* of the death, and yet, *no moral answers*. Why? Because as brilliant as these scientists are in their field, none of them could conduct a study, look under a microscope, and—*based on their scientific analysis*—say, "Ah! What this young man did was *morally wrong*. It says so right here in the petri dish!"

Now, I'm not saying these scientists didn't *know* what the young man did was immoral, but I am saying they didn't need to look under a microscope to *know* it. This is because, at best, science could only tell them what *is* the case, but it couldn't tell them what *ought* to be the case.[78] It could only describe what happened, *but could not prescribe what should* have happened. As atheist philosopher of science Dr. Michael Ruse explains, "science does not ask certain questions, and so it is no surprise that it does not give [certain] answers."[79]

For this reason, questions regarding morality or ethics move us beyond the realm of science and into the field of philosophy. Hence, science becomes impotent for answering moral questions (i.e., a category fallacy) and thus, providing a scientific analysis could never suffice for a moral one.

RESPONDING TO AN OBJECTION

Suppose a person objects to our thought experiment by arguing that causing pain is immoral, and science can show us what causes pain in the body. Thus, "according to science," we should avoid causing pain to others. Using *The Lazy Approach*, let's expose the problems with the objection.

1. Identifying the Fallacies

Recall the variation of tactical tool #4, "That's Not an Argument," where we discern the difference between an *actual* argument and a combination of claims presented *as if* it were an argument. In this case, the purported "objection" is the latter. To see why, consider the three claims implicit in the "objection."

1. Causing pain is immoral.
2. Science can show us how pain harms the body.
3. Therefore, causing pain is wrong.

First, this isn't a valid argument but merely a **tautology**—repeating the same thing twice in a different way. Here, the words "immoral" and "wrong" are being used as synonyms. Thus, the person is essentially saying, "Causing pain is wrong, therefore, causing pain is wrong," or, "causing pain is immoral, therefore, causing pain is immoral." Again, this is not an argument but a tautology that does nothing to advance the conversation.

Third, this results in the person committing the fallacy of **begging the question** by way of **circular reasoning**, two fallacies that often go together. Evident by the tautology, the argument is circular: "Causing pain is immoral because it's wrong. Therefore, it's wrong to cause pain because it's immoral." Concerning the fallacy of **begging the question**, this occurs when a person does not argue for the truth of their position but presents it by simply *assuming* it's true. In this example, the person begins with the claim, "causing pain is immoral," but doesn't provide a justification as to *why* it's immoral. Instead, they simply assume it (i.e., begging the question).

Granted, I'd agree that, all things being equal, causing pain is immoral. However, by what objective standard can the advocate of scientism judge *any* behavior as immoral? As we saw in the previous section, the assessment of moral knowledge, given scientism, becomes impossible.

Finally, not only is scientism impotent for gaining knowledge about morality, but as with postmodernism, reduces to absurdity by implicitly allowing for morally reprehensible behaviors that are logically consistent within its worldview. As before, we can propose a moral dilemma and offer an undesirable solution that, while abhorrent, is logically compatible with the objection (tactical tool #5: a *reductio ad absurdum*).

2. Exposing the Absurd Implications of Scientism

Note how the justification for the moral judgment that "causing pain is wrong" focuses on the experience of pain. Hence, we can reword the objection as follows: "An act is immoral if and only if it causes a person to experience pain." This would imply that if no pain is experienced, then the same act, according to the objection, cannot be judged immoral. So (utilizing tactical tools #2, #3, and #5), consider the following thought experiment as a *reductio ad absurdum* counterexample.

We can all affirm that cutting someone slowly with a knife for fun is immoral, and indeed, science can verify the pain this causes. Nevertheless, the same science that shows us how pain is identified in the body is the same science that can show us how to eliminate the presence of pain altogether. Thus, we can offer the same scenario but propose using anesthesia (much like a doctor would use in surgery), knocking the person out, eliminating the pain, and patching the person up after we've had our fun. Given that the victim will never experience an ounce of pain (or remember the encounter), we can now ask if the act remains immoral. And here is where the inadequacy of assessing ethical behavior within scientism becomes apparent.

First, while science can answer the question of *how* pain is caused, it *cannot* answer whether causing the pain is immoral (hence, the fallacy of begging the question). Or, more to the point, whether removing the presence of pain equally removes the immoral nature of the act. Second, although the advocate of scientism may believe the act *remains* immoral, their justification will no longer be rooted in "science," but in arguing the philosophy of ethics. Unfortunately, however, if philosophical explanations are rejected within scientism (see the beginning of this chapter), then they must be rejected for answering moral dilemmas, as well.

For this reason, if the person concedes that the act remains immoral (although their justification of pain has been removed), then they must now concede that scientism is both impotent (because it cannot answer the moral dilemma) and false (because the act is morally compatible with the objection when we all know it's wrong). Therefore, by demonstrating why these abhorrent, though logically consistent, and thus, implicitly permissible practices within a worldview should be rejected, we've demonstrated why the worldview of scientism must be rejected as well.

SCIENCE VS. FAITH: RESPONDING TO THE CLAIMS OF SCIENTISM

Recall that a culture permeated with scientism tends to assume the false dichotomy between science and "faith." To address this mentality, consider two popular claims that stem from this stronghold: 1) Christianity is anti-science, and 2) Science explains everything: God explains nothing.

1. "Christianity Is Anti-Science"

We've all heard the mantra that Christianity is opposed to science. However, nothing can be further from the truth. Historically, the scientific revolution exploded around the 16th and 17th centuries, primarily in the West and not the East. Why then and there? Because these early scientists in the West possessed a foundational belief that the East did not have. Namely, the belief that one could discover rational intelligibility in the universe *because a rational, intelligent creator designed it.*

By way of analogy, no one studies a scattered heap of garbage expecting to discover intentional order, design, or purpose to its structure. Similarly, if there's no God, there'd be no reason to study the universe's structure—expecting to discover intentional order, design, or purpose to its existence. Why look for design or purpose where there is none? However, if there *is* a God who created, ordered, and designed the universe, then with excitement, there's much to find through scientific investigation! As C. S. Lewis summarized, "Men became scientific because they expected law in nature, and they expected law in nature because they believed in a lawgiver."[80]

As an example of this, consider the words of astronomer Johannes Kepler, a key figure in the 17th-century scientific revolution:

> The chief aim of all investigations of the external world should be to discover the rational order which has been imposed on it by God, and which he revealed to us in the language of mathematics.[81]

Indeed, Kepler famously described the scientific endeavor as "thinking God's thoughts after him."[82] Or consider Francis Bacon (1564-1626), regarded by many as the father of modern science (developing the scientific method itself), when he proclaims that God has given us two books: the book of Nature and the book of the Bible, and that "to be properly educated, one should give one's mind to studying both."[83]

As Oxford historian of science, John Brooke, observes, "the particular conceptions of science held by its pioneers were often informed by theological and metaphysical beliefs."[84] And as Nobel Prize winner in biochemistry Melvin Calvin explains, "This monotheistic view seems to be the historical foundation for modern science."[85]

In his book, *Has Science Buried God?*, Dr. John Lennox provides a list of prominent scientists who were pivotal in the historical rise of science *because* of their belief in God. In chronological order, these were Galileo (1564–1642), Kepler (1571–1630), Pascal (1623–1662), Boyle (1627–1691), Newton (1642–1727), Faraday (1791–1867), Babbage (1791–1871), Mendel (1822–1884), Pasteur (1822–1895), Kelvin (1824–1907) and Clerk Maxwell (1831–1879). Reflecting on this prestigious list, Lennox writes,

> Far from hindering the rise of modern science, *faith in God was one of the motors that drove it.* I therefore regard it as a privilege and an honour, not an embarrassment, to be both a scientist and a Christian.[86]

Hence, Christianity never was, nor has it ever been, a hindrance to science, but was the very foundation of it!

2. "Science Explains Everything, God Explains Nothing"

Another popular claim stemming from this stronghold is the idea that "we don't need God to explain anything because we have science!" As a result, many nonbelievers assume that any argument for God as an explanation for something must be an **argument from ignorance**, or more popularly known as a "**God of the gaps**" fallacy. That is, using God as an explanation when a scientific explanation cannot be found. Such an accusation is typically presented by comparing belief in God to the belief in Thor, the god of thunder.

When ancient man saw lightning and couldn't explain it, they invented a god of thunder, called him "Thor," and devoted an entire day of the week to honor him: Thursday (literally, "Thor's Day"). Yet, no one today believes that the existence of Thor serves as an explanation for lightning. Why not? Because of science! Given modern science, we now understand how electrical charges operate and thus, Thor as an explanation is unnecessary.

By the same token (argues the atheist), when Christians cannot explain something scientifically, we use God as an explanation (i.e., an excuse) to "fill in the gaps" of our scientific ignorance. But much like these superstitious, ancient civilizations, we're committing a "god of the gaps" fallacy. Nevertheless, just as science did away with Thor's existence as an explanation for thunder, Christians should realize it has done away with God's existence as an explanation for anything.

Exposing the Fallacies

Though popular, this argument fails for various reasons. First, it assumes that belief in God as an explanation for something hinders the flourishing of science. This was addressed in the previous section. Second, it assumes that arguments for the existence of God ignore what we know about the universe—a "God of the gaps" argument from ignorance. But as we'll see in Part 4 of this book, the best arguments for God aren't rooted in what we *don't know* but in what we *do know*. Hence, the Thor "god of the gaps" analogy doesn't apply. Now consider the fallacies.

A False Dichotomy: Origin vs Operation

As with most claims of scientism, the argument becomes a false dichotomy fallacy. In this case, the nonbeliever presents God and science as two mutually exclusive explanations, assuming it must be one or the other, not both. But consider how this erroneously confuses two categories of explanations: *origin* and *operation.*

To illustrate, suppose a Ford motorcar is put before you, and you are asked to explain it with only two options: Henry Ford or the physics of internal combustion?[87] In response to this challenge, we can begin by asking, "an explanation for what?" Because on the one hand, while the physics of internal combustion may explain the *operation* of the car, it cannot explain its origin. For that, you need an agent—Henry Ford himself. On the other hand, while Henry Ford may explain the *origin* of the car (why it exists), his existence cannot explain its operation. For that, you need the laws of physics. Hence, the false dichotomy. Ford, as an agent, explains its origin, not its operation, and the laws of physics explain its operation, not its origin.[88] Both categories of explanation are needed and, thus, cannot be mutually exclusive.

A Category Fallacy: The Mechanics Do Not Disprove a Mechanic

Pushing the objection further, some claim that modern scientific discoveries can now disprove the existence of God. But note that because of their ignorance of this false dichotomy, they now commit a category fallacy. Why? Because God is not an opposing explanation to science, just as Henry Ford is not an opposing explanation to the laws of physics. Hence, scientific discoveries could never be used to "disprove" the existence of God, just as discovering the physics of internal combustion could never be used to disprove the existence of Henry Ford. To argue otherwise is not only a false dichotomy but a category fallacy.

As Oxford philosophy professor Dr. Richard Swinburne explains,

> I am not postulating a "God of the gaps", a god merely to explain the things that science has not yet explained. I am postulating a God to explain why science explains; I do not deny that science explains, but I postulate God to explain why science explains.[89]

In other words, arguments for the existence of God are explanations of *origin* that deal with ontology (the reason for which something *exists*), whereas scientific discoveries are explanations of *operation* that deal with epistemology (a way of *knowing* the thing that exists). Thus, one can *know* the laws of physics (the operation) without believing in Henry Ford, but without Henry Ford (the origin), there would be no car to operate. Similarly, one need not believe in God to discover the operations of science, but without God, there would be no science to discover. As Lennox remarks:

> When Sir Isaac Newton discovered the universal law of gravitation he did not say, "I have discovered a mechanism that accounts for planetary motion, therefore there is no agent God who designed it." Quite the opposite: precisely because he understood how it worked, he was moved to increased admiration for the God who had designed it that way.[90]

Conclusion and Summary

With the information provided in this chapter, you are now equipped with the knowledge and tools for explaining why scientism is:

- Self-refuting (because scientism is philosophy, not science).
- A category fallacy concerning the question of God (science is limited to the physical, God is immaterial).
- Subordinate to philosophy (presupposing philosophical truths that it cannot prove).
- Impotent for addressing moral dilemmas (because these are questions of philosophy, not science).
- A false dichotomy concerning origin and operation (Henry Ford vs. physics, God vs. science).
- And most importantly, demonstrably false (cannot account for the existence of truth or the laws of logic, both of which are needed to do science in the first place).

In the next chapter, we begin addressing the stronghold of naturalism by using questions to tease out and identify the view in conversation. Because there is overlap between these two (scientism and naturalism), much of what will be presented there could equally apply to scientism (and vice versa).

Chapter 15

Responding to Naturalism

Let me summarize my views on what modern evolutionary biology tells us loud and clear... There are no gods, no purposeful forces of any kind, no life after death... There is no ultimate foundation for ethics, no ultimate meaning in life, and no free will for humans, either.[91]

–William Provine, Cornell professor, and naturalist

Reviewing Naturalism

In Chapter 8 we unpacked three key features for identifying naturalism: *empiricism*, *reductionism*, and *physicalism*. Empiricism was presented as the naturalist epistemology, limiting knowledge strictly to the five senses. Reductionism was presented as how a naturalist (appealing strictly to physical processes) may seek to explain everything by reducing some entity "X" to *nothing but* or *nothing more than* some entity "Y." Finally, physicalism was the naturalist ontology applied to human beings, reducing persons to *nothing more than* physical objects. Hence, within naturalism as a worldview, nothing immaterial exists, nor is it needed to explain anything.

This meant that if naturalism is true, then neither the soul nor God (being immaterial entities) can exist, the resurrection would be impossible, and thus, Christianity would be false. Hence, adequately addressing this stronghold is essential. To do this, we'll take each feature individually, unpack their problems, expose the fallacies, and demonstrate how the logical entailments of naturalism as a whole lead to irrational, undesirable conclusions.

EXPOSING THE PROBLEMS WITH EMPIRICISM

1. Empiricism Is Self-Defeating

As previously mentioned, we don't want to assume the nonbeliever holds to the features just mentioned. Instead, we want to identify them by paying careful attention to the kind of evidence they request.

- What *scientific evidence* do you have for God?
- What is the *proof* for God?
- Can you *demonstrate* God's existence (or the evidence)?
- How can you *test* this evidence?
- What *method* can be used to investigate God's existence?

In each of these, there's a hint of these features, but this may not be evident at face value. Given that two people can use the same term but have entirely different meanings, getting them to define their terms is essential. Thus, we can ask what the person means by "evidence," "proof," "demonstrate," "test," or "method." The most common responses seem to be (but are not limited to) the following:

- *Scientific* evidence
- *Empirical* evidence/investigation
- *Demonstrable* evidence
- *Testable* evidence

It may appear that the person has answered the question, but in actuality, they've only shortened their answers. Nothing has been defined. This typically occurs for two reasons. First, the person may not know what they *mean* by "empirical," "demonstrable," or "testable." They've always used these words authoritatively but have never been challenged on their meaning. Nine times out of ten, they mean something physical.

Second, the person may genuinely believe that scientific, empirical investigation is the only evidence available to us. Being so ingrained in their worldview, they haven't considered the possibility of accepting anything other than "scientific, empirical evidence" (e.g., it's beyond their plausibility structure). For this reason, it would be helpful to press forward by using a variation of our two questions within *The Lazy Approach*: "What do you mean by that?" and "How did you come to that conclusion?" Consider the following examples:

Example #1

Nonbeliever: What proof is there for God?

Eric: What do you mean by proof?

Nonbeliever: The only proof that is available to us. Scientific!

Eric: Are you implying that scientific evidence is the only way to gain knowledge about reality?

Nonbeliever: Of course!

Eric: And how did you come to that conclusion?

From here, one can use what we've learned in the last chapter and show how scientism is ultimately self-defeating.

Example #2

I once debated the well-known atheist and self-proclaimed skeptic Matt Dillahunty on the topic, "Does the Soul Exist?" In our debate, he claimed I needed a "method" to demonstrate the truth of my position.[92] This stems from the skeptic's epistemic view known as **methodism** (the epistemological position, not the church denomination!) which assumes that a "method" or "demonstration" is needed to justify the truth of *every possible claim*.

Matt: But first you must demonstrate that you have a method [for "investigating" the soul] that is reliable.

Eric: You keep asserting that I must present a method to justify every claim I make. But if that's the case, then what *method* did you use to discover that we need methods?

Note, my strategy wasn't to offer a "method" to his challenge (indeed, I disagreed with his methodism) but to provide a rebuttal against his position (tactical tool #3). Why? Because if a method is needed to justify the truth of *every* claim, then it follows that the claim, "a method is needed to justify the truth of every claim," requires a method to justify it. However, once a purported method is given, then according to his skepticism, a method would be needed to justify the claim that was used to justify the initial methodological claim to begin with.

In other words, if his methodological approach were correct, it would lead to an **infinite regress** (requiring a method for a method for a method), and no claim could ever be justified. Hence, because I disagreed with the assumption behind his question, I didn't provide a direct answer. Instead, I questioned the question and exposed the *reductio ad absurdum* of his position (tactical tools #1 and #5).

Example #3

In my debate with popular internet atheist Aron Ra, he claimed that the only "rational evidence" was *necessarily* empirical evidence.

Aron: What rational evidence do you have for God?

Eric: What do you mean by rational evidence?

Aron: Empirical, verifiable evidence.

Eric: Are you implying that the only "rational evidence" one can have for a position is *necessarily* empirical?

Aron: Of course. What else is there?

Eric: I see. And what *empirical evidence* did you use to verify that empirical evidence is the only rational evidence available?

This response is similar to the approach for exposing scientism as self-refuting (tactical tools #1 and #2). Here, the empiricist assumes that every starting point for discovering truth must begin with empiricism. Yet, such an assumption is a starting point that's philosophical, *not* empirical. Therefore, his claim was false at best and, at worst, self-defeating.

2. Examining Professor P's Ploy

Suppose you were in my shoes when Professor P argued against the soul. Though we have yet to respond to this objection, we can use what we've learned and begin asking some questions. Remember, with *The Lazy Approach*, you don't need to know all the right answers, you just need to know how to ask the right questions.

Tactical Tool #4: Argument or Assertion?

To begin with, Professor P never gave an *actual argument* for his belief that physicalism is true (i.e., there is no soul). All he did was ask rhetorical questions, make a few statements, and then assert (not provide a case or argument) that the soul did not exist. Did you catch this? If not, go back and read it for yourself.

Recall that one of the tools within *The Lazy Approach* is identifying whether someone is making an actual argument or merely making an assertion, declarative statement, or expressing their opinion. What my professor did was the latter, just with a sense of rhetorical elegance and confidence. However, rhetorical elegance and confidence cannot justify the truth of a position. After all, a person can be rhetorical, elegant, and confident—but still be rhetorically, elegantly, and confidently wrong.

If you encounter this in conversation, respond in a way that helps you identify and expose the problem. Utilizing *The Lazy Approach*, you can ask a probing question, reword the position, and place the burden of proof back on their shoulders (tactical tools #1 and #2).

- Are you implying that if we cannot "find the soul" under a microscope, it doesn't exist?
- But if the soul existed, wouldn't it be non-physical? Why should we use physical means of investigation to try and "find it?"
- Is this not assuming that the soul (or God) has a physical location, weight, mass, or shape? Why would we apply these physical characteristics to something that is, by definition, non-physical? (i.e., a category fallacy)

- How did you come to the conclusion that consciousness is physical?

Tactical Tool #5: Question Begging and Circular Reasoning

In addition, given that an argument was never presented for his objection, it commits the fallacies of being both question-begging and circular. Using Professor P's own words (as presented in chapter 8), let's unpack this approach in a hypothetical conversation.

Eric: How do you know everything that exists is physical?

Naturalist: Because every time we've investigated claims of souls or the supernatural, the explanation has always been nothing more than physics and chemistry.

Eric: So, if I understand you correctly (tactical tool #2), you're saying that every time we study the physical, we only find something physical?

Naturalist: Exactly.

Eric: And how does studying the physical, which you admitted can only show us the physical, prove that something immaterial *cannot* exist?

Remember, if an argument is not given (or if we disagree with the underlining assumption), then we have nothing to rebut (much less refute), and the burden of proof should be placed back on them. Again, the one making the claim bears the burden, and it's not our job to prove them wrong; it's their job to prove they're right.

3. Looking for the Invisible Man: A Category Fallacy

In the previous chapter, we learned how scientism involves a category fallacy when applied to the question of God. Concerning empiricism and the soul, the same principle applies. To illustrate, suppose you overhear two of your neighbors arguing and, being the peacemaking Christian you are, you stop to see if you can help settle the dispute. After a few minutes of inquiring about the situation, you learn the following.

Neighbor #1 claims there's an invisible man in his house and Neighbor #2, being skeptical of this, offered to investigate. However, after five hours of investigation, Neighbor #2 accused Neighbor #1 of lying. Thus, their argument ensued. Trying not to take sides, you ask Neighbor #2 why he thinks Neighbor #1 is lying. Here's his response:

> This guy claims there's an invisible man in his house, but after five hours of searching, I never *saw him anywhere*! And trust me, I *looked* everywhere. I *looked* in the closet, I *looked* under the beds, and I even *looked* in the bathroom. But not once did I ever *see* this invisible man myself!

With an angry but puzzled look, Neighbor #1 pulls at his hair and shouts, "Well, of course you didn't see him. He's *invisible*!"

Now, whatever the truth may be, no one can deny that what Neighbor #1 has said in his defense is correct. Granted, this wouldn't prove he's right, but it would prove that Neighbor #2's inability to *"visibly see"* an *invisible* man cannot be used to argue that the invisible man doesn't exist. After all, being unable to see something invisible would, at the very least, be logically consistent with the claim and thus, cannot be an argument against it.

In the same way, if the soul exists and is immaterial, then one cannot use empirical means of investigation (like studying the brain or body under a microscope and not "finding" or "seeing" a soul—as my professor insinuated) to argue against it. It's simply the wrong tool for the assessment and thus, a category fallacy. Therefore, appealing to empiricism as an objection to the soul is incredibly misguided and fallacious—even if done by a philosophy professor who should've known better.

ADDRESSING REDUCTIONISM AND PHYSICALISM

Within naturalism, *physicalism* (the view that human beings are purely physical objects) is logically entailed by *reductionism* (the view that everything is reducible and explainable in terms of chemistry and physics). One follows the other as a byproduct of a *logically consistent* naturalist worldview, and effectively addressing these features requires that we better understand their relation.

A Philosophical Preface: Epistemic Chains

When it comes to the study of epistemology, consider how a **base belief** will logically imply further beliefs that a person must hold to if they wish to be logically consistent. For example, if a person believes all dogs are mammals (a *base* belief), they must further believe the next dog they encounter will be a mammal (the *implied* belief). Hence, if the former *base belief* is true (all dogs are mammals), then the ***implied belief*** (the next dog I encounter will be a mammal) must also be true.

In philosophical terms, when some *base belief* "A" entails an *implied belief* "B," we have the beginning of an **epistemic chain** (the notion that a base belief can and will imply a further chain of beliefs that are logically entailed by the previous). Such a chain can be illustrated as follows:

A → B → C → D... (and so forth)

Now consider how a base belief can be *directly* or *indirectly* proven false by addressing the implied beliefs within the chain. This can be done in one of two ways.

1. Attacking the Truth of an Implied Belief (The Direct Way)

The first way is to attack the truth of an implied belief *directly*. This is because if belief A implies belief B, but belief B is proven false, then it would logically follow that belief A must be false, as well. Pulling from the first example, if a person believes all dogs are brown (base belief A), then they must further believe that the next dog they encounter will be brown (the implied belief B). However, if the next dog they encounter is *not* brown (proving the implied belief B is false), it would follow that their base belief A (all dogs are brown) must be false. In an argument, this can be written as follows:

1. If A is true, then B is true.
2. B is not true.
3. Therefore, A is false.

2. Attacking the Logical Coherence of the Chain (The Indirect Way)

The second approach to proving that a base belief is false is by exposing the logical incoherence or inconsistency of the chain as a whole. To grasp this approach, consider that a base belief can imply two beliefs that branch into two separate chains.

```
   B...→ X
  ↗
A
  ↘
   C...→Y
```

To illustrate, suppose that some base belief A implied two separate beliefs: B) an immovable object exists, and C) an unstoppable force exists. Note that both B and C, when taken in isolation, could be true *independently*. Indeed, there's nothing logically inconsistent or incoherent with *either* an immovable object (implied belief B) or an unstoppable force (implied belief C) existing. Hence, our first approach wouldn't apply.

However, if it can be demonstrated that the implied beliefs, while *possibly true* in isolation, *cannot possibly* be true when taken as a whole, then it would follow that the base belief A is false given that it produced a logically incoherent, inconsistent set of beliefs. Hence, our second approach: showing that the implied set of beliefs cannot be true *holistically*.

After all, if an immovable object existed and was confronted by an unstoppable force, then either the immovable object would move (meaning it wasn't immovable) or the unstoppable force would stop (meaning it wasn't unstoppable). And note that we don't need to know which of the two outcomes will occur. All we need to know is that these implied beliefs, while possibly true *independently*, cannot possibly be true *simultaneously*. Therefore, if two or more implied beliefs cannot be true together, then the base belief which produced them must be false. In an argument, this can be written as follows:

1. If A is true, then both B and C are true.
2. Taken together, both B and C cannot possibly be true.
3. Therefore, A cannot possibly be true.

4. Therefore, A is false.

The Epistemic Chains of Naturalism

Allow me to explain why understanding this is foundational for evangelism. Due to plausibility structures, some nonbelievers are unwilling to entertain the idea that their base belief (God does not exist) or even their first implied belief (naturalism) is *possibly* false. However, their implied beliefs further down the chain (e.g., that consciousness is physical or that free will doesn't exist—more on this later) are not as dogmatically held. For this reason, if we can learn to formulate questions or arguments that demonstrate how the implied beliefs of their worldview must be false, it would suffice to demonstrate why their base belief (naturalism or atheism) must be false, as well. To grasp this approach for naturalism, consider the following epistemic chain:

Consciousness is physical
↗
Naturalism → Reductionism → Physicalism → No Soul
↘
Freewill cannot exist

My aim here is to introduce you to the practice of learning to look at a worldview holistically, as opposed to taking individual claims, arguments, or positions in isolation—as if such beliefs are disconnected without ramifications. We've already seen how a lack of holistic thinking concerning the Christian worldview led to the unchecked infiltration of these strongholds in the church—such as believing the brain thinks while failing to consider that we serve (and are made in the image of) a God that has no brain and thinks just fine.

Nevertheless, with this understanding before us, we can now address the features of physicalism and reductionism by evaluating the logical coherence of the chain as a whole. To be clear, we'll still be using *The Lazy Approach* for our responses, but as foreshadowed in chapter 11, there's nothing inherently lazy about it. As demonstrated in the previous chapters, knowing how to maneuver our approach for each stronghold required some philosophical understanding. But now that the "hard work" has been done, implementing the approach becomes a "lazy man's" task.

Break Every Chain

To reiterate the chain once more, if naturalism is true and everything that exists is physical, then it follows that every aspect of reality can and must be *reducible* to (and explained by) something physical. When applied to human beings, this led to physicalism; the view that human persons are purely physical objects (no soul exists). As a result, if the naturalist wants to be logically consistent within their worldview, then at least two branches must follow in their chain of beliefs. Namely, that:

1. Consciousness, *if it exists*, must be reducible or identical to something physical.
2. Free will cannot exist, and determinism must be true.

Our focus in addressing these will be brief, emphasizing only a *small* portion of the points that could be made about these topics. For the sake of space, we'll use the first for addressing physicalism and the second for addressing reductionism.

1. PHYSICALISM: MIND AND MATTER

Leibniz's Law: A Test for Identity

If physicalism is true, then consciousness, if it exists, must be *reducible* and/or *identical* to something physical like the brain. In philosophy, when we say that X is **identical** to Y, we simply mean that X is *literally the same thing as* Y. For example, if I said that Eric Hernandez is *identical to* the author of this book, then I'm referring to one person, not two, because Eric Hernandez and the author of this book are the same person. Hence, I'm using two labels to refer to one thing.

As a test for identity, this is known as ***Leibniz's Law of the Indiscernibility of Identicals***, but for brevity's sake, we'll simply refer to this as "**Leibniz's Law.**" According to Leibniz's Law, if two things in question are identical, say, some X and Y, then whatever is true of X will *necessarily* be true of Y (and vice versa). Conversely, if we can find *one thing* true of X that is not true of Y (or vice versa), then they cannot be the same thing (i.e., they cannot be identical).

To illustrate, suppose you walk into a lab and see two bottles of clear fluids. One bottle is labeled "Water," and the other is "Chemical X," but the label was worn out and illegible. Applying Leibnitz's Law, you want to know if these are the same substance because, as far as you can tell, they're identical. Both are fluids, both are clear, and thus, may be the same substance. However, you turn over the bottle of Chemical X and find a label that reads, "Caution: Flammable." Given that water is not flammable, but Chemical X is, you conclude that the two cannot be the same substance. Therefore, even if you don't know what Chemical X is, you now know that, given Leibnitz's Law, they cannot be identical.

Addressing Professor P's "Argument"

Recall that Professor P's "argument" for physicalism revolved around the assumption that the mind is *nothing more than* (i.e., identical to) the brain. If true, this would mean that whatever is true of the mind must be true of the brain and vice versa. However, this would also mean that if we can find *one thing* true of the mind that's not true of the brain (or vice versa), then given Leibnitz's Law, they cannot be the same thing. And here is where the existence of consciousness becomes a problem for the naturalist.

If we can demonstrate that consciousness is not physical (attacking the implied belief), then physicalism (and by default, the base belief of naturalism) cannot be true. So, to address the purported "argument" in favor of physicalism, we can begin by asking, "Does Professor P's argument satisfy Leibniz's Law?" That is, did he show that the mind and brain are the same thing? No, and this brings us to our first response via a rebuttal.

The Rebuttal: Identity or Mere Correlation?

In defense of physicalism, many naturalists point to the cause-effect or dependency relationship between the mind and brain. For example, we know from neuroscience that when a mental state occurs (e.g., a thought or belief), there will be a correlating brain state (i.e., neurons firing). In cases of brain damage (such as Alzheimer's), certain regions of the brain are directly correlated with certain functions of the mind (such as memory). As a result, damage to these regions has a direct effect on one's ability to recall memories. This would suffice to demonstrate two things:

1. A cause-and-effect relationship between the mind and brain.
2. A dependence relationship between specified regions of the brain and specified functions of the mind.

Because of this (argues the naturalist), the mind and brain must be the same thing. But is this truly the case? Has neuroscience provided the final nail in the Christian worldview coffin? No, and for one simple reason: *cause and effect or dependency does not establish identity*.

To illustrate why this popular argument fails, consider the relationship between a musician and his instrument. A guitarist knows that to successfully play the note C, he must press down and strum the specific group of correlated strings. Similarly, he knows that if these correlating groups of strings were damaged, he could no longer play the note. This establishes two things:

1. A cause-and-effect relationship between the guitarist and his guitar.
2. A dependence relationship between specified regions of the guitar for specified functions of the notes.

But what follows from this? Nothing important or profound.

No one would say that because a guitarist depends on his guitar, therefore, he is identical to his guitar, or that the note C and its correlated strings are reducible to one another. But if establishing a cause and effect, dependency relationship between musicians, their instruments, and its notes cannot establish identity, then how could the same line of reasoning be used in defense of physicalism?

Considering the anti-depressant pill that Professor P presented for his argument, the medication can indeed affect the states of my brain, which, in turn, affect the states of my mind. But what follows from this? That my mental states are *identical, reducible*, or, *located within* the physical regions of my brain? No. Not any more than detuning a guitar (which affects the pitch and sound of the music) proves the note C is *identical, reducible*, or, *located within* a physical region of the guitar. Again, *establishing a cause and effect or dependency relation does not establish identity.*

Granted, this rebuttal doesn't prove that Professor P is wrong, and that consciousness is immaterial, but it does prove that such correlations cannot be used to prove that Professor P is right. Using Leibniz's Law, we can now provide a refutation.

The Refutation: The Non-identity of Mind and Matter

"Breaking the chains" of naturalism for this point simply requires that we show the non-identity of mind and matter (i.e., that the mind and brain are not the same thing). Unfortunately for the naturalist, this is trivially easy to do, and mind you, we only need *one example*. Using Leibniz's Law, here are three examples demonstrating that the mind and brain are not the same thing.

1. *A belief is a mental state that can be true or false, but no state of my brain can be true or false*. To argue otherwise is a category fallacy (after all, what would it mean to say that one group of neurons firing is true while another group of neurons firing is false?). Therefore, if a belief can be true or false, but its correlating neurons cannot, then the mind and brain cannot be the same thing.
2. *My brain can weigh three pounds, but my thought that grass is green does not weigh three pounds*. While you may be having heavy thoughts reading this chapter, it will not require a neck

brace. Therefore, if my brain possesses weight, but my thoughts do not, they cannot be the same thing.

3. *My brain can measure seven inches long, but the smell of a rose or the taste of a banana (which are states of my mind) is not seven inches long.* Again, saying otherwise is a category fallacy (smells and tastes have neither weight nor length). Therefore, if my brain can have a length but my mental states do not, they cannot be the same thing.

So, in conclusion, if all the states and properties of my brain are physical, but all the states and properties of my mind are not physical, then it follows that consciousness is neither reducible nor identical to anything physical like the brain. However, if consciousness exists and cannot be physical, then consequently, physicalism (and by default, naturalism) cannot be true.

To demonstrate this refutation using **deductive logic** (a conclusion deduced from previously established points), we can formulate the argument into a **syllogism**: a set of premises (the statements in an argument) that lead to a specified conclusion. For this argument, the syllogism can be written as follows:

1. If naturalism is true (the base belief), then consciousness must be physical (the implied belief of physicalism).
2. Consciousness is not physical (i.e., physicalism is false).
3. Therefore, naturalism is false.[93]

A Price Tag for Naturalism: Exposing the Logical Incoherence of Physicalism

In philosophy, a **price tag** is the "intellectual price" one must pay to be logically consistent while maintaining the implications of their worldview. Given what's been demonstrated above, if the naturalist wishes to be logically consistent, he must now pay the price tag of denying that consciousness exists (otherwise, the existence of consciousness—being non-physical—would entail that physicalism is false). In an attempt to preserve the "integrity" of their worldview, some naturalists have willingly paid this price, and with this, the lazy approach easily comes into play.

Take the atheist philosopher Daniel Dennett as an example. In his book, *Consciousness Explained*, Dennett argues that consciousness is just an illusion. But here's the irony: consciousness must exist for illusions to be possible! Using The Lazy Approach, we can show the self-refuting nature of this position (tactical tool #5) with a syllogism:

1. If physicalism is true, then consciousness cannot exist.
2. I am consciously aware of this dilemma.
3. Therefore, consciousness exists.
4. Therefore, physicalism is false.

Moreover, consider the fact that if consciousness does not exist, then the states of consciousness, such as a belief, cannot exist either. Therefore, if a person denies that consciousness exists, they are essentially making the self-defeating claim that *they believe that beliefs do not exist*! As before, this can be exposed in a syllogism:

1. If physicalism is true, then beliefs do not exist.
2. I believe this.
3. Therefore, beliefs exist.
4. Therefore, physicalism is false.

For this reason, learning how to analyze the epistemic chain of a stronghold becomes crucial for evangelism, and knowing how or when to move the conversation in this direction (addressing beliefs that are entailed further down the chain) becomes a powerful tool for tearing down strongholds.

2. REDUCTIONISM: THE IMPLICATIONS OF DETERMINISM

For our purposes here, **determinism** can be defined as the view that all the thoughts, beliefs, actions, and decisions of human beings are *causally determined* by prior, external factors beyond our control. Given the (ontological) implications of reductionism, many naturalists have come to accept that if physicalism is true, then free will cannot exist, and instead, determinism must be true. What are these implications? We'll briefly name two.

First, if physicalism is true and there is no soul, then human beings are reducible to purely physical objects composed of physical properties and parts. Second, purely physical objects do not act on their own but are caused to act by external forces governed by the laws of chemistry and physics. For instance, water does not "freely choose" to freeze at 32 degrees Fahrenheit, a bullet cannot "choose" to disobey Newton's laws of motion (deciding to swerve left or right instead of straight), and after putting a dollar into a Coke machine, it cannot "choose" to sing you a song instead of dropping a Coke. Why? Because purely physical objects don't *freely* act on their own, but are *causally determined* to act by external, prior factors. Hence, purely physical objects aren't free but determined.[94]

Therefore, if physicalism is true and human beings are reducible to purely physical objects, then the same principle applies—all beliefs, actions, and decisions are casually determined by external, prior factors beyond our control. Thus, another price tag that the naturalist must pay to be logically consistent within his worldview: denying free will and affirming determinism.

An Inherent Price Tag, Rebuttal, and Self-Refutation

As before, not only have some naturalists come to embrace this price tag but have even written books to defend it. Take atheist philosopher and neuroscientist Sam Harris who, in his book, *Free Will*, argues that because determinism is true, human freedom is impossible. Harris writes:

> We know that determinism, in every sense relevant to human behavior, is true. Unconscious neural events determine our thoughts and actions–and are themselves determined by prior causes of which we are subjectively unaware.[95]

It should be stated upfront that our goal here will not be to try and prove that free will exists, but instead, use *The Lazy Approach* to expose the logical implications of determinism (tactical tool #3).

With this in mind, two points can be made here, and the first is quite ironic. If Harris truly believes that determinism is true and human freedom is impossible, then why write an entire book arguing there is no free will unless, of course, he believed that human beings possessed the freedom to read it in the first place? Perhaps he was hoping we were all determined to buy it? Regardless of the reason, I can applaud his boldness and bravery in attempting to be logically consistent with his worldview. However, boldness and bravery do not make determinism true.

The second concerns the contradictory paradox of trying to convince someone free will does not exist while simultaneously believing they lack the freedom to change their mind.[96] This is because if determinism is true, then the other person's ability to *freely* change their mind is impossible. So ironically, any successful demonstration of *freely* convincing someone that determinism is true only becomes a successful demonstration that determinism is false. Clearly, this is self-defeating.

TWO FURTHER IMPLICATIONS OF NATURALISM

If naturalism implies determinism via physicalism and free will does not exist, then two further implicit price tags are worth unpacking—both of which can be incredibly powerful when conversing with nonbelievers. Namely, that moral responsibility and intellectual integrity become impossible.

1. The Price Tag of Moral Responsibility

Consider that if external factors beyond one's control causally determine a person's beliefs, behaviors, and decisions, then *we could never hold anyone morally responsible for their actions.* To illustrate, suppose a gun was used in a murder. In this **chain of events**, the gun fired the bullet, penetrated the victim's heart, and caused the person's death.

Gun → Bullet → Death

But note, although the bullet was the *direct cause* of death, neither the bullet nor gun is held morally responsible for the crime. Why? Because neither acted on its own but was *caused* to act by a prior event—the person pulling the trigger. Put differently, the bullet and gun were intermediate, **secondary movers,** whereas the one pulling the trigger was the primary, **first mover**. Hence, to find moral blame, we must follow the chain of events until we arrive at the *first mover*.

Person (the first mover) → Gun → Bullet → Death

But consider the implications of this for naturalism given determinism.

If human beings are purely physical objects, then much like the gun or bullet, the person becomes *nothing more than* an intermediate, secondary mover in this causal chain of events. Why? Because if determinism is true, then this person didn't choose to act on his own but, like the gun or bullet, *was causally determined to act by some prior event beyond his control.*

Event X (the first mover) → Person → Gun → Bullet → Death

Consequently then, if we cannot blame the gun or bullet (because they were intermediate, secondary movers), then we cannot blame the person either. All three were purely physical objects (reductionism), neither of which were the source of their actions (determinism), and thus, neither can be held morally responsible. Hence, the price tag: either determinism is true and human beings *are not morally responsible for their actions*, or human beings are (and should be held) morally responsible for their actions, and, thus, determinism is false. In a syllogism, the price tag can be written as follows:

1. If naturalism is true, then determinism is true.
2. If determinism is true, then human beings are not morally responsible for their actions.
3. Human beings *are* morally responsible for their actions.
4. Therefore, determinism is false.
5. Therefore (based on 1 and 4), naturalism is false.

As before, by showing why the implications of a worldview must be rejected, we've simultaneously shown why the worldview must be rejected as well.

2. The Price Tag of Intellectual Integrity

By **intellectual integrity,** I mean the idea that a person has come to believe something based on the evidence in a rationally responsible way. That is, one's beliefs were formed through a process of rigorous research, analyzing the evidence, and then freely coming to one's own logical conclusion. If this is done, a person can claim a sense of intellectual integrity with respect to their beliefs (be it atheism or theism).

However, this notion of intellectual integrity assumes that one is *rationally responsible* for their beliefs and, in some sense, possess the freedom to do so. Yet, given what we've discussed so far, if naturalism cannot allow for the possibility of human freedom, then it cannot allow for the possibility of intellectual integrity via rational responsibility either. To grasp the detriment of this price tag, consider that many atheists call themselves "free thinkers," meaning they are "enlightened," unbound, and not "brainwashed" by the shackles of religion. Hence, they're "free to think" for themselves. But note the inconsistency here.

If the atheist holds to naturalism and acknowledges that free will does not exist, they must equally acknowledge that none of their thoughts or beliefs were ever free, to begin with. Yet, if none of their thoughts or beliefs were ever free, then by their own standards, the last thing they could possibly call themselves is a "free thinker." As an argument against atheism, consider the following syllogism:

1. If atheism is true, then free will does not exist.
2. Because of the evidence, I freely chose to become an atheist.
3. Therefore, free will exists.
4. Therefore, atheism is false.

USING WHAT WE'VE LEARNED IN CONVERSATION

As you'll discover, many nonbelievers are willingly eager to share their views with believers, and it only takes providing the opportunity to do so. To illustrate, I was once invited to a friend's company Christmas party. As I mingled with some of the guests, one employee felt the need to inform me that he used to be a Christian but, after studying the evidence for himself, decided to become an atheist. Intrigued by this, I asked why, and in a short amount of time, he provided *a lot* of information.

He began by explaining how he's always aimed to be logically consistent and rational in his beliefs. Next, he claimed that religion led to immoral behavior, such as war, terrorism (e.g., 9/11), and what he called "homosexual persecution" and the suppression of "women's rights" (referring to abortion). Additionally, he said the pivotal point for him was realizing that free will did not exist. Not wanting to assume the connection (though I had an idea), I asked him to elaborate ("how did you come to that conclusion?").

He explained that belief in God is predominantly determined by where a person is born, their upbringing, and their parents. Moreover, neuroscience has studied the effects of religion on the brain and discovered that religious people possess similar brain patterns. Hence, no one is ever "free" to believe in God and thus, atheism became the most rational conclusion to embrace.

Now, there were plenty of ways that I could have responded, but given we were in a friendly Christmas party environment, I implemented *The Lazy Approach* to keep the conversation cordial.

Eric: This is interesting. It seems two main factors drove you to reject Christianity. The first is that religious beliefs lead to immoral behavior, and the second is that free will does not exist. Is that correct?

Atheist: Yes, exactly.

Eric: And being a person who aims to be logically consistent and rational, these factors were sufficient for embracing atheism as the most logically consistent, rational position to take?

Atheist: Of course. We must always follow the evidence where it leads, no matter what we want to be true.

Eric: Oh, I certainly agree with that. But would you mind if I asked you a few questions regarding what you've said?

Atheist: Yes, of course. Most Christians usually get upset with me at this point.

Eric: I'm sorry to hear that.

Atheist: It's okay. I'm just happy to finally discuss these issues with a believer in a respectful way. What would you like to ask?

Eric: Well, first, it seems you feel that people should be held morally accountable for their behavior. But you also explained how the realization that free will didn't exist was partly why you gave up believing in God. Yet, if free will doesn't exist, then what these religious people did was simply something they were determined to do and didn't have the freedom to do otherwise. So, given our mutual commitment to logical consistency, rationality, and following the evidence where it leads, here's the question. Given your view, how can we hold anyone morally responsible for their actions?

His eyebrows lifted in surprise as if the thought had never crossed his mind. He'd never made this connection before, nor had anyone made it for him. I continued.

Eric: Concerning my second question, you seem to attribute your atheism to a sense of intellectual integrity, devoting hours to rigorous research and rationally following the evidence to its most logical conclusion. But again, if free will doesn't exist, then I'm wondering if you genuinely feel this was the result of logical consistency, rationality, and intellectual integrity, or, if this was something you were merely determined to believe—even if this belief was false—and you didn't have the free will to believe otherwise. In other words, if you believe that free will does not exist, then I can't help but ask if you freely came to believe this.

Atheist: Wow. I honestly don't know. I've never thought about this before...I'm not sure what to say.

I could almost see the scales falling from his eyes as the strongholds began to crumble. As before, there was no altercation, and nothing became heated. I simply listened attentively, took the information he provided, and strategically asked questions. Moreover, note that my approach was implemented from a holistic point of view. I began by reiterating his position, ensuring I had not misunderstood it, and this allowed me to set up my final questions, giving them a more powerful impact at the end (tactical tools #1, #2, and #5).

Again, *anyone can do this*. It simply takes patience, attentive listening, having *the eyes to see* the holistic implications, and asking a few tactical questions. As Scripture explains, "let every person be quick to hear, slow to speak," because "the wise of heart is called discerning, and sweetness of speech increases persuasiveness" (James 1:19; Proverbs 16:21, ESV).

Summary and Conclusion

Much like scientism, empiricism becomes epistemically self-defeating and, when applied to the question of God or the soul, a category fallacy (e.g., using one's eyes to look for an invisible man). Concerning reductionism and physicalism, these were taken as byproducts of a larger, holistic chain within the naturalist worldview. Using *The Lazy Approach*, we learned to address this chain in two ways. First, by attacking the truth of an implied belief—if A implies B but B is false, then A must be false, as well. Second, by attacking the coherence of the chain as a whole—if A implied B and C, but B and C couldn't possibly be true together, then A must be false.

With this, we addressed the naturalist's view of physicalism by attacking its implied belief that consciousness, if it exists, must be physical. Beginning with a rebuttal, we demonstrated that a cause-and-effect or dependence relation between the mind and brain cannot establish identity. Next, we used Leibniz's Law to show that because there are things true of the mind that are not true of the brain (and vice versa), they cannot be the same thing. This served as the refutation, demonstrating that if consciousness exists, it cannot be physical, and if it cannot be physical, then physicalism is false.

In addressing reductionism, we looked at the holistic implications of the chain, noting how physicalism implied a belief in determinism, leading to self-defeating, logical incoherence and inconsistencies. From here, we examined two further implications concerning the impossibility of moral responsibility and intellectual integrity as price tags. Namely, that if naturalism is true, then no atheist could ever 1) hold anyone morally responsible for their actions, and 2) claim rational responsibility for their atheism. Finally, we took what we learned and applied *The Lazy Approach* for tearing down the stronghold in a casual conversation, keeping the discussion environment calm and cordial the entire time.

Chapter 16

The Art and Discipline of Identifying Logical Fallacies

Having read this far, you are now equipped with the necessary knowledge and tools for tearing down the three dominant strongholds that permeate our culture: *postmodernism*, *scientism*, and *naturalism*. In this chapter, we expand our approach by examining the most common logical fallacies you may encounter (tactical tool #5). Doing so will help conduct more fruitful discussions while avoiding unnecessary debates. I cannot overemphasize how useful this tool can be when dealing with those who are hostile, uncharitable, or if you find yourself with limited time.

Biblical Basis: Proverbs 26:4-5

Do not answer a fool according to his folly, or you yourself will be just like him. Answer a fool according to his folly, or he will be wise in his own eyes.

In this passage, we read what appears to be a contradiction that revolves around whether we should "answer a fool according to their folly." In the first verse, we are instructed not to, only to immediately be required to do so in the next. So, what gives? The answer lies in the reasons provided for each.

To begin with, the term "folly" entails the notion of foolishness or lacking good sense. When conversing with a nonbeliever, the first verse instructs us not to respond with answers that are just as fallacious as their claims. The idea of childish arguments comes to mind, such as, "I know you are, but what am I?" when responding to an insult. Here, the person is being just as childish (or foolish) as the other. We are instructed to avoid this "lest we become like him." In the second verse, we are instructed to "answer the fool according to his folly," but in this sense, it's for offering a correction to the foolishness, *not* an invitation to participate in it.

Two Rules for Conversing with Nonbelievers

With this biblical basis, we now have two "rules" for conversing with nonbelievers:

> **Rule #1:** Do not engage in fallacious reasoning (lest you be like him).
>
> **Rule #2:** Point out and correct their fallacious reasoning (lest he thinks he's right).

This becomes apparent when we read it in the Amplified Bible.

> *Do not answer [nor pretend to agree with the frivolous comments of] a [closed-minded] fool according to his folly, otherwise you, even you, will be like him. Answer [and correct the erroneous concepts of] a fool according to his folly, otherwise he will be wise in his own eyes [if he thinks you agree with him].*

Concerning the first rule, this means that when discussing, answering, or providing a defense of Christianity, we should not commit logical fallacies like the other person. We serve a God of reason and rationality, the foundation of logic itself. Hence, our case and defense of Christianity must always be logically consistent, rationally coherent, and biblical. We give God no glory when we, as believers, utter irrational nonsense, logical fallacies, or provide biblically incoherent answers.

The second rule, "correct the erroneous concepts of a fool according to his folly" means that when we are presented with logical fallacies, we are to voice our disagreement and respond with the intent of offering a correction, be it in the form of a rebuttal, a refutation, or both. Learning to incorporate these rules will be the emphasis of this chapter.

IDENTIFYING LOGICAL FALLACIES: THE EXAMPLE OF JESUS

In the most basic sense, a **logical fallacy** is an error in logic or reason that either "breaks" a law of logic (a **formal logical fallacy**) or contains a fault in reasoning to a conclusion (an **informal logical fallacy**). In the previous chapters, we've learned to identify and expose fallacies such as *a reductio ad absurdum*, a *false dichotomy,* and *begging the question* via a false presupposition (to name a few). For each of these, we used questions to voice our disagreement and expose their problems.

*S*uffice it to say, Jesus was a master at this! Although you'll be hard-pressed to find the phrase "logical fallacy" or "false dichotomy" coming from the mouth of Jesus in any of the gospels, we can examine one instance (among many) in which Jesus employed this tool brilliantly.

Jesus Engages with the Sadducees

In Matthew 22:23-33, a group of Sadducees approach Jesus to question his belief in the resurrection. Before we look at their argument, some background context is needed.

To begin with, the Sadducees were a group of Jewish leaders and priests that followed God but denied commonly held theological beliefs, such as the existence of angels, the soul, and most notably, the resurrection of the dead (Acts 23:6-8). Hence, they're described as "those who say there is no resurrection of the dead." This further entailed a denial of two beliefs relevant to the situation: 1) the afterlife and 2) what is known in theology as the **intermediate state**—where a person continues to exist as a disembodied soul after death but prior to the final, bodily resurrection (which again, they denied).

For this reason, they'll present Jesus with a thought experiment with the intent of exposing His belief in the resurrection (and, by default, His belief in the afterlife and the intermediate state)[97] as a ***reductio ad ab-***

surdum fallacy. Their goal will be to show that if what Jesus believes is true, it'll ultimately leads to absurd conclusions.

The Argument From the Sadducees (verses 24-28)

In a paraphrased fashion, their argument can be summarized as follows:

> Jesus, we don't believe in an afterlife, but you do, and here's the problem. Suppose a woman has seven husbands throughout her lifetime (marrying each one after the previous passes). When she dies and is resurrected, whose wife will she be in heaven? Because if what you believe is true, then it seems you only have two options–both of which lead to absurdity. If you say she's only married to the first, then she commits adultery against the other six. If you say she's married to all seven, then she commits polygamy. Either way, both options are prohibited by God, which is precisely the problem with your position. Your beliefs reduce to absurdity and, therefore, must be rejected.

Two Responses From Jesus

To understand the approach Jesus is about to take, two more things must be understood for context. First, the Sadducees were experts in Jewish law who *prided themselves in knowing and memorizing* Scripture. Second, Sadducees often had disciples that followed them around to sit under their teachings. Given that this was a premeditated attempt to publicly humiliate Jesus as ignorant and unbiblical (showing that their "intellect" was superior to His), there would've been a large group of their students with them.

Additionally, much like middle school students running to see a fight in the cafeteria, a sizable crowd would've gathered as they saw this group approaching Jesus. This was understandably a public challenge in this culture.[98] and the people were eager to see this fight happen. With this contextual picture in your mind, consider the two ways in which Jesus responds.

1. The Rebuttal (verses 29-30)

In His first response, Jesus begins by publicly calling out their ignorance, telling them, "You are all wrong because you don't know the Scriptures." Given their pride in *devoting their lives* to *knowing and memorizing* Scripture (and given the social context of the situation), this was *a public insult to* their perceived intelligence (again, think of the cafeteria scene). The crowd would've lost their minds!

Next, He points out how their argument rests entirely on the assumption that there's marriage in Heaven. Given that He rejects this false presupposition, their objection fails and is exposed as a false dichotomy. Hence, His rebuttal:

> You are all wrong because you do not know the Scriptures or the power of God. At the resurrection people will neither marry nor be given in marriage.

At this point, He's successfully demolished their argument. But consider the brilliance of His next response as He segues into a refutation.

2. The Refutation (verses 31-32)

As before, He begins with an insult but adds a pinch of snark and sarcasm. "But about the resurrection of the dead—have you not read what God has said to you?" Again, the crowd goes wild! Now consider the reasoning behind this move. First, the foundation of Christianity rests entirely on the truth of the resurrection, which entails a belief in the afterlife and intermediate state of existence.[99] Hence, Sadducean teaching was antithetical to the reception of the gospel, and this had a detrimental impact on their students.

Second, recall the large crowd that would've been present. Jesus was not only addressing the Sadducees, but wording His response in such a way as to reach the audience. Given that they looked up to the intellectual arrogance of the Sadducees, undermining their intelligence would've simultaneously undermined their authority.[100] While space does not permit further elaboration on this approach, suffice it to say that there's a time and place for this when foundational issues are on the table. Removing the intellectual authority of an influencer of such strongholds aided in shifting the plausibility structure within that culture.

Next, He begins His refutation by appealing to the authority of Scripture, quoting from Exodus 3:6, "I am the God of Abraham, and the God of Isaac, and the God of Jacob." But note, this verse does nothing to prove an afterlife, much less a disembodied soul that will receive a final resurrection. Hence, He adds to the verse by stating, "He is not the God of the dead but of the living!" Nevertheless, this is an odd move to make. After all, if He wanted to appeal to the authority of Scripture for proving resurrection, there are far better verses to use, such as Isaiah 26:19 or Daniel 12:2. So, what gives? Did these verses slip His mind? Was Jesus having a bad day? Or was there, as they say, a "method behind the madness?" Indeed, there was.

For the Sadducees, only the Torah (the first five books of the Bible) was regarded as "God's authoritative word,"[101] and Jesus knew that quoting from Isaiah or Daniel would only devolve into a debate about the overall authority of Scripture. They didn't care what these other books had to say. For this reason, He quotes Exodus (a book they regarded as authoritative) and, note—*intentionally avoids the debate about biblical authority altogether*. Did you catch that? Because it bears repeating. In this instance, *Jesus chooses not to debate biblical reliability or the authority of Scripture.*

Recall our discussion of "theological triage." Jesus doesn't waste time on issues non-essential to the reception of the gospel. Instead, He *keeps the-main-thing-the-main-thing* (the truth of an afterlife and bodily resurrection). Moreover, recall that with *The Lazy Approach*, one can concede for the sake of argument that the other person's belief *may be* true but still show how their overall position is false. Hence, Jesus is not conceding what they believed about the rest of Scripture, but is conceding that *even if* what they believe about Scripture is true, His view would still be correct.

Thus, He quotes from Exodus 3:6, "I am the God of Abraham, and the God of Isaac, and the God of Jacob" (which was one of their favorite verses to quote![102]), and then adds, "He is not the God of the dead but of the living!" But what does that mean? Simply this; if God is the God of Abraham, Isaac, and Jacob, and He's not the God of the dead, but of the living, then *based on their own Scriptures*, it must follow that despite their physical death, Abraham, Isaac, and Jacob are still alive today—proving an intermediate state of continued existence that awaits a final resurrection. Hence, "He is not the God of the dead but the living!"

Summarizing the Response

With this background context in mind, we can now re-examine Jesus' response to the Sadducees and fully appreciate how He identified, rebutted, and refuted their logical fallacies. In a "modern tone" fashion, consider the following paraphrase:

> Guys, look, I know you're trying to make my belief in the resurrection look like a *reductio ad absurdum* fallacy. But the problem is that *you just don't know the Scriptures*. Don't you know there's no marriage in Heaven? Which means your entire case is based on a false presupposition about marriage that has resulted in this false dichotomy. So, the fallacy isn't with my view but yours. But now that I've dismantled your argument, let's talk about the resurrection. *Haven't you guys read your own Scriptures*? I mean, come on; you've only got five books to memorize–and you're supposed to be the experts! Doesn't your favorite passage in Exodus say that God *is* the God of Abraham, Isaac, and Jacob, and don't you know that He's the God of the living, not the dead? But given your view, if Abraham, Isaac, and Jacob are dead and have ceased to exist, how can He be their God? Yet, if He's *still* their God–as the Scriptures imply–and is the God of the living, then it must follow that they continue to exist after death and are still alive today. Therefore, *even by your own standards of Scripture*, my view is still correct, your view cannot possibly be true, and thus, your rejection of the afterlife, the intermediate state, and the final resurrection must be false.

It's no wonder that Scripture states, "when the crowds heard this, they were astonished... Jesus had silenced the Sadducees . . . No one could say a word in reply, and from that day on no one dared to ask him any more questions" (Matthew 22:33-34, 48). This is the example and brilliance of Jesus, and we must strive to be like Him!

THE FOOL HAS COMMITTED A LOGICAL FALLACY IN HIS HEART: NAMES, DEFINITIONS, AND EXAMPLES

With the two rules presented to us in the beginning of this chapter, let's examine the most common logical fallacies you'll encounter when witnessing to nonbelievers. This is because when the fool commits a logical fallacy in his heart (Psalms 14:1; 53:1), strongholds are birthed, and Scripture commands that we identify, expose, and destroy them (2 Corinthians 10:4-5). Again, we aim to destroy ideas, not people. We are to give a defense, but with gentleness and respect (1 Peter 3:15).

Unfortunately, most (if not all) of these fallacies are committed by believers as well. So, following the command of Matthew 7:5 (in a modified version), "we must first learn to take the logical fallacy out of our own eye so we can see clearly to remove the logical fallacy from another's." To do this, we'll learn what they are (names and definitions), how they're committed (by both believers and nonbelievers), and how to respond accordingly (while avoiding them ourselves). As a warmup, we begin by reviewing the fallacies already covered in this book.

A Self-defeating Statement: A statement that refutes itself by failing to meet its own standard. This is a *formal fallacy* (i.e., it breaks a law of logic) and occurs when a person has made a claim that proves itself false.

Examples: *"There is no absolute truth." "You shouldn't judge anyone." "No one should be intolerant of other beliefs." "Don't force your moral point of view on others."*

Responses:

- Is that absolutely true?
- Then why are you judging me for judging?
- Then why are you not tolerant of my beliefs?
- Then why are you forcing your moral point of view on me?

A Category Fallacy: Mistaking or attributing two categories that do not belong together. Given this does not break a law of logic, it's an *informal fallacy*.

Examples: *How many pounds does the taste of banana weigh? What does the color blue smell like? Show me scientific evidence for God.*

Responses: Although a banana is a physical object that has weight, the taste of a banana does not. While a blue flower may smell sweet, its color does not. Regarding the last example, we've discussed how the question is *implicitly* a category fallacy. Science can only study the physical, and God is non-physical.

A *Reductio Ad Absurdum*: This occurs when a person holds a view that implicitly or holistically leads to irrational, illogical, and absurd conclusions.

Example: *If we don't allow women to have abortions, they'll do so illegally and be harmed in the process.*

Response: Reword the principle of the position to "remove the fluff" and demonstrate the absurdity of the view (see chapter 11).

A Logical Contradiction: A logical incompatibility or contradiction between two or more statements. There are two ways in which something can be logically contradictory: by *definition* or by *implication*.

Contradiction by Definition: *Who is the bachelor married to?*

Response: A married person is, by definition, not single, and a bachelor is, by definition, not married. Hence, a "married bachelor" is a logical contradiction. Note how asking this question also becomes a category fallacy. As you'll discover, some fallacies are often the result of others.

Contradiction by Implication (when taken together as a whole): *The existence of an immovable object and an unstoppable force.*

Response: Although an immovable object or an unstoppable force can exist independently, they cannot possibly exist simultaneously (see chapter 15). This also becomes a *reductio ad absurdum*.

Example From Believers: *God Can Do the "Logically Impossible"*

To grasp why this statement is a logical contradiction, ask yourself, can God make a "married bachelor" come into existence? No. As we just learned, this is a logical contradiction by definition and, thus, cannot exist. Does this trouble you? If so, allow me to try a different approach. Ask yourself the following:

- Can God do *anything*?
- Is there anything I can do that God *cannot*?

Most believers respond by saying yes, God can do anything, and no, there's nothing I can do that God cannot. If this was your response, two more questions follow:

- Can God sin?
- Can God learn?

The obvious answer is "No," God can neither sin nor learn. However, we can sin and learn. Therefore, God cannot do anything, and we've established two things we can do that God cannot. But consider the reasons behind this.

Concerning the former, Hebrews 6:18 states that it's impossible for God to lie, and this sentiment is conveyed throughout Scripture (Numbers 23:19; Titus 1:2). This is because a God that is morally *perfect* cannot, by definition, do something morally *imperfect*. Thus, it's logically impossible for God to sin.

Concerning the latter, the same principle applies. Scripture teaches that His understanding is infinite and He knows all things (Psalms 147:5; 1 John 3:20). In philosophical, theological terminology, this means God is **omniscient**. Hence, if God knows all things, He lacks no knowledge, and if He lacks no knowledge, there's nothing left for Him to learn.

For this reason, when we say God *cannot* do the logically impossible, it's not due to a deficiency or lack of strength—as if God needed to lift more weights to gain the power to do these logically impossible acts. Rather, it's that logically impossible acts entail a contradiction in terms that cannot be done in the first place. Now consider the application.

God's "inability" to sin or learn becomes a reflection of His perfection, whereas our ability to do both is nothing to brag about. We can sin because we lack something, but God cannot because He lacks nothing. Additionally, our ability to learn demonstrates our ignorance, whereas God's "inability" to learn only demonstrates His omniscience. This should not trouble our faith but increase it. So, let's glorify God in knowing He cannot do the logically impossible!

Example From a Nonbeliever: *If God is omnipotent, can He create a rock so heavy He cannot lift?*

This popular question presents an alleged objection against the notion of God's omnipotence, attempting to show a logical contradiction by implication. However, the logical contradiction here isn't in God's nature but in the question. Historically, **omnipotence** has been defined as God's *ability to bring about a logically possible state of affairs*. As we saw above, this doesn't mean the ability to do the logically impossible.

Put differently, omnipotence is not the power to do anything, but is *the ability to do anything that power can do*. Hence, God cannot create a "married bachelor," a "squared circle," or "a rock so heavy He cannot lift." These are not logically possible states of affairs but contradictions, and no amount of power can make logical contradictions possible. So no, God cannot create a rock so heavy He cannot lift any more than He can beat Himself in a wrestling match. The question itself is a logically incoherent contradiction, which becomes an infringement, not against God, but logic.

Begging the Question: Implying, assuming, or presenting something as true without argument or justification. This always involves a **presupposition** (pre-supposing something is true beforehand).

Example: *Have you stopped beating your wife?*

The underlying presupposition here is that the person beats their spouse (and is married). With this fallacy, we've learned not to answer the question directly, but address the **false presupposition** by questioning the question: "Why would you assume I beat my wife?" or, "Why would you assume I'm married?"

Example From a Believer: *God exists because the Bible says so.*

This example has no *false* presupposition, but it's still a question-begging fallacy. Note the underlying presupposition; whatever the Bible says is true. This isn't a question begging fallacy because it's false, but because it erroneously assumes that the nonbeliever agrees with your view.

To illustrate, suppose that a Muslim wanted to convert you by quoting three verses from the Quran and declaring it as Allah's holy, authoritative word. Would you drop to your knees with tears of repentance and devote your life to Allah? No, because you disagree with his underlying presupposition—whatever the Qur'an says is true (and is God's holy, authoritative word). Hence, it commits the fallacy of begging the question. And if his approach didn't work for you, why expect it to work for the atheist when quoting the Bible?

Example From a Nonbeliever: *God doesn't exist because evolution is true.*

There are two question-begging assumptions within this statement. 1) Evolution is true, and 2) if evolution is true, God cannot exist. Recall the notion of theological triage and note that with a rebuttal, we can focus on demonstrating how the overall argument (the second assumption) fails *even if* the first assumption (evolution) is true.

Response: *But if God exists, couldn't He use evolution to bring about our species?*

Given that the obvious answer is yes, their argument collapses (hence, the rebuttal). This is no different from the approach Jesus took with the Sadducees, demonstrating how their argument failed *even if* what they believed about Scripture was true.

Circular Reasoning: Using two or more reasons that assume each other to be true; I believe "X" because of "Y," and I believe "Y" because of "X." This often involves a question-begging assumption.

Example: *I'm the smartest person in the world because this book I wrote says so.*

In this example, the person believes they're the smartest person in the world, and this belief is based on a book they've written, making the belief (along with its justification) a fallacy of circular reasoning. However, this may not always be apparent, and the person may be unaware that their reasoning is circular. Using the same example, consider the following conversation:

John: I believe I'm the smartest person in the world.

Jane: How did you come to that conclusion?

John: Because this book says so right here.

Jane: I see. Who wrote the book?

John: I did!

Additionally, consider that when an *informal* fallacy is committed, it doesn't automatically mean the conclusion is false. The person may be "the smartest person in the world," but the way they've justified this conclusion is still fallaciously circular.

Example From a Believer:

Christian: I believe God exists.

Nonbeliever: Why?

Christian: Because the Bible says so.

Nonbeliever: I see. And who wrote the Bible?

Christian: God did!

Note that a logical fallacy doesn't become logical when we use spiritual language. Although we know the conclusion of this argument is true, we must present and defend it in non-fallacious ways.

Example From a Nonbeliever:

Nonbeliever: God doesn't exist.

Eric: Why?

Nonbeliever: Because He isn't real.

Eric: And why do you believe He isn't real?

Nonbeliever: Because He doesn't exist.

In this example, the fallacy now involves a **tautology**: repeating the same thing twice with different words that mean the same thing. With tautologies, no new information is provided to further the discussion. Consider a less obvious example.

Less Obvious Example: *We have no empirical method for testing supernatural claims, and we only discover natural explanations every time we study the physical world.*

This argument commits a handful of fallacies. (1) It *begs the question*—assuming we need "empirical methods" for testing supernatural claims. This is (2) a *category fallacy*. Additionally, the words "physical" and "natural" are being used as synonyms, which can be reworded (tactical tool #2) as follows: "Every time we study the physical, we only discover the physical" or "studying the natural world only demonstrates something natural." This is (3) a *tautology*.

Given the tautology, we can now identify (4) the circular reasoning. This person implicitly believes that supernatural claims cannot be *empirically* validated because we can only study the natural world, but then believes we can only study the natural world because supernatural claims cannot be *empirically* validated (which, again, is a category fallacy). Hence, the entire argument is a tautological claim based on circular reasoning.

For the sake of space, we'll focus on how the nonbeliever commits the remaining fallacies and learn how to respond accordingly.

A *Non-sequitur*: This fallacy (Latin for "it does not follow") occurs when a person implies or directly states a conclusion that *does not logically follow* from what they've said.

Example: *She's wearing red shoes. Therefore, her favorite color must be red.*

Again, with informal fallacies, the conclusion *might* be true. Nevertheless, it *doesn't logically follow* that her favorite color is red *simply because* she's wearing red shoes. Hence, it's a *non-sequitur*.

Example From a Nonbeliever: *Belief in God is for people who don't understand science.*

A general rule for identifying this fallacy is determining where the word "therefore" should be placed in their statement. This is because the word "therefore" implies that something *must follow* based on what's been said. If their conclusion does not follow, it's a *non-sequitur*.

Response: *So, belief in God is for people who don't understand science. Therefore, what?*

At this point, the ball is back in their court. If they say, "therefore, God doesn't exist," you can point out how their conclusion doesn't logically follow from their claim. While it's true that *some* believers don't understand science, it's also true that some *unbelievers* don't understand science either. "So what?" Nothing relevant follows from the assertion (tactical tool #4: "go on" or "so what?").

The Genetic Fallacy: Attempting to falsify a belief by showing its origin.

Example #1: *People believe in God because of fear and ignorance.*

In this example, the person tries to falsify belief in God by showing (or more appropriately, assuming) where the belief came from. However, showing where a belief *may have* originated doesn't prove the belief is false. For instance, suppose a person believes everything they read in a fortune cookie. Their next fortune cookie reads "2+2=4," and on this basis, they come to believe it. Although they've arrived at this belief in an unusual way, it's nonetheless true. Similarly, *even if* we concede that belief in God is the product of "fear and ignorance," it doesn't prove that belief in God is false.

Example #2: *You're only a Christian because you were born in America. You'd be a Muslim if you were born in the Middle East!*

Again, even if we conceded the point, it wouldn't prove that Christianity is false. Arguing otherwise is not only a genetic fallacy but a *non-sequitur*. Hence, we could reply with a "therefore?," "go on," or "so what?" (tactical tool #4). Additionally, we can take the principle of the claim and apply it to their position (tactical tool #2).

Eric: Are you an atheist simply because of where you were born?

Atheist: No, of course not!

Eric: So, why does your claim only apply to my position but not yours?

Appeal to Authority Fallacy: Attempting to prove something solely because an authoritative figure (especially one that's not in the relevant field) says so.

Examples:

- No serious, respectable scientist believes in God.
- My doctor doesn't believe in prayer, only in medicine.
- Theoretical physicist and cosmologist Stephen Hawkins says philosophy is dead.

It's important to understand that not every appeal to authority is an *appeal to authority fallacy*. For instance, if a person claimed that Christians shouldn't believe a historic Christian doctrine, then one could point to the authority of Scripture to show how they're factually incorrect. This is neither question-begging, circular, nor an appeal to authority fallacy. Why not? Because if the person is attacking a belief *within* the Christian worldview, then Scripture *is the appropriate authority* for settling the dispute.

By contrast, none of the authority figures in the examples above are the appropriate authorities to consult regarding the beliefs in question. Hence, the first two examples are implicit category fallacies. Asking a scientist or doctor what they believe about God or prayer is like asking a plumber what he thinks about dentistry. This isn't an insult to either profession. It's simply pointing out how the nature of these professions isn't *directly relevant* to the belief in question. The same applies to the last example, but with an additional fallacy. Saying that philosophy is dead is itself a philosophical statement and thus, self-defeating.

Finally, note the caveat presented in the first example, "No *serious, respectable* scientist believes in God." This arbitrary standard is an example of a **No True Scotsman fallacy**. The name is derived from a Scotsman claiming that "no Scotsman puts sugar on his porridge!" only to hear a fellow Scotsman say, "But I'm a Scotsman, and I put sugar on my porridge." In raging disbelief, he pounds the table and shouts, "Well, *no true* Scotsman puts sugar on his porridge!"

Similarly, claiming that "no serious, respectable" scientist believes in God fails to recognize the history of science and, more pertinently, that many serious, respectable scientists believe in God today. Hence, we can ask what they mean by "serious" or "respectable." If they mean no *atheist* scientist, they've further committed the fallacies of begging the question (assuming only atheists can be "serious" scientists) and circular reasoning (believing that only atheists are "respectable" scientists because the only respectable scientists are atheists).

An *Ad Hominem* Fallacy: This fallacy (Latin for "against the man") occurs when a person attempts to falsify a belief by attacking the person's behavior or character.

Example: *Don't listen to that doctor. I hear he drinks and smokes!*

In this instance, the person wants to demean the doctor's advice, not by appealing to his authority but to his behavior. However, if a doctor told a person to refrain from drinking and smoking, the advice isn't invalidated if the doctor drank and smoked himself. At best, his advice is hypocritical but not false.

Example From a Nonbeliever: "*Your suit looks expensive.*"

During the Q&A portion of a public debate, an atheist approached the microphone with a Bible to ask me a question. After reading a passage about frugality, he said:

> Your suit looks expensive, and while it's a nice suit, I could never afford something like that. So, how can you expect us to trust in God when clearly, you trust more in your money?

The audience (comprised of Christians and atheists) began to laugh at the question, but they weren't laughing for the same reason. Those who know me personally know I buy all my suits from thrift stores. So, with a smile on my face, I responded:

> Well, I genuinely appreciate the compliment because (examining my suit) I agree, it's a nice suit that *looks* expensive. However, I bought this for only $15 at a thrift store, and if you honestly feel you couldn't afford it, I'd be happy to buy one for you. Nevertheless, we should keep in mind that the topic of tonight's debate is "Does God Exist," and not "Is Eric's Suit too Expensive."

Blushing with embarrassment, the atheist thanked me for my response and quietly returned to his seat.

To be clear, not every assertion or complaint merits a response. However, given that his "objection" was attempting to muddy the waters against my character, not only did I refute his claim (the suit was only

$15 from a thrift store) but offered a rebuttal that *even if* my suit were expensive, it wouldn't invalidate the truth of my arguments. Hence, the objection was an *ad hominem* fallacy (and a *non-sequitur*).

A Red Herring Fallacy: This fallacy occurs when a person diverts the conversation by changing the subject to non-related, irrelevant issues. The phrase "red herring" comes from the practice of escaped convicts who used the blood of fish to divert dogs away from their scent, leading the authorities to track the smell of the fish rather than him.

When conversing with nonbelievers, we want our conversations to "stay on track," keeping the focus on the existence of God and the truth of Christianity. If we take the bait, we allow the conversation to veer off into non-central issues. Hence, we must learn to avoid red herrings.

Atheist: Well, I don't believe in God *because* I don't believe in fairytales.

Eric: Great, me either.

[awkward silence]

Atheist: But you *do* believe in fairytales. Doesn't the Bible mention talking snakes? That's a fairytale!

Eric: If you're referring to Genesis, it says serpent. But we can go with "snake" if you prefer. Still, I don't see your point. If God exists, couldn't He allow a "snake" to talk?

Atheist: But I don't believe in God.

Eric: I understand. But follow me here. I'm simply asking *if* God existed, could He allow a snake to talk?

Atheist: Well, sure, but that's *only* if He existed.

Eric: Right. So, it seems that our central question shouldn't be whether snakes can talk but whether God exists. So, if you don't mind, let's address that question first, and maybe we can get to "talking snakes" later.

A Strawman Fallacy: A misrepresentation of a person's position or argument.

Suppose John puts a picture of Bill's face on a scarecrow, knocks it down, and claims victory. In this illustration, John didn't defeat Bill, but a *strawman* of Bill. Similarly, a nonbeliever may misrepresent certain beliefs within Christianity (or an argument you've just given in defense of Christianity) but note, when they "refute" the mischaracterization, they're not refuting Christianity but a *strawman* of it.

Example: *Christians believe in a magical sky daddy that grants them wishes, but no such being exists!*

Given that no doctrine within Christianity teaches such a thing, this is a strawman. Thus, we can respond by agreeing with the person that no such "magical sky daddy" exists.

As a side note, it may be possible to proactively prevent this fallacy at the beginning of the conversation by asking some questions. For example, if someone says they don't believe in God, you can ask them to describe the God they don't believe in. Chances are, they're denying a God the Bible doesn't describe.

Nevertheless, responding to this fallacy will depend on the strawman you are presented with, which may not be obvious. Consider these examples:

- If God exists, why doesn't He heal amputees?
- If Christianity is true, why did this person die of cancer?
- If God exists, why doesn't He remove all the evil in the world?

Note how these questions are implicit strawmen (that also beg the question) regarding *an assumed view* of God or Christianity. These implicit strawmen seem to be that:

A) God is some genie that must grant all prayer requests.
B) God's existence depends on how *we view* our quality of life.

C) We are like God's pets, and it's His job to keep us healthy and happy.

D) All of the above.

In response, we can begin uncovering these assumptions by turning their implicit accusations into questions. Using what the person has said to fill in the blanks, consider the following:

- Are you saying that if God existed, then He must _________?
- Are you implying that if God exists, then it's His job to _________?
- Are you under the impression that if Christianity were true, then _________?
- Are you arguing that the truth of Christianity depends entirely on ________?

Additionally, recall that the beliefs within a worldview must be considered holistically. Christianity is no exception, and in these instances, we use it to our advantage. For instance, if Christianity is true, then are not those in Heaven receiving the ultimate healing? Moreover, if Christianity is true, will God not one day rid the world of evil? And if Christianity is true, isn't it our job to feed the poor, visit the sick, and help those in need? Because not only does Christianity accurately predict these problems, but if true, adequately provides answers to them!

Conclusion

Knowing how to identify and respond to logical fallacies is an effective way to avoid unnecessary debates, diffuse potentially heated conversations, and bring the focus back to the heart of the issue. In Proverbs 26:4-5 we're given two rules for conversing with nonbelievers:

Rule #1: Do not engage in fallacious reasoning (don't be like him).

Rule #2: Point out and correct their fallacious reasoning (don't let him think he's right).

As an exercise, I encourage you to gather with a group, write down a list of questions, accusations, or objections you've heard from nonbelievers, and identify how they've committed one or more of the fallacies from this chapter. As you grow in this discipline, your conversations with nonbelievers will be more productive, less time-consuming, and make you a better ambassador for Christ.

PART 4

HOW Can We Reach Them? Presenting the Evidence

Chapter 17

A Biblical Basis for Presenting Evidence

Evidence, Arguments, and *Knowing* vs. *Showing*

Although presenting arguments and evidence is a crucial component when witnessing to nonbelievers, two preliminary remarks are in order. First, the word "argument" here should be understood in the technical sense as used in philosophy or law. To "give an argument" simply means presenting the person with a case—reasons and evidence for the truth of what one believes. The second is understanding the distinction between ***knowing*** *that* Christianity is true and ***showing*** *that* Christianity is true. This aligns with the questions from chapter one: 1) Why are you a Christian? and 2) Why should somebody else be a Christian?

Recall that while a personal testimony may be sufficient for *knowing that* Christianity is true (the first question), it may be insufficient for *showing that* Christianity is true (the second question). By analogy, not only do I *know that* my wife loves me, but I can also *show that* my wife loves me. However, the way I *know* my wife loves me may not be the same way I can *show that* my wife loves me to another person. While the two may overlap, they're not the same task. For this reason, presenting arguments and evidence becomes a key component for *showing that* Christianity is true to the nonbeliever.

A BIBLICAL BASIS FOR ARGUMENTS AND EVIDENCE

Unfortunately, some Christians object to this approach, which typically arises from 1) a misconceived notion of "faith" (e.g., fideism) and 2) a failure to understand the biblical basis for presenting evidence. As we learned in chapter one, the biblical definition of faith is an active trust or confidence *based on knowledge*, which is itself based on evidence and reason. Moreover, we learned that fideism (the belief that faith is separate from and incompatible with evidence or reason) is not only false but unbiblical. Given that we've covered this in previous chapters, we'll focus on addressing the second: a biblical basis for presenting evidence.

The Example of Jesus: "*Believe on the Evidence*"

When Jesus was confronted by those who refused to believe He was the Messiah, He didn't say, "just have more faith" or "pray harder," but pointed to the evidence that demonstrated it.

> "...How long will you keep us in suspense? If you are the Messiah, tell us plainly." Jesus answered them, "I have told you so, yet you do not believe. The works that I do in My Father's name ... they are My credentials and **the evidence** declaring who I am ... even though you do not believe me, **believe the works**, that you may **know and understand**" (John 10:24-25, 38, AMP).

> "Believe me when I say that I am in the Father and the Father is in me; or **at least believe on the evidence of the works themselves"** (John 14:11).

In defense of His divinity as the Messiah, Jesus essentially says, "don't take my word for it; look at the evidence!"

A similar response is found in Matthew 11:2-5 when John the Baptist begins to doubt and asks, "Are you the one who is to come, or should we expect someone else?" In response, Jesus points him to the evidence. "Go back and report to John what you hear and see: the blind receive sight, the lame walk, those who have leprosy are cleansed, the deaf hear, the dead are raised, and the good news is proclaimed to the poor."[103]

In all this, we see a perfect illustration of the distinction between *knowing* versus *showing*. Although Jesus *knew* He was the Messiah, they didn't, so he began *showing* the evidence for it. Hence, "Believe me... **or at least believe on the evidence**."

"Just Show Them More Love"?

Despite this, some have taught that our lives as nice, heartfelt loving Christians *alone* is a sufficient testimony to the truth of Christianity. Yet, Jesus never claimed they should believe Him because of His character as a gentle, heartfelt loving "Christian." While the Bible may teach this aspect of evangelism elsewhere, that's not the case here.

> ...But Jesus said to them, "I have shown you many good works from the Father. For which of these do you stone me?" "We are not stoning you for any **good work**," they replied, "but for **blasphemy**, because you, a mere man, claim to be God" (John 10:31-33).

Note, they weren't refusing to believe Him because He was being rude or "un-Christ-like," but because *they regarded His views as blasphemous and false*. Yes, we should love others as Christ loved them, but if Christ did this and they *still* refused to believe, then it must follow that *love alone* is insufficient. Granted, developing loving relationships with nonbelievers is a *fundamental component* of evangelism, but it's not *the only component* of evangelism.

"But You Can't Argue Someone into the Kingdom!"

Another common objection against presenting arguments and evidence is that you "cannot argue someone into the kingdom." This can mean one of two things. First, it can mean that arguments, evidence, or reason cannot be used to bring someone to salvation. But this is simply false. I've done it myself, and the apostle Paul (not to mention Jesus) exemplified this approach throughout his ministry.

- And according to Paul's custom, he visited them, and for three Sabbaths **reasoned with them** from the Scriptures,

explaining and giving evidence... and **some of them were persuaded** (Acts 17:2-4, NASB).

- And he **reasoned and debated** in the synagogue every Sabbath, trying to **persuade** Jews and Greeks (Acts 18:4, AMP).

- And he went into the synagogue and for three months spoke boldly, **reasoning** and **arguing** and **persuading** them about the kingdom of God... This continued for two years, so that all the inhabitants...heard the word of the Lord [concerning eternal salvation through faith in Christ] (Acts 19:8,10, AMP).

Second, this "objection" could also mean that argumentation and evidence *alone* cannot bring someone to salvation, and, in this sense, I wholeheartedly agree! Salvation is the work of God alone "through the sanctifying work of the Spirit" (2 Thessalonians 2:13). However, this principle cuts both ways. So sure, we cannot "argue someone into the kingdom," but this also means we cannot "love someone into the kingdom" either.

Nevertheless, acknowledging that neither love nor evidence *alone* is sufficient to bring someone to salvation, it doesn't follow that neither plays a role in evangelism. It's God's prerogative to bring the gospel by any means He wishes, and, as is evident through Scripture, we're commanded to use both.

PRESENTING EVIDENCE AND DEALING WITH THOSE WHO DOUBT

Biblical Basis: "*Be merciful to those who doubt***...."** (Jude 1:22,).

"Doubting Thomas"

John 20:24-29 is often referred to as the story of "doubting Thomas." Sadly, this passage has been used to teach that we shouldn't present evidence to doubters or nonbelievers but instead, tell them to "just believe" or "have more faith" (as if faith is whimsically blind and non-evidence based). Yet, this passage teaches the exact opposite.

Still, this sentiment is justified by one of the most misapplied, misinterpreted verses in Scripture, "Blessed are those who have not seen and yet have believed." Unfortunately, this widespread misunderstanding is held by both believers and nonbelievers alike. As atheist and scientist, Richard Dawkins writes:

> Another member of the religious meme complex is called faith. It means blind trust, in the absence of evidence, even in the teeth of evidence. The story of Doubting Thomas is told, not so that we shall admire Thomas, but so that we can admire the other apostles in comparison. Thomas demanded evidence... The other apostles, whose faith was so strong that they did not need evidence, are held to us as worthy of imitation.[104]

Similarly, in my debate with atheist popularizer Aron Ra, he proudly wore a shirt that read, "Walking by Sight, NOT Faith!" Suffice it to say that if faith the size of a mustard seed can move mountains, then perhaps an understanding of faith the size of a mustard seed can prevent them, as well.

Examining How Jesus Responded to Doubt

Returning to our passage, Thomas finds himself in a predicament. The other disciples testify that Jesus has risen from the dead, but Thomas refuses to believe unless he sees and touches the evidence himself. How does Jesus respond? In two ways, but most (if not all) sermons I've heard only focus on the second, "Blessed are those who have not seen and yet have believed." Because the emphasis is typically on this response, many assume that Jesus is referring to the other disciples who, unlike Thomas, didn't demand to see and touch the evidence of His wounds. But note the context.

In verses 19-20 (ten whole verses before Jesus' second response), He appears to the disciples and *shows them* His hands and side, and verse 24 clarifies that Thomas *was not present at this time*. Meaning that Thomas' request to see the evidence for himself was not without context. He was merely asking to see what the other disciples had the privilege of *already seeing* firsthand. Hence, this second response, "blessed are those who have not seen and yet have believed," cannot be referring to the other disciples, given that they also *believed by seeing*. Instead, it likely refers to those who would receive the gospel after He ascended, accurately describing most Christians today who follow Jesus and yet, have not seen Him with their own eyes.

Therefore, the more significant reading for evangelism from this passage should emphasize the first way Jesus responded to Thomas's instance of doubt. And what was this initial response? Presenting Thomas with the very thing he was asking for. He presented the evidence.

> Then he said to Thomas, "Put your finger here, and see my hands; and put out your hand, and place it in my side. Do not disbelieve, but believe." Thomas answered him, "My Lord and my God!" (verses 27-28, ESV).

The fact that this was Jesus' initial response is important for a few reasons.

First, if we focus only on the second response, we convey the misconceived idea that Jesus is somehow upset with doubters. This causes those who struggle with doubt in the church to feel shame or embarrassment, forcing them to hide their doubt in fear of being ostracized from a church that should be answering their questions, not avoiding them. I've witnessed this effect firsthand (see the introduction of this book).

Second, this provides a profound picture for dealing with those who struggle with doubt. Note, Jesus did not scold, condemn, or hit Thomas over the head with a Bible. Instead, He acknowledged Thomas's doubt, showed His hands, lifted His robe, and said, "touch." "Put your finger here, put out your hand, and place it in my side," all so Thomas would "not disbelieve, but believe." Hence, when Jesus encountered a friend who struggled with doubt and asked for evidence, His initial response was to provide it!

The Application for Evangelism

Consider the simple yet profound application this has for apologetics in evangelism. Like Jesus, we must not look down on those who doubt but stand beside and help them wrestle with their questions. As Christ did with Thomas, we should provide evidence, arguments, and answers to those we're trying to reach. This is the principle of apologetics (1 Peter 3:15).

For this reason, asking the initial "why" question becomes essential when evangelizing nonbelievers (see chapter 4). This allows us to identify the strongholds and recognize the reasons behind their doubt. This isn't to win an argument (though that may happen) but to show genuine concern for their questions. Hence, we shouldn't patronize others with insensitive comments like, "Just have more faith!" but lend an attentive, caring ear to better understand their struggle. If we want to share Christ and show love in a culture filled with "doubting Thomases," then let's do one of the most loving things that any believer can do for those struggling with doubt: present them with the evidence. Jesus did this with His friend, and we should strive to be more like Jesus!

A PREFACE FOR THE REMAINING CHAPTERS

In the remainder of this book, we'll look at five arguments that can be presented as evidence for *showing that* Christianity is true. The first four provide a case for theism—the belief that God exists. Chapter 18 deals with the question of our existence, chapter 19 with the beginning of the universe, chapter 20 with the question of morality, and chapter 21 with the existence of evil. Each is an incredibly powerful argument for the existence of God that may suffice for bringing a person from atheism (or agnosticism) to theism. However, two final questions would remain: Which God, and which religion? The last section of this book answers this by looking at a fifth argument: the resurrection of Jesus. This is because if the resurrection is an actual, historical event, then all bets are off—Christianity is true.

Chapter 18

The Argument From Contingency

Biblical Basis: Romans 1:20

> *For ever since the creation of the world His invisible attributes, His eternal power and divine nature, have been clearly seen, being understood through His workmanship [all His creation, the wonderful things that He has made], so that they [who fail to believe and trust in Him] are without excuse and without defense* (AMP).

In this passage, we find what appears to be an oxymoron. Namely that "God's *invisible attributes*... have been *clearly seen*." But note the reason: "being understood through His workmanship, all His creation, the wonderful things that He has made." According to Scripture, this means that we can logically deduce the invisible attributes of God's nature simply by examining the nature of creation itself. Hence, what cannot be seen is clearly seen, and what was once invisible becomes visible.

By way of analogy, if we study the parts and functions of a car, we learn about the mind of the mechanic that designed it. Thus, the more we know about the car, the more we learn about the mechanic. The same principle applies to God and creation. As Psalm 19:1 states, "the heavens declare the glory of God; the skies proclaim the work of his hands." Therefore, creation becomes a visible testimony to God's majesty, power, and divine nature. This is precisely what we find in our first two arguments.

LAYING THE FOUNDATION

In this chapter, we begin our endeavors by examining how the nature of existence itself provides a powerful argument for the existence of God. To do this, we first lay a foundation for understanding 1) the nature of existence and 2) how one must approach an explanation for it.

1. The Nature of Existence: Necessity vs. Contingency

In the words of German Philosopher, mathematician, and logician G. W. Leibniz (1646-1716), "The first question which should rightly be asked is why is there something rather than nothing."[105] That is, why does anything at all exist? As Leibniz observed, everything that exists falls under one of two categories: that which exists *necessarily* and that which exists *contingently*.

Briefly, the notion of **necessity** is of something that must exist or be true by its very nature. It is something that *must be* the case, and its non-existence is *logically impossible*.[106] By contrast, **contingency** entails the notion that something is the case but *did not have to be* the case, and thus, its *non-existence* is a logical possibility. For example, I exist, but my existence is contingent, not necessary. Had my parents never met, I would not exist. Hence, I did not "have to be," and my existence *contingently depended on* something external and prior to myself. We can simplify our understanding as follows:

Necessity:

- Something that "must be" by its very nature.
- Its non-existence is logically impossible.
- It *could not* have been otherwise.

Contingency:

- Something that "does not have to be" (depending on something external to itself).
- Its non-existence is logically possible.
- It *could have* been otherwise.

2. The Explanation: Borrowing Lenders vs. Owning Lenders[107]

As Leibniz also understood, everything that exists will have an explanation for its existence, and that explanation will be found in something that exists *necessarily* or something that exists *contingently*.[108] To grasp this principle of explanation, consider the following illustration.

Suppose Person A needs five dollars and approaches Person B to borrow the money. Unfortunately, Person B doesn't have the money but writes a check and asks that Person A not cash it until tomorrow. Thankfully, Person B remembers that Person C owes him five dollars and approaches him for the money. However, Person C doesn't have the money either, but as before, writes Person B a check in good faith. Person C then goes to Person D, but again, the same problem arises, and the same solution is proposed. So far, this chain can be illustrated as follows:

A → B → C → D...

At this point, everyone in the chain is what we may call a **borrowing lender**, seeking to *borrow* in order *to lend what they do not possess*. But note the problem. If the chain continues in this way, then no matter how many *borrowing lenders* we add, Person A will never receive the money.

But suppose the next day that, all things being equal, Person A successfully cashes the funds from Person B's check. This would imply that, at some point, the chain must have ended with what we may call an **owning lender**. Namely, someone who *already possessed* the funds and *didn't need to borrow it from someone prior*. We'll call him Person Z.

A ← B ← C ← D...?... ← Z

Concerning explanations, we can see that persons B-D were insufficient given that borrowing lenders cannot lend what they do not yet possess. Hence, unless the chain stopped with an *owning lender*, Person A's check would've bounced. Therefore, given that Person A received the money, it logically followed that an owning lender must have existed. Thus, persons B-D were *contingent explanations*, whereas Person Z was *necessary*.

THE ARGUMENT FROM CONTINGENCY

With these foundations in mind, we can begin the argument by asking, why do I exist? As previously stated, I exist, but my existence is contingent. So, to explain my *contingent existence,* I must point to something external and prior to myself—namely, my parents. Hence, I "borrowed existence" from my parents.

However, given that my parents are also contingent, I must now explain their existence in order to adequately explain mine. Why? Because explaining the existence of something contingent by way of another contingent thing doesn't provide a complete explanation of the chain. So, we can explain their existence by pointing to their parents. But once again, the same problem arises. Thus far, we can see the formation of the following chain:

ME → PARENTS → GRANDPARENTS → GREAT GRANDPARENTS....?

At this point, every member in the chain is merely a *contingent "borrowing lender."* Borrowing existence from persons prior and lending it to the next. But as before, if this causal chain of *contingent beings* continues to regress without end, I would not exist. Yet, I DO exist! This means that, much like the check analogy, there *must be* an owning lender at the beginning of the chain. Now consider the logical implications.

This would have to be an own *owning lender with respect to existence itself.* That is, a being that never came into existence but has *always existed.* A being that is *self-existent, non-contingent,* and *necessary.* A being that *must be, cannot fail* to be, and *didn't need to borrow existence* in order to be. A being that serves as the necessary explanation and foundation for everything else that exists and, thus, a being whose nonexistence is logically impossible—namely, God.[109]

ME ← PARENTS ← GRANDPARENTS ← GREAT GRANDPARENTS... ← GOD

Therefore, given the nature of existence itself, it would logically follow that *if anything contingent exists,* then God *must exist necessarily.* Put differently, if God did not exist, then *nothing* would exist because everything owes its existence to God in one way or another.[110] As the opening chapter of John states:

> In the beginning was the Word, and the Word was with God, and the Word was God. He was in the beginning with God. **All things came into being through Him, and apart from Him not even one thing came into being that has come into being** (John 1:1-3, NASB).

Objection: The Universe Is Necessary, Not God

At this point, the nonbeliever may claim that just as my parents are sufficient to explain my existence, the universe is sufficient to explain everything within it. If I couldn't exist without my parents, and they couldn't exist without the universe, then it must follow that the universe, not God, is the logically necessary starting point that explains everything else. Hence, the chain would be as follows:

ME ← PARENTS ← GRANDPARENTS ← GREAT GRANDPARENTS... ← THE UNIVERSE

In response to this objection, we can begin by asking—is the universe necessary or contingent? Recall the attributes of necessity, and let's see if they apply to the universe.

1. Is the universe's non-existence *logically impossible*?
2. Did this universe *have* to exist?
3. Is the universe *eternal*?
4. Did the universe have a *beginning*?

Concerning the first two, the answer is clearly "no." First, the universe's non-existence is *not* logically impossible. It could have failed to exist. Second, the universe, as it exists, did not *have to exist* in this way. Any other universe could've popped into existence with a different arrangement of stars or galaxies.

The last two questions go together, and we'll deal with them in detail in the next chapter. For now, suffice it to say that if the universe had a beginning, then it cannot be eternal, and if it cannot be eternal, then it cannot be necessary. Therefore, given that the universe fails to meet the attributes of necessity, it follows that its existence must be contingent, not necessary.

Subsequently, the objection only adds another contingent link into our chain of explanations. But as with the first analogy, adding more "hot checks" into the chain cannot "put the money in the bank." We still require a *necessary* Being that serves as the foundation for all contingently existing things. That is, an *owning lender of existence* itself that can lend existence to everything else without borrowing from something prior. Hence, we still need God.

ME ← PARENTS ← GRANDPARENTS .... ← THE UNIVERSE ← GOD

The Argument from Contingency

This was at the heart of Leibniz's conclusion for what has been called **The Argument from Contingency**. In a syllogistic format, the argument goes as follows:

1. Every contingent thing has an explanation of its existence.
2. If the universe has an explanation of its existence, that explanation is God.
3. The universe is a contingent thing.
4. Therefore, the universe has an explanation of its existence.
5. Therefore, the explanation of the universe is God.

Given that this is a structurally valid, sound argument (i.e., an argument with true premises), the conclusion becomes logically unavoidable. It wouldn't matter if the person didn't like the argument or had other reasons for being an atheist.[111] It logically follows that if the universe exists and is contingent (along with all contingent things that exist within it), *God must exist necessarily.*

Natural Theology: Listing the Attributes of God From the Argument

In our opening verse, we learned that one can logically deduce certain attributes of God simply by reflecting on the nature of creation. In philosophy, this is known as **natural theology** (inferring knowledge of God apart from divine revelation) and is precisely what we've done in this chapter. From these arguments alone, we can logically deduce that if *anything* contingent exists, then there must exist a *logically necessary, non-contingent, self-existent, eternal being* whose *nonexistence is logically impossible* and is the *foundation*, *explanation*, and *reason* for which anything at all exists; the universe and everything in it.

Therefore, if you exist, God must exist. If the universe exists, God must exist. And ironically, if the atheist exists, then once again, God must exist necessarily, and His nonexistence is logically impossible. As Scripture explains:

> For by Him all things were created, both in the heavens and on earth, visible and invisible, whether thrones, or dominions, or rulers, or authorities–all things have been created through Him and for Him. He is before all things, and in Him all things hold together (Colossians 1:16-17, NASB).

Chapter 19

The Kalam Cosmological Argument

Our next argument for the existence of God comes from the fact that the universe had a beginning. One of the best-known proponents of this is philosopher and theologian Dr. William Lane Craig, who calls this version of the argument **The Kalam Cosmological Argument**. Although the name is a mouthful, the argument is relatively simple, and I've shared it with others in about thirty seconds or less.

30 Seconds or Less

As I was catching up on emails and waiting to get my oil changed, a lady began nervously pacing back and forth in front of me. Finally, she stopped and said, "Can I ask you a question? Do you believe in God?" With a smile, I responded, "Absolutely! And not only do I *believe* God exists, I *know* God exists." Her eyes widened. "But isn't it all about faith? I mean, I believe in God too, but how can you show someone else that God exists?" Excited at the opportunity, I took out a pen, grabbed the nearest napkin, and wrote down the argument. With just two premises and a conclusion, the argument goes as follows:

The Kalam Cosmological Argument

1. Everything that begins to exist has a cause.
2. The universe began to exist.
3. Therefore, the universe has a cause.

UNPACKING THE ARGUMENT

To begin unpacking the profundity of the argument, we must first understand the three things that came into existence at the universe's inception. Namely, *time*, *space*, and *matter*.

To put the point differently, we can say that if there were no universe, there would be no time, no space, and no matter. Now, if everything that begins to exist has a cause, and if time, space, and matter began, then it logically follows that time, space, and matter must have had a cause.

The next step is explaining the (ontological) relationship between causes and their effects. Put succinctly, causes logically precede, can be greater than, and are external to their effects. For example, the person that *caused* my laptop to exist does not reside within it. As the cause of my laptop, his existence was logically prior to, greater than, and external to it. Similarly, if time, space, and matter had a beginning and thus, needed a cause, then based on a logical deduction, it follows that **the cause** of time, space, and matter must have been *timeless*, *spaceless*, and *immaterial*.

At this point, a nonbeliever may interject and claim that the universe's cause need not be God. Although we have yet to mention Him, it's evident to anyone that these attributes fall under the historic Christian concept of God. Nevertheless, this nonbeliever argues that the universe's cause could've been something natural. But note the problem here. If the universe had a beginning that encompassed all of nature, *then nature had a beginning*, and thus, it too, must have a cause. Yet, to argue that something *natural* caused all of nature is to argue that "*nature existed*

prior to its existence in order to *bring itself into existence*," which is a logical absurdity.

Therefore, if nature had a beginning, then the cause of all things natural must be something *greater than* and *external to* the natural world. Something transcendent: beyond nature, outside of the natural, and, oh wait, there's a word for that: *super-natural.* Literally, beyond the natural! Hence, the nonbeliever has only added to our list of attributes for this cause, and we can now say that if the universe began to exist, then a *timeless, spaceless, immaterial*, and (thanks to the objection) *supernatural* Being must exist. Moreover, given that this Cause of the universe would've had to create *everything* out of *absolutely nothing*, an additional attribute must be that this supernatural Being is *unimaginably powerful*.

Furthermore, in the last chapter, we learned that the universe is a contingent thing that didn't have to exist. It was caused to exist, and this implies that its existence was the result of a *personal, free* decision. Why? Because inanimate material objects do not make *free* decisions (see chapter 15). Moreover, decisions stem from wills, wills come from minds, and the paradigm cases of minds are grounded in persons. Therefore, if the universe was caused to exist and is contingent, then the cause of its existence must have been the result of a *personal* Being endowed with freedom of the will. Hence, we now have the implicit attributes of a cause that is both *personal, free,* and relative to the last argument—*logically necessary*.

So, based on the logical deduction from this argument alone, we can now say that if the universe began to exist (take a deep breath for dramatic effect when presenting this), then there must exist a *timeless, spaceless, immaterial, unimaginably powerful, transcendent, supernatural, logically necessary, personal, free* Being—and I just call him God for short. Therefore, if the universe began to exist, then God *must* exist.

RESPONDING TO OBJECTIONS

Recall that when an argument is structurally valid and sound, the conclusion becomes logically unavoidable. Therefore, if a person wishes to reject the conclusion, they must do so by attacking one of the premises. Because we cannot cover every objection (and we don't need to do), I refer you to a lecture video by Dr. William Lane Craig entitled "Objections So Bad I Couldn't Have Made Them Up (Or, The World's Ten Worst Objections to The Kalam Cosmological Argument)."[112] For our purposes here, we'll only focus on a handful of objections.[113]

Objections and Defense of Premise One

1. Getting Something from Nothing

Any objection to premise one must deny that *everything that begins to exist has a cause*. Yet, this is a fundamental principle of **metaphysics** (the branch of philosophy that studies the nature of being and ultimate reality[114]), which essentially states *you cannot get something from nothing*. That is, *you cannot get being from non-being*. As Craig explains:

> To claim that something can come into being from nothing is worse than magic. When a magician pulls a rabbit out of a hat, at least you've got the magician, not to mention the hat! But if you deny premise 1, you've got to think that the whole universe just appeared at some point in the past for no reason whatsoever... This is simply the faith of an atheist. In fact, I think this represents a greater leap of faith than belief in the existence of God. For it is, I repeat, literally worse than magic. If this is the alternative to belief in God, then unbelievers can never accuse believers of irrationality, for what could be more evidently irrational than this?[115]

2. "Quantum Mechanics"

Despite this, some attempt to object to premise one by alluding to the science of quantum mechanics. This "quantum mechanics card" seems to be the nonbeliever's "ace in the hole" when they want to deny a fundamental principle of metaphysics. This approach grew in popularity when atheist physicist Lawrence Krauss released his book, *A Universe From Nothing: Why Is There Something Rather Than Nothing?*

Implied by the subtitle, this was Krauss' attempt to answer Leibniz's question, but without God and in the name of science. According to Krauss:

> There's a plausible case for understanding precisely how a universe full of stuff, like the universe we live in, could result literally from nothing by natural processes... Nothing can create something all the time due to the laws of quantum mechanics, and it's fascinatingly interesting...literally, whole universes can pop out of nothing.[116]

In brief, the argument goes something like this: in quantum mechanics, virtual particles pop in and out of existence, uncaused and out of nothing all the time. If this can happen with subatomic particles, then why not the universe? By alluding to quantum mechanics, we can now prove that the universe was uncaused and popped into existence out of nothing—God is not needed. Hence, according to Krauss, the universe's cause wasn't God but "nothing."

Now admittedly, I'm no scientist, whereas Krauss has a Ph.D. in science. However, one doesn't need a Ph.D. to know when a scientist engages in logical fallacies and poor philosophy. Using *The Lazy Approach*, we can begin by asking Krauss a straightforward question, "What do you mean by '*nothing*?'" Luckily for us, he's provided some answers. "By nothing, I don't mean nothing. I mean *nothing*."[117] Profound. Undeniably, Krauss is a deep thinker.

Elsewhere, he states that "nothing is unstable" and that "nothing" can have weight and mass. Recognizing the absurdity of these statements, he adds:

> Now that sounds ridiculous. Why should nothing weigh something? ...The answer is, nothing isn't nothing anymore in physics. Because of the laws of Quantum mechanics and special relativity, on extremely small scales, "nothing" is really a boiling bubbling brew of virtual particles that are popping in and out of existence in a time scale so short you can't see them.[118]

I'm reminded of that famous line from *The Princess Bride* where Inigo Montoya, with a look of suspicion, says, "You keep using that word. I don't think it means what you think it means."

In philosophy, Krauss commits what is known as the **fallacy of equivocation**: using a word that means one thing but referring to something entirely different. For instance, if I said I had *nothing* for lunch today, it wouldn't make sense to ask, "And what did it taste like?" or "How many calories were in it?" This is because the word "nothing" (literally, "no-thing") means the absence of everything. Hence, if something has taste, weight, or mass, then we aren't referring to *nothing* but *something*!

So, what is Krauss referring to when he uses the word "nothing?" Essentially, a "quantum vacuum"—a sea of fluctuating energy. Understanding this phrase is not relevant to the point. Instead, the relevant point is understanding that when Krauss uses the word "*no-thing*," he's actually referring to "*some-thing*." Namely, a quantum vacuum. Therefore, even if we granted his argument (tactical tool #3), he's not proving that the universe came from nothing, but something! Thus, the title of his book shouldn't be *A Universe From Nothing*, but more appropriately, "A Universe From *Something*." Ironically for Krauss, in an attempt to deny God by redefining the word "nothing," nothing has been proven.

As if this elementary philosophical mistake weren't embarrassing enough, consider the response given by fellow atheist and theoretical physicist Dr. David Albert. In a published review by *The New York Times*, Dr. Albert explains how Krauss's argument of "something popping into existence out of nothing" is like arguing that rearranging one's fingers can make a fist pop into existence out of "no fists." Unpacking the absurdity, Albert states:

> That's just not right ... the fact that particles can pop in and out of existence, over time, as those fields rearrange themselves, is not a whit more mysterious than the fact that fists can pop in and out of existence, over time, as my fingers rearrange themselves. And none of these poppings–if you look at them aright–amount to anything even remotely in the neighborhood of a creation from nothing.[119]

Again, Albert is an atheist (*not* a Christian) with no dog in this fight. Yet, he concludes by stating, "But all there is to say about this, as far as I can see, is that Krauss is dead wrong and his religious and philosophical critics are absolutely right."[120]

Objections and Defense of Premise Two

At this point, if the nonbeliever wishes to deny the conclusion, then his only hope is to deny premise two: *the universe began to exist*. However, a defense of this premise is easily provided in two academic fields: science and philosophy.

1. A Scientific Defense

Recall that using science to answer metaphysical questions (such as the existence of God) is a category fallacy. However, premise two is not inherently a claim of metaphysics but science. Thus, although science cannot *directly* answer the God question, it can provide evidence *in support of* a premise that logically leads to the conclusion that God exists. Let's briefly unpack two scientific discoveries that support this premise.

1.1 The Second Law of Thermodynamics

According to the second law of thermodynamics, the universe is running out of usable energy. To grasp why this scientific discovery supports the second premise, consider two analogies. First analogy, imagine a car with a full tank of gas. After running the car for a few days, you'll inevitably run out. In the same way, the universe is running out of usable energy. Had it been here forever, it would've inevitably run out of energy by now. Since it has not, it follows that the universe cannot be eternal and, thus, had an absolute beginning.

Second analogy, if we spin a quarter on a table, we know it cannot continue to spin forever. At some point, it'll run out of "spinning energy." Thus, if the universe continues to have its "spinning energy," then we know it hasn't been here forever. Put differently, we can say that if the universe is slowly winding down, then something (or, more pertinently, *someone*) must've "wound it up." Therefore, based on the second law of thermodynamics, we know that the universe cannot be past eternal but must have had a definite beginning.

1.2 The Universe Is Expanding

One of the most remarkable discoveries in modern cosmology is that the universe has been expanding throughout its history. As a result, we can now trace its expansion back to a singular beginning. Think of this like a cone on its side. The initial singularity to the left representing its beginning, and the expanding section to the right representing the present.

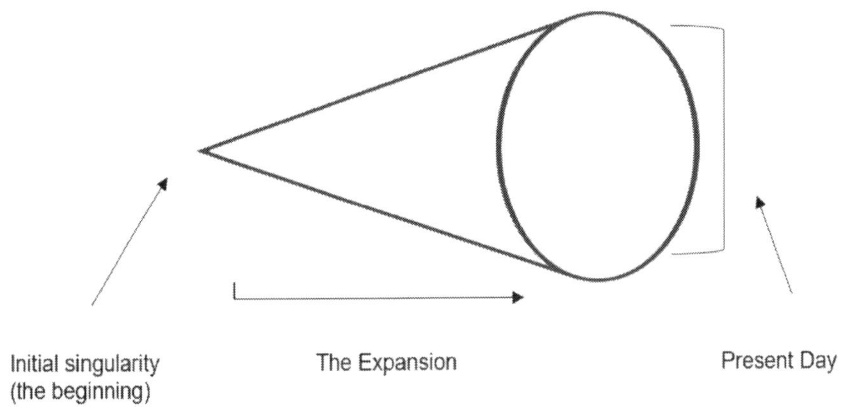

This scientific discovery made it clear; if we have an expanding universe, then we have a universe with a beginning.

In 2003, the work of leading cosmologists Arvin Borde, Alan Guth, and Alexander Vilenkin provided further evidence of this in what is known as the "BGV theorem." Given the evidence, they concluded that "any universe which has on average been expanding throughout its history cannot be eternal in the past but must have an absolute beginning."[121][122]

The "Big Bang" Had a Banger

The scientific discoveries listed above typically fall under what is known as "Big Bang Cosmology." Although some believers have a "knee jerk" reaction to this phrase, consider the history behind its name. The term "Big Bang" was first coined by atheist cosmologist Fred Hoyle (1945-2001), who *didn't believe* the universe had a beginning. At the time, Hoyle's view (known as "The Steady State Theory") was the dominating theory held by most atheist scientists, believing the universe to be eternal and without beginning.

However, a Christian theist—physicist, astronomer, and priest named Georges Lemaître discovered the evidence for the (now prevailing) theory that the universe had a beginning, not Hoyle. So, why did this atheist scientist coin the name for a view he neither believed nor discovered? Because he wanted to publicly ridicule the idea and those who held to it. But why all the animosity and mockery toward this new "Big Bang" theory?

The answer can be found in the reaction of atheist scientist John Maddox who had complained how a universe with a beginning gave creationists "ample justification" for their beliefs.[123] As Lennox paraphrases Maddox, "we mustn't give into this idea of a beginning because it will give too much leverage to people who believe the Bible."[124] But what was this "leverage" that Maddox was referring to? Simply the first sentence of the first verse in the first book of the Bible, which states, "*In the beginning*." And if the Bible got the first part right, what else did it get right?

Ironically, Christians are often accused of fighting or denying "science" because of our "privatized, personal beliefs." Yet, here is a clear, historical example where a large sect of the atheist community resisted science, not because of the evidence, *but because of their own privatized, personal beliefs* in atheism! But as leading cosmologist and theoretical physicist Alexander Vilenkin explains:

> With the proof now in place, cosmologists can no longer hide behind the possibility of a past eternal universe. There is no escape: they have to face the problem of a cosmic beginning.[125]

2. A Philosophical Defense: You Cannot Cross Infinity

Our second defense of premise two comes from the logical impossibility of crossing infinity. To grasp this point, ask yourself, "how many numbers would it take to count *past* infinity?" Clearly, it's a logically impossibility. There's no set of numbers we could count to reach infinity, *much less cross it*. But note, just as we cannot *count to* infinity, we cannot *count down from* infinity, either. And this is precisely the problem with denying that the universe had a beginning.

To illustrate, consider that the series of days within the existence of the universe have been formed by adding one day after. Think of this like a line of dominoes falling successively until the present day is reached, and let's call today "domino 0." As illustrated below, reaching today required that we first crossed domino -1, and before that, -2, and before that, -3, and so on.

... - 3 → - 2 → - 1→ 0 (Present Day)

However, if the number of past "domino days" is infinite, we would've never arrived at today. Why not? Because again, if we cannot *count to* infinity, then we cannot *count down from* infinity (much less cross it!). Hence, if the past number of days is infinite, then reaching today becomes a logical impossibility. Yet here we are! Therefore, if today has been reached, then it follows that the series of past days cannot be infinite, but must have had a definite beginning.

Putting the problem differently, reaching the present day by crossing infinity would be like trying to jump out of an infinitely tall well. It simply cannot be done, and denying the universe's beginning only makes the problem worse. *This* would be like trying to jump out of an infinitely tall well that's bottomless. Not only could it never be done, but the attempt itself becomes impossible.[126]

Final Objection: But What Caused God?

After presenting the argument, don't be surprised if you hear the age-old, tiresome objection, "but where did God come from?" Amusingly, this objection is often presented with a smug attitude, as if the nonbeliever has just uttered some profound epiphany that no Christian scholar or philosopher has ever considered (much less answered!) in the past two thousand-plus years. It's the typical go-to objection that's held in the highest esteem. The final nail in the coffin. A checkmate. The silver bullet to Christianity. Actually, it's one of the worst objections I've ever heard.

Actual Objection or Strawman?

Predictably, the objection is presented by asking, "If everything that exists has a cause, then what caused God?" But did you catch the implicit strawman in the question? Note that the first premise is, "Everything that ***begins*** *to exist* has a cause," and not, "*Everything that exists* has a cause." Hence, the objection is a strawman. This is where tactical tool #2 in "reverse" applies.

Recall that reiterating a person's position back to them is first to ensure that we've not misunderstood their view. This type of etiquette should work both ways. Thus, if I feel that a person's objection stems from misunderstanding my argument, I ask them to repeat it. If they can articulate it accurately, then perhaps I've misunderstood their objection.

By contrast, if they cannot reiterate (or at least paraphrase) the argument, then I have no problem asking why they're responding to an argument they've not taken the time to understand. You'd be surprised how humbling this can be for them, and rightly so. Not only does this bring some humility toward their attitude, but it forces them to try and understand what you've presented. Again, the first premise states, "everything that *begins to exist* has a cause," and not "*everything that exists* has a cause." So, asking them to reiterate the argument can be a respectful way to expose the strawman in their objection.

Responding to the Objection

In his book, *On Guard: Defending Your Faith With Reason and Precision*, Craig succinctly responds to this misguided objection: "Something that is eternal wouldn't need a cause, since it never came into being."[127] Given what we've learned in this chapter, we can elaborate in the following way:

> If time began at the universe's inception and God is its cause, then it follows that God was timeless. If God was timeless, then he must be eternal. If eternal, then he has no beginning, and if he has no beginning, then he needs no cause.

Therefore, to ask "what caused God" is essentially asking the question, "*What caused the uncaused cause of the universe which, by definition, has no cause to begin with?*" It's simply a nonsensical question.

Moreover, recall how the question "who is the bachelor married to?" is a category fallacy. If a bachelor is single by definition, then it makes no sense to inquire about his spouse. Similarly, if God is uncaused and eternal by nature, then it makes no sense to ask for the thing that caused Him. For this reason, God has traditionally been understood as the *uncaused,* ***first cause*** of the universe, and there is no cause prior to the first (otherwise, it wouldn't be the first cause but a second or third). Thus, we can simplify our response further:

> If God is timeless, then He is eternal, and if eternal, then had no beginning, and if He had no beginning, then He has no cause, and if He has no cause, then it follows that God must be the uncaused, first cause and Creator of the universe.

Therefore, we can conclude once more that if the universe began to exist, then there must exist a *timeless, spaceless, immaterial, supernatural, unimaginably powerful, free, personal, logically necessary, self-existent, non-contingent, eternal, beginningless, uncaused-first cause, Creator* and *Sustainer* of the universe—and again, I just call him God for short.

Chapter 20

The Argument From Morality

Concerning the question of God's existence, some may retort, "Who cares, and why does it matter? Can't we all be good people, feed the homeless, and care for one another? Why do we need God to be moral? Can't we be good because it's the right thing to do?" But not so fast. What is "goodness?" And "right" according to whom? To assert these ideas is to beg the question that "right," "wrong," and "good" or "bad" are genuine features of reality to begin with. Yet, if morality is merely a social construct invented by our society (e.g., relativism), then, strictly speaking, nothing could ever be objectively "right" or "wrong," "good," or "bad." Hence, the preliminary question before us is this: does morality exist, and if so, what grounding does it have in reality?

The Moral Argument

In this chapter, our argument for the existence of God comes from the existence of morality. As before, the argument is relatively easy to memorize and can be presented in a syllogistic format with just two premises and a conclusion.[128]

1. If God does not exist, then objective moral values and duties do not exist.
2. Objective moral values and duties do exist.
3. Therefore, God exists.

To unpack the argument, we can begin by identifying key features of morality itself. This is needed for two reasons. First, although everyone may be familiar with the notion of moral values and duties, articulating their definition may be difficult (especially if one has not thought deeply about moral philosophy). Put differently, while we can point to things that are right or wrong, understanding the nature of *what makes something right or wrong* is the more profound question one must begin with.

Second, morality is a question of metaphysics—immaterial, beyond the physical, and concerns the nature of ultimate reality. By studying the nature of morality, it will ultimately point us to the kind of things that can possess it and, more pertinently, the very thing that grounds its existence. This is similar to our approach concerning the nature of consciousness in chapter 15. If the properties of consciousness are immaterial, then it requires an immaterial substance (i.e., a soul) to possess and ground its existence. The same principle applies to understanding the ontology of morality (i.e., the reason it exists in the first place).

UNPACKING THE NATURE OF MORALITY

Objective vs. Subjective

To begin with, if morality exists, then it's either objective or subjective. **Objective morality** is the notion that morality is *universally valid, binding*, and *independent of* human thought or opinion. Consider the acts of murder, slavery, or the Holocaust. Are these *objectively* wrong? Absolutely. Would their moral status change if everyone thought they were objectively right? Absolutely not. Thus, if morality exists and is objective, it is *universally binding* for *all people* at *all times* and in *all places*. It is independent of universal agreement and remains true even if no one else believes it.

By contrast, **subjective morality** entails the notion that **moral values** (something being good or bad) and **moral duties** (actions being right or wrong) *subjectively depend* on a person's thought or opinion. With this view, murder, slavery, or the Holocaust are not *inherently* or *necessarily* wrong, but depend on whom you're asking and during the era you're asking it. Hence, if morality is subjective, then moral values, duties, or obligations are *not universally valid* or binding to all people at all times and in all places. Instead, their moral status largely depends on the person carrying out the action and thus, becomes *dependent on* human thought or opinion.

So, which is it? Does morality exist, and if so, is it *objective* or *subjective*?[129] For any rational, sincere seeker of truth, morality, if it exists, must be objective. That is to say, it cannot be dependent on, much less, *grounded in*, something like the human mind, for the human mind is contingent, not necessary. To grasp this implication, consider how the number two being even is a *necessary, objective* truth that's *independent of and not grounded in* the human mind. If no one existed, it would still be true that the number two is even. Thus, its existence and truth are independent of our acknowledgment, acceptance, or concept of it. It was true before we existed and will be true long after.

Similarly, if morality exists and is objective, it cannot be grounded in us. Otherwise, it becomes subjectively contingent and dependent upon our existence, thoughts, and opinions of it.[130] Yet, slavery didn't become wrong two hundred years ago but *was always wrong*, even if others thought it was right. For this reason, morality's existence, necessity, and objectivity cannot be grounded something contingent that had a beginning but instead, must be grounded in something *transcendent, necessarily existent*, and *eternal*. From this alone, we can see how the existence of objective morality requires the existence of God. Still, our case becomes stronger by unpacking additional features of morality that equally require God as an *ontological* foundation.

Additional Features of Morality

To begin with, the notion of a **moral duty** entails that there exist moral obligations. Hence, I have a moral duty (i.e., obligation) to feed my children, love my wife, and help those in need. Additionally, a universal obligation entails that there must exist a *universal command, order*, and *moral law*, which further entails there must be a universal *moral law giver*.

Moreover, consider that **moral values** such as loyalty, love, kindness, and so forth are properties that are intrinsic to persons, not objects. Rocks, tables, and chairs cannot possess the virtues of being loyal, loving, or kind, nor can they be morally obligated to do so. Hence, that which grounds these additional moral features must also be *sentient, rational, morally perfect*, and *personal*.[131]

Therefore, given all the features we've discussed, we can now conclude that if morality exists and is objective, then it must be grounded in something that is *transcendent, necessarily existent, eternal, sentient, rational, morally perfect*, and *personal*—namely, God. Thus, by unpacking the nature of morality, we see that if God does not exist, then objective moral values and duties would not exist. Or, put in the affirmative, if objective morality exists, then God must exist. Hence, the moral argument:

1. If God does not exist, then objective moral values and duties do not exist.
2. Objective moral values and duties do exist.
3. Therefore, God exists.

RESPONDING TO OBJECTIONS

"But I Can Be Good Without God!"

We begin with some common misconceptions about the argument that you'll likely hear conveyed with the following responses:

- But I can be good without believing in God!
- Are you saying all atheists are bad people?
- I don't need God to know right from wrong!

Note, these aren't objections to the argument but strawmen of it. To understand why, let's clearly state what the argument is *not* saying (in a conversation, this can be a point of using tactical #2 in reverse, asking the other person to reword the argument back to you).

Given the argument, we are <u>*not*</u> saying:

– One must <u>*believe*</u> in God to live a moral life.

- Atheists cannot recognize morality without *belief* in God.
- One cannot formulate a system of ethics without *referring* to God.

Instead, we're simply saying that without God *as the ontological foundation*, objective morality cannot exist. Thus, it's not *belief in God* that's necessary for objective morality, but *the existence of God.*[132] Granted, some atheists may be more moral than some Christians, but again, this misses the point of the argument that without God, *objective morality cannot exist.*

Moral Ontology vs. Moral Epistemology

To avoid this confusion, it may be necessary to explain the distinction between what is known as *moral ontology* and *moral epistemology.*

Moral ontology: *the existence* of morality.

Moral epistemology: *the knowledge* of morality.

As presented, **moral ontology** deals with *the existence* of morality (the *reason* and *grounding* for which morality *exists* in the first place), whereas **moral epistemology** deals with *the knowledge* of morality (how a person comes to *believe or know* moral truths).

To illustrate this distinction with an analogy, a person can read a book without believing in the existence of authors. However, if it weren't for authors, there'd be no book to read. Granted, one can explain how they came to know about the book (epistemology), but *knowledge* about the book does nothing to explain *why* the book *exists* (ontology). For that, you need an author. Similarly, a person can *know* that objective morality exists without *believing* in God. But once again, if God does not exist, then objective morality would not exist, to begin with. Hence, the moral argument is a concern of *moral ontology*, not *moral epistemology*, and we shouldn't confuse the two.

For this reason, we're not arguing that nonbelievers are bad, evil, or immoral people. Rather, we're arguing that if there is no God, then in principle, *no one could ever be objectively* bad, evil, or immoral in the first place. Hence, to say "God doesn't exist, but I can still be good" would be like saying, "We're all out of bread, so I'll just have a slice of toast instead." If there is no bread, there can be no toast, and if there is no God, there can be no objective morality.

Objections and Defense of Premise One

"We Don't Need God for Morality"

Recall that denying the conclusion of a syllogism requires a refutation or rebuttal to one of the premises. For premise one, this would require a demonstration that objective morality can exist even if God does not. This is typically done by appealing to science and evolution. Allegedly, if science can explain the existence of objective morality via the evolutionary process, then God as an ontological foundation is unnecessary.

Science and Evolution

Coincidentally, my professor mentioned in chapter 8 was my philosophy of ethics professor. During one class, he argued that given evolution, our survival objectively entailed that we get along with, not own, and be civilly "good" to one another. As a thought experiment, he imagined a caveman stealing meat from his tribe out of greed but was consequently beaten to death. This evolutionary process of trial and error taught us that a **utilitarian** perspective (the view that something is moral if and only if it benefits the majority) was most beneficial to our survival as a species. Thus, morality evolved into what it is now, and indeed, science can confirm what is *objectively conducive* to the flourishing of human beings. Therefore, "science and evolution" is the basis for demonstrating where morality came from. God is not needed.

Response

Using *The Lazy Approach*, consider five reasons why this "science and evolution" argument fails as both an explanation and objection. First, even if we grant this (tactical tool #3), evolution wouldn't give us an *ontological foundation* for the *existence* of objective morality. At best, it would only show *how we learned* about morality. Thus, it confuses moral ontology with moral epistemology.

Second, this still doesn't give us a universally binding, *objective moral standard*. While the principle of "not stealing meat" may work for this tribe, what *universally binding value* does it have to a bigger, stronger tribe that could murder the weaker tribe and steal the meat for themselves? After all, this would certainly be conducive to the stronger tribe's survival (tactical tool #5: *reductio ad absurdum*). Hence, we're ultimately left with a *subjective* morality that is not binding to *all tribes* at *all times* and for *all places* but is instead, subjectively contingent upon a "weaker tribe" mentality.

Third, the existence of morality is a metaphysical question that cannot be settled scientifically. As previously discussed, you won't find moral values in a test tube, and you cannot study the moral status of "stealing meat" under a microscope. Again, this is a category fallacy—and one that stems from the stronghold of scientism (tactical tool #5).

Fourth, the argument implicitly commits the fallacy of circular reasoning. This can be exposed by rewording the conclusion of the argument (tactical tools #2 and #5) as follows: "Given the evolutionary process, science can confirm that the flourishing of human beings is good, and the flourishing of human beings is good because science can confirm it given the evolutionary process." So essentially, "this is good because we're told it is good, and we're told it is good because it is good" (this also becomes a tautology).

Fifth, this further commits a question-begging fallacy (assuming that human flourishing is a virtuous moral imperative) that leads to **speciesism**, which is having an unjustified bias toward your own species. But if God does not exist, then what makes us so special? Why must *anything* revolve around the flourishing and survival of our species? We're not the strongest, fastest, or biggest animal (and, for some, not the brightest). So, why place the value on us?

As a thought experiment, suppose an alien race invaded earth and began to slaughter, enslave, and rape the human species. What logical argument could we give to demonstrate the immoral nature of their actions? Sure, we could say we don't like it or that what they're doing is immoral on our planet. But they could easily reply that what *we deem* immoral is merely the byproduct of our evolutionary history. This is how morality has evolved on *this* planet, but such a mentality is primitive, outdated, and, more importantly, doesn't apply on theirs.

To them, we'd be nothing more than a weed in their cosmic garden, a nuisance that must be eradicated for the survival of their species. And who struggles with a moral dilemma when pulling a weed from a garden? After all, they're bigger, stronger, and far more advanced. Therefore, it's the survival of their species that matters, not ours. Again, what makes us so special?

Suffice it to say if there's no transcendent, necessary, eternal, universally binding, and maximally perfect standard to ground objective morality (i.e., God), then there's simply no reason to favor the flourishing survival of our species over another. If there is no God, our existence has no objective meaning, purpose, or value. As atheist philosopher of science Michael Ruse explains:

> The position of the modern evolutionist is that humans have an awareness of morality... because such an awareness is of biological worth. Morality is a biological adaptation, no less than our hands and feet and teeth... Morality is just an aid to survival and reproduction ... and any deeper meaning is illusory.[133]

Objections and Defense of Premise Two

"Morality *is* Relative"

Many nonbelieving scholars have come to realize that if there is no God, then *objective* morality cannot exist.[134] Thus, denying premise two often becomes an attempt to double down in defense of moral relativism. To support this view, some have pointed to the fact that various cultures around the world don't *universally agree* on what is right or wrong. If morality were objective (they argue), then everyone would agree. Since they don't, morality must, therefore, be relative.

Before addressing the view, consider the problems with the objection (tactical tool #5). First, the existence of objective morality is *not dependent upon* universal agreement. After all, it's objectively true that the world is round even if some cultures have believed otherwise. Second, this also confuses moral epistemology (beliefs) with moral ontology (existence). Again, we're not asking who *believes* the right moral values but rather, *why* moral values *exist* in the first place. Third, this assertion is false; disagreement about *moral values* among cultures is not as widespread as the argument assumes.

To illustrate, some people in Eastern religions would rather starve than eat a cow, believing the latter is immoral. Why? Because if reincarnation is true, then eating a cow could literally be eating grandma. Now, although I, as a Christian, don't believe in reincarnation, I'd certainly agree that eating grandma is immoral. But note, this becomes a difference, not of moral values, but facts. In other words, I don't eat cows because I believe eating grandma is morally permissible. Instead, I eat cows because I don't think it could possibly be grandma to begin with. Hence, this ultimately becomes a disagreement of facts, *not moral values.*

Exposing the Implications of Moral Relativism

Still, a nonbeliever could stand firm in asserting that objective morality does not exist and adopt a position of cultural/moral relativism—the view that each person (or culture) must choose their own set of moral standards to live by. On this view, although nothing is ever *objectively* right or wrong, we can still act in accordance with the guidelines that help our society function and flourish. But consider three implications of this position that serve as a *reductio ad absurdum* (tactical tool #5).

1. Wholly Subjective, Non-binding Preferences

With moral or cultural relativism, morality reduces to subjectively non-binding, arbitrary preferences. For instance, some people eat peas with a spoon, others prefer a fork, and I may detest peas altogether. However, my distaste for peas doesn't oblige you not to eat peas. Why should my preference override yours? Similarly, you may not rape or murder, others don't like it, and some prefer to do so only on the weekends. But again, why should your non-binding, subjective preference apply to someone else? The nonbeliever may argue, "But this wouldn't be beneficial to our society, and you can't compare rape and murder to food!" I agree. However, this retort only makes sense if *objective* morality exists and moral relativism is false.

Recall the alien invasion thought experiment. Again, we could yell, "Stop, you can't do this to us! It's wrong!" And they could always reply, "Well, that's just *your* preferential guidelines according to *your* society's morality. But this is what is best for our society, and your arbitrary morality is not binding to the societies on our planet." If morality is not objective but a mere preference, then why should *any* society be obliged to follow our society's *arbitrary* standards? As Russian writer Fyodor Dostoyevsky observed, if God does not exist, then nothing would be immoral, and all things would be lawful.

2. There Can Be No Moral Progress, Only Neutral Change

The high school I attended required a strict dress code where students could only wear blue or white collared shirts. Clearly, this was a social convention relative to the school, and there was nothing *inherently* or *objectively* immoral about wearing a different color shirt. Thus, when they eventually lightened the rules to include more choices, it wasn't a *moral improvement* but an arbitrary, morally *neutral change*. This is because the notion of moral progress entails moving toward an *objective moral standard*. Yet, if there is no objective moral standard, then moral progress becomes impossible. Now consider the implications of this as it relates to moral relativism.

The laws in the U. S. have legalized same-sex marriage, and many nonbelievers claim this was genuine moral progress toward equality, much like the abolition of slavery. But given moral relativism, permitting slavery or disallowing same-sex marriage was no more "immoral" than wearing the wrong color shirt to school. As before, if an objective moral standard does not exist, then *any* changes to our laws cannot be taken as genuine moral improvements but, again, become arbitrary, neutral changes. *Nothing was ever objectively moral or immoral to begin with.*

Note, the point here isn't to argue whether same-sex marriage is moral or immoral. Instead, the point here is to demonstrate that if the nonbeliever wants to affirm the existence of *any* moral progress, then they must first affirm the existence of an objective moral standard. However, if they affirm the existence of an objective moral standard, then they must now affirm the conclusion that, therefore, God must exist. Hence, the price tag. If God does not exist, then moral progress is impossible. Conversely, if moral progress *is* possible, then God *must* exist.

3. Moral Relativism Is Unlivable

Despite this, a moral relativist could argue that no one should "force their morality onto other people." As was pointed out with *The Lazy Approach*, this is self-defeating. Moreover, consider that if moral relativism is true, we could never hold a person to an "ethical preference" they reject. Yet if someone thought it was morally permissible to steal the moral relativist's stuff, would they honestly say, "Although I think stealing is wrong, I won't force my morality onto you. So go ahead, steal away, and let me get the door for you!" No, because this not only reduces to absurdity, but is pragmatically unlivable.

Final Objection: The "Euthyphro Dilemma"

One of the most popular objections you may hear raised against the moral argument is known as the **Euthyphro Dilemma**, which goes something like this: "*Is something good because God wills it? Or does God will something because it's good*?" If we say something is good because God wills it, then morality becomes subjectively dependent upon Him (in this case, God could command something morally reprehensible and yet, this would become obligatory). If we say God wills something because *it is* good, then the standard of goodness becomes external to and independent of His existence. Hence, there are only two options: either subjectivity that is based on God or objectivity that is independent of God. Either way, if objective morality exists, God isn't necessary for it.

Response

First, note how the objection presents a false dichotomy by assuming only two options exist when there's a third. Namely, *God's very nature is* the foundational standard of goodness itself; thus, He wills something *because He is good.*[135] Second, this objection seems to implicitly attack an *epistemic way of knowing* the good when, again, our argument revolves around God as the *ontological grounding of* goodness itself.

To illustrate the problem, suppose we conducted a contest to see who could draw the best picture of the New York skyline, and our standard for judging the winner will be based on the New York skyline itself. But imagine someone challenged the results by asking, "but what makes the New York skyline look like the New York skyline?" Clearly, this is absurd. There is no standard beyond the New York skyline to judge whether it is, in fact, the New York skyline. It looks like the New York skyline *because that's precisely what it is by its very nature.*

In the same way, if God is the ontological foundation of objective morality, then there can be no standard beyond His nature. Much like existence itself requires a foundation (see chapter 18), the grounding of morality equally requires one.[136] Otherwise, there would be an infinite regress (asking for a standard of the standard of the standard), and consequently, no ultimate, objective standard could exist. Hence, the buck must stop somewhere. And given its features, this foundation could only be grounded in a *transcendent, necessary, eternal, intrinsically unchanging, sentient, rational, maximally perfect,* and *personal* being—namely, God. Hence, God wills something because *He is the good,* and just as there is no standard beyond the New York skyline, there is no objective standard for morality beyond Himself.

Chapter 21

The Argument From the Existence of Evil

It's been said that one of the strongest arguments against the existence of God is the existence of evil and, pushing the objection further—nonbelievers criticize religion for committing evil acts in the name of God. Moreover, some argue that in the Bible, God Himself commanded others to carry out evil acts, pointing at passages that allegedly prove their case. Never mind the context, ancient culture, or whether they've understood the passage. The point is, they're using the existence of evil as an objection against the existence of God.

The most well-known formulation of these type of arguments is known as "The Epicurean Riddle." According to this objection, the concept of an all-loving, all-powerful God is logically incompatible with the existence of evil, pain, and suffering in the world. While we'll address this objection at the end of the chapter, suffice it to say that all these arguments fall under what is known as "**The Problem of Evil**."

Now, I present these upfront to demonstrate the weight a nonbeliever must place on the existence of evil in order to use it as an objection against the existence of God. However, the purpose of this chapter will not be to show that God and evil can coexist (though that will be demonstrated) but to show that atheism and evil cannot.

THE PRESUPPOSITIONS OF EVIL

To begin with, consider that the truth of some propositions will be logically dependent on the truth of prior assumptions. For example, take the claim that John got fired from his job. For this claim to be true, we must first assume that John had a job to begin with. This is because if the prior assumption that "John had a job" is false, then the claim "John got fired from his job" couldn't possibly be true, given that John cannot lose something he never had. Hence, the truth of the initial claim logically depends on the truth of the assumption embedded within the claim itself (i.e., that John had a job).[137]

Two Prerequisites for Evil to Exist

Similarly, if the nonbeliever wants to argue against the existence of God via the existence of evil, then he must first assume that evil exists. However, if he assumes evil exists, then at least two prerequisite assumptions must be true. Namely, that:

1. An objective moral standard of goodness exists.
2. There is teleology to life in the natural world.

In other words, if evil exists, then both presuppositions must be true and, more pertinently, must be accounted for within an atheistic worldview. However, if either condition cannot be true within an atheistic worldview, then evil cannot exist and, thus, could never be used as an argument against God, but instead, becomes an argument against atheism. To unpack this problem, let's review these presuppositions individually.

1. An Objective Moral Standard of Goodness

A Lie Is a Deviation from Truth

Consider the logical relationship between the existence of a lie and the existence of truth. If I accuse someone of lying, then I'm insinuating there's a truth from which they're deviating. Hence, the existence of a lie is *logically dependent on* the existence of truth. But note, this doesn't work the other way around. For instance, if everyone in the world told the truth, then lies would not exist. Yet, for a lie to even be possible, there must first be a truth from which it deviates. Therefore, truth can exist without lies, but lies cannot exist without truth; truth doesn't depend on the existence of lies but lies *logically* and *necessarily* depend on the existence of truth.

Evil Is a Deviation from the Good

Concerning an objective moral standard, the same logical principle applies to evil and goodness. Goodness itself exists and doesn't depend on the existence of evil. However, if evil exists, then it's logically dependent on the existence of objective good. Much like a lie can only exist as a deviation from truth, so too, evil exists only as a deviation from the good. Hence, you can have good without evil, but you cannot have evil without the good. Evil depends on an objective moral standard, but an objective moral standard doesn't depend on the existence of evil.

For this reason, if an objection from the nonbeliever assumes evil exists, they must further assume that an objective moral standard of goodness exists. But as we learned in the last chapter, such a moral standard cannot exist in an atheist worldview, and here is where the first problem arises.

Using the Objection from Evil in The Moral Argument

Recall the syllogism from The Moral Argument, which concluded that if objective morality exists, then necessarily, God must exist. However, the atheist here argues against belief in God by presenting evil as an objection. But note, this does nothing to undermine the argument but only reinforces it with an additional premise. Namely, that evil exists! So, given that the nonbeliever is granting the existence of evil, we can now reformulate the argument as follows:

1. If God does not exist, then an objective moral standard does not exist.

2. Evil exists!
3. Therefore, an objective moral standard (i.e., from which the evil is deviating) exists.
4. Therefore, God exists.

In other words, to claim that *anything* is evil is to assume an objective moral standard from which it's deviating. Hence, the objection from evil only serves to imply that an objective moral standard of goodness exists. Thus, by appealing to the existence of evil as an objection to the existence of God, the atheist has logically led himself to the conclusion that, therefore, God must exist!

So, the irony of the objection is this: to prove that atheism is true because evil exists, one must first assume that atheism is false. Such an objection is holistically and internally self-defeating. Hence, if the atheist worldview cannot assume the existence of God, then it cannot assume the existence of evil, either.

The Existence of Evil: A Price Tag for Atheism

At this point, the price tag becomes an argument against atheism that can be presented in the following syllogism:

1. If atheism is true, then evil does not exist.
2. Evil does exist.
3. Therefore, atheism is false.

If the atheist wishes to avoid this conclusion, he must deny that evil exists. Yet, he's already conceded that religion has done evil in the name of God. However, if evil has been done in the name of God, then it follows that evil exists, and thus, atheism is false.

Due to his own objection, the atheist must now choose between two awkward price tags. If he wants to affirm atheism is true, then he must deny the assumption that evil exists. By contrast, if he wants to affirm evil exists, then he must assume atheism is false. Regardless of his decision, one thing is certain; he cannot continue holding to both. Either atheism is true and evil does not exist, or evil exists, and atheism is false. Logically speaking, there is no alternative.

2. Teleology to Life in the Natural World

The second requirement for evil to exist entails the presupposition that there is teleology to life in the natural world. Put succinctly, **teleology** is the notion which entails that there is a ***final cause***—an objective *purpose*, *goal*, or end *for the sake of* which something *ought to function* and *flourish*. To illustrate, suppose I said I had a bad phone. In doing so, I would presuppose the notion of teleology in a few ways.

First, a "bad phone" assumes a dysfunction, which implies that the phone is deviating from its *proper function*. That is to say, there's something my phone *ought* to be doing (receiving calls or texts), but it's not. Second, this would assume there's a *final cause*—an *objective goal* or *purpose* for *the sake of which* my phone was made. Hence, in presupposing the existence of "bad phones," we simultaneously presuppose the existence of teleology.

From this, two further implications follow: namely, that there is (1) a specified *design* to the phone which, by default, implies (2) there must be a *designer*. Why? Because if my phone was made for something, then we are assuming that it has a *design plan*, and by assuming a design plan, we are further assuming it must've had a *designer*. So, in summation, "bad phones" presuppose teleology, teleology presupposes a design plan, and a design plan presupposes a designer. This chain of implications can be illustrated as follows:

Bad Phone → Dysfunction →
- Proper function → Teleology → Design Plan → Designer
- Ought
- Final Cause
- Objective Goal or Purpose

When applied to the question of morality, the existence of "bad phones" are like evil in the natural world, given that we're assuming *proper functions*, *oughts*, and *final causes* (end goals and purposes). However, if evil (much like a "bad phone") entails the notion of teleology, then the same implications follow. Namely, that the evil in question is deviating from a specified *design plan* which, by default, entails that there must be a transcendent *Designer* to life in the natural world. This obviously becomes a problem for any atheist that offers evil as an objection.

The Problem of Teleology for Atheism

If atheism is true, then naturalistic, Darwinian evolution becomes the only mechanism that can account for our existence, and evolution is no designer. Inherently, it's a mechanism that seeks to explain our existence *without invoking a designer to life*. Hence, if naturalistic evolution is true, then no designer was ever needed. Fair enough. But as a result, it must now follow that on atheism, any description or explanation of our existence must be devoid of teleological notions such as *final causes*, *oughts*, or *proper functions*. Otherwise, a designer is needed, and on atheism, there can be no such thing.

Now consider an objection from evil against the existence of God based on a child born with a fatally weakened heart due to a disease. To expose the problem with this objection from an atheist worldview, let's apply the notions of *proper function*, *oughts*, and *final causes*—all of which assume teleology.

1. The Problem of Proper Function

A disease, by definition, is a *disorder* of *structure* or *function* which automatically assumes there is a *proper function* to begin with. But if atheism is true and there is no teleology, then by default, *there can be no proper function to life in the natural world*. Consequently, this means an objection from evil based on a biological dysfunction (which assumes a proper function) cannot exist either.

2. The Problem of Oughts

Moreover, if the objector assumes children *ought* to not have diseases, then he is appealing to teleology which, again, cannot exist within an atheist worldview. As the atheist philosopher David Hume concluded, you cannot get an "*ought*" from an "*is*." For instance, no one looks at a rock and says, "this rock *is* bumpy, but it *ought* to be round," or "this rock has three points, but it *ought* to have four." Why? Because there is no teleological design, goal, or purpose when it comes to the points or texture of a rock. Rocks just are what they are, and there is no "ought" to their structure.

Similarly, if a child's heart stops beating because of a disease, then according to Hume, we can only say the heart *is* not beating, but we cannot conclude that, therefore, the child's heart *ought to* beat. Granted, one may try and save the child's life, but on atheism, this would be no different than "saving" a round rock from being bumpy. If atheism is true and teleology cannot exist, then there can be no obligatory moral acts that we *ought* to do.

3. The Problem of a Final Cause to Life

Recall that a final cause entails the notion of something being done *for the sake of* reaching an *end goal* or *purpose*. Yet, if atheism is true, then our existence cannot be explained or derived from a *final cause*, as if we existed (or are evolving) *for the sake of* reaching some objective *end goal* or *purpose*. Therefore, it cannot be said that on atheism, hearts beat *for the sake of* sustaining life. Otherwise, one must invoke a final cause to life that further invokes a *designer*. Henceforth, if there can be no objective final causes in an atheist worldview, there can be no teleology, and if there can be no teleology, there can be no evil.

As Dawkins explains:

> In a universe of blind physical forces and genetic replication, some people are going to get hurt, other people are going to get lucky, and you won't find any rhyme or reason in it, nor any justice. The universe we observe has precisely the properties we should expect if there is, at bottom, no design, no purpose, no evil and no good, nothing but blind, pitiless indifference.[138]

If God does not exist, then things just are what they are, and there is no final cause. We aren't evolving *for the sake of* anything, and there are no end goals or purposes to our existence. No matter what the atheist may want to say at this point, one thing he cannot say is this: a child born with a fatally weakened heart due to a disease is objectively evil. Rocks fall and kill people, mutations happen and kill children, and there is no rhyme or reason to it. There is no evil.

Summarizing the Teleological Problem

We can now summarize this teleological problem for atheism in the following way: if an objection from evil assumes dysfunction, and if dysfunction assumes *proper function*, and if proper function assumes *oughts* and *final causes*, then we are inevitably assuming a teleological *design* plan to life in the natural world, which further assumes a teleological *Designer*—namely, God.

Disease → Dysfunction → Teleology to Life → Design Plan → Designer → God

As a result, the atheist is left with two price tags for his objection:

1. No God → No Teleology→ No Evil.
2. Evil → Teleology → God Must Exist.

If there is no God, there can be no teleology and, thus, no evil. However, if evil exists, there must be teleology, and therefore, God must exist.

OBJECTION: THE EPICUREAN RIDDLE

As previously mentioned, the Epicurean Riddle is an argument attempting to demonstrate that if evil exists, then an all-powerful, all-loving God cannot. This argument is typically presented as follows:

> If God is willing to prevent evil but not able, then He is not all-powerful. If He is able but not willing, then He is not all-loving. But if He is both willing and able, then how can evil exist? However, if He is neither able nor willing, then why call Him God?

A similar (though less sophisticated) case of this argument was presented in chapter 11, which assumed a logical contradiction between the existence of God and the existence of evil. As before, no explanation for this assumption has been provided (no different than saying that if grass is green, then the sky shouldn't be blue). Again, without an explicit explanation, no response is needed.

Furthermore, this entire chapter serves an indirect response to the objection. How so? Because the objection assumes it's logically impossible for God and evil to coexist. Yet, we've seen that if evil exists, then God *must* exist! For this reason, the argument can only "work" as an internal critique against Christianity, *not as an argument for atheism*. Setting these two points aside, let's briefly examine some possible rebuttals (tactical tool #3).

1. Morally Sufficient Reasons

Note that if God exists and is not only all-powerful and all-loving but also *all-knowing* (omniscient), then He could have morally sufficient reasons for allowing the pain and suffering that exists today. This is similar to the response provided in chapter 11 regarding the compatibility of me being an "all-loving" father while allowing pain and suffering in my children's lives. My knowledge of the outcome provided the overriding, morally sufficient reasons for permitting the pain and suffering that would occur.

2. God, Omniscience, and Utilitarianism

Additionally, recall the **utilitarian** view of ethics which grants that an action is morally permissible *if and only if* it benefits the greatest number of people.[139] This is a favored position among nonbelievers. Although utilitarianism is insufficient for an adequate moral framework, the principle still carries some weight, but with a caveat. Because see, to know which actions would (or would not) benefit the greatest number of people, one would have to *exhaustively know* the logical outcome of every step, calculate the long-term benefits, and grant the action appropriately. Thus, to adequately apply a utilitarian view of ethics, *one would have to be omniscient!*

Unfortunately for the nonbeliever, only God would be in a position to carry out such a goal. Therefore, if the atheist wants to appeal to a utilitarian view of ethics, then his only hope for the view is God! Hence, the principle backfires, and still, God is required for an adequate moral framework.

3. Pain Is Teleological

Still, a person may object by arguing that an all-loving, all-powerful God could (and should) remove any pain a person may feel in any situation. But suffice it to say that the existence of pain is teleological (it has an end goal, purpose, and proper function) and, as such, is actually a good thing. While this may sound counterintuitive, consider that the same water, which nourishes us, can also drown us, and the same fire that warms us may also burn us. Hence, pain becomes the teleological factor that warns, guides, and informs us against such danger. But imagine if this were not so.

By way of example, consider the rare medical condition known as *congenital insensitivity to pain*. Such is the case for Gabby Gingras, famously known as "the girl who feels no pain," and is a condition that's virtually impossible to detect at birth. In her case, it was recognized as she began teething—mutilating her mouth and chewing on her tongue "like it was bubble gum."[140] For safety concerns, this led to the permanent removal of her teeth. Additionally, the doctors had to sew her eyes shut for a time because, unable to feel pain, she nearly went blind, clawing her eyes out while trying to scratch an itch.

Moreover, consider that when a child touches a stove, the immense pain informs them never to do it again. This was not so with Gabby. Unlike the average child, there were many things she couldn't do because of her condition, and according to her mother, her one big wish was to "bite an apple" like everyone else. Suffice it to say that while pain may be a nuisance to us, for Gabby, it would be a teleological blessing, and she'd gladly trade places. Remember this the next time you bite into an apple.

Nevertheless, if the nonbeliever claims that because such horrid conditions exist, God must not exist, they're only reinforcing the argument from this chapter. As we've seen, if God does not exist, then evil and biological dysfunctions cannot exist. Given that evil and biological dysfunctions do exist, it follows that, therefore, God *must* exist. Hence, the inescapable weight and force of the argument.

4. The Existence of Human Freedom

A final point to consider concerning the existence of God and evil is the existence of human freedom. It's easy to see that most of the evil and suffering today is the direct (or indirect) byproduct of human freedom. This includes everything from murder and rape to choosing to live in hazardous areas known for flooding (such as beachfront houses). Each of these not only contains evil and suffering but also the free decisions of human beings.

Furthermore, consider how the abuse of human freedom and power may force people to live in unsuitable environments with no essential provisions. This is the case with governmental oppression in foreign countries. Such evil is not a result of God's will, but the abuse and corruption of the human will. As philosopher and theologian Dr. Norman Geisler explains, "God is responsible for the fact of freedom, but human beings are responsible for their acts of freedom."[141]

In philosophy, this is known as the **free will defense** against the problem of evil.[142] But note, such a defense cannot be accounted for in an atheist worldview. As we learned in chapter 15, if atheism is true, then given naturalism, free will and moral responsibility cannot exist. So, without God, there's no evil, no freedom, and, thus, no one to blame. If this upsets the nonbeliever, then at best, they can be angry at God. However, if atheism is true and there's neither God nor evil, then there's no justification to be angry. Either atheism is true and evil is impossible, or evil does exist, humans are responsible, and therefore, atheism is false.

PART 5

WHERE Do We Point Them To? The Risen Jesus

Chapter 22

The Truth of Christianity and the Resurrection

In the last few chapters, we surveyed four arguments for the existence of God, each of which can be used independently as a witnessing tool and, when taken together, present a strong, cumulative case for the reality of God's nature. Nevertheless, a person may claim that up to this point, we've only provided evidence for the existence of *some God*, but not *the Christian God* in particular. This will be our focus for the remainder of the book.

But Which God, Which Religion?

Recall that two things are needed to demonstrate the truth of Christianity: the existence of God and the resurrection of Jesus. This can be seen as the two-step process of 1) showing that God exists (bringing the nonbeliever from atheism or agnosticism to theism), and 2) showing that Christianity is true via the resurrection (bringing them from theism to Christianity). Thus far, we've only accomplished the first step, leaving the person to ask, "But which God exists? Which religion is true?" And consider how our first four arguments implicitly address this by severely limiting the possibilities.

If we were to compile a list of all the attributes we've logically deduced thus far, we're ultimately left with the three religions that affirm classical monotheism: Islam, Judaism, and Christianity. This would mean that all gods which lack one or more of these attributes can be scratched off the list. Take Thor as an example. Even if we granted his existence, his existence: 1) would not be necessary but contingent (the first argument), 2) would be neither immaterial nor spaceless (the second argument), 3) could not serve as the ontological foundation of objective morality (the third argument), and 4) could not be the reason for teleology to life in the natural world (the fourth argument). This would equally exclude Eastern religions, such as Buddhism and Hinduism.

Hence, we're ultimately left with the three religions that affirm classical monotheism: Islam, Judaism, and Christianity, and this is where the second step comes into play. While it's beyond the scope of this book to address these religions individually, given the nature of truth and logic, we don't have to. In chapter 14, we learned about the law of excluded middle, which essentially states that if X is true, then any answer contrary to X must be false by default. Given the same rules of logic, if it can be demonstrated that Christianity is true via the resurrection, then any other answer to the question, "Which God, which religion?" would either be inadequate (Judaism) or false (Islam), by default.

THE IMPLICATIONS OF THE RESURRECTION

Biblical Basis: 1 Corinthians 15:12-19

> **...And if Christ has not been raised**, then our preaching is vain [useless, amounting to nothing], and your faith is also vain [imaginary, unfounded, devoid of value and benefit–not based on truth]...**and if Christ has not been raised**, your faith is worthless and powerless [mere delusion]; you are still in your sins [and under the control and penalty of sin]...If we who are [abiding] in Christ have hoped only in this life [and this is all there is], **then we are of all people most miserable and to be pitied** (AMP).

According to Scripture, the truth of Christ's resurrection is necessary for Christianity to be true. If Christ *did not* rise from the dead, then Christianity is false and our faith is "worthless and powerless." By contrast, if Christ *did* rise from the dead, then all bets are off—Christianity is true.

The remaining chapters will be dedicated to this case, but for now, consider its implications.

1. The Truth of Christianity Is Testable

Unlike any other religion throughout history, the resurrection provides an explicit test for the truth of Christianity that can be *objectively verified in an external way*. By contrast, consider the "test of truth" for Mormonism from two of their canonical books:

> ... ask God, the Eternal Father, in the name of Christ, if these things are not true; and if ye shall ask with a sincere heart, with real intent, having faith in Christ, he will manifest the truth of it unto you, by the power of the Holy Ghost (Book of Mormon. Moroni 10:4)
>
> ...then you must ask me if it be right, and if it is right I will cause that your bosom shall burn within you; therefore, you shall feel that it is right (D&C 9:8).

Note how the first test places a suspicious emphasis on asking with a "sincere heart" with "real intent" and "having faith in Christ." If you pray and don't get the answer that Mormonism is true, then it's alleged that you didn't have a "sincere heart" with "real intent" and "faith in Christ." In the second, the test for truth comes by "*feeling* that it is right," what's often referred to as the "burning in the bosom" (allegedly given by the "Holy Ghost"). Yet, neither of these "tests" can be verified objectively or externally but instead, rely on internal, privatized, subjective experiences and personal testimonies. Now consider the test of truth for Christianity according to the Bible:

> ...He has given proof of this to everyone by raising him from the dead (Acts 17:31).
>
> ...If Christ has not been raised, then our preaching is in vain ... your faith is also vain [imaginary, unfounded, devoid of value and benefit–not based on truth] ... your faith is worthless and powerless [mere delusion] ... then we are of all people most miserable and to be pitied (1 Corinthians 15:12-19, AMP).

So, in summation, if you want to know whether Mormonism is true, then look for the internal, privatized, *subjective feelings* or personal testimony. But if you want to know whether Christianity is true, then look for the external, *objectively verifiable* evidence of the resurrection. While more can be said here, ask yourself: have our evangelistic approaches been more in line with Mormonism or biblical Christianity?

2. A Test Against Fraud

A second implication of the resurrection becomes a test against fraud. Given the existence of spurious religions *claiming to be* Christian (i.e., Jehovah's Witnesses or Mormonism), some have argued this undermines *any* view of Christianity. But this is simply false.

By analogy, consider that when a person trains to identify counterfeit bills, they do so by knowing and studying *the original*. Hence, when an expert comes across a counterfeit bill he's never seen before, he can immediately identify the problem—not because he's familiar with the counterfeit, but because he knows the original. He may have no idea how many fraudulent $20 bills are in circulation, but he doesn't have to. He only needs to know what the real $20 bill looks like, and if it doesn't match the original, then it must be a counterfeit.

Similarly, if we can demonstrate the truth of *historic Christianity* via the resurrection, then we have and know what the "real deal" looks like. Thus, *any claim, belief, or religion* that doesn't match *biblical Christianity* is a fraudulent, counterfeit religion by default. Therefore, if the existence of counterfeit, fraudulent bills does nothing to undermine the existence of a real $20 bill, then the existence of "counterfeit, fraudulent" religions does nothing to undermine the truth of biblical Christianity. Ironically (if anything), the existence of counterfeits implies there must be a true, original one to begin with.

3. A Test for Truth in Times of Doubt

Finally, the resurrection implicitly becomes a practical test for truth in times of doubt for every believer. For instance, some passages in Scripture are admittedly difficult to understand, while others contain some "hard pills to swallow." Without the relevant training in historical context, ancient culture, or Greek language, wrestling with these issues is amplified, and doubt about Christianity may creep in.

But note that while these issues may be *emotionally* problematic, they do nothing to override the truth of the resurrection. Why? Because the truth of Christianity is not dependent upon our ability to exegete every difficult passage, reconcile every alleged discrepancy, or contingent upon our emotional experiences (thank God!). Instead, the truth of Christianity rests entirely on the simple fact that *God exists and raised Jesus from the dead*. Hence, if the resurrection is true, then Christianity is true and, not just any God exists, but specifically the Christian God, and no amount of difficult passages, alleged discrepancies, or emotional struggles could ever change this fact.

The "Baltimore Call"

This concept clicked for me on the day I heard Dr. Michael Licona, one of the world's leading scholars on the resurrection, share about his own struggles with doubt as a believer. Licona openly admits that he's skeptical by nature, second-guessing virtually every decision (including a cologne he once bought!) and doubting almost every belief he's held to—Christianity included. Because of this, early in his career, he sought the help of Dr. Gary Habermas, arguably the world's leading scholar on the resurrection.

According to Licona, there were periods in his life where he experienced a crisis of faith, wrestling with what he considered debilitating questions, such as the authorship of the gospels, alleged contradictions, and other difficult passages. One day, the weight of these doubts was too overwhelming to bear alone, and as usual, called Dr. Habermas for counsel. In Licona's own words, the conversation (which Habermas later labeled the "Baltimore Call") went something like this:[143]

> "Doc! You know, many scholars don't think that Matthew, Mark, Luke, and John wrote the gospels. They say we don't know who wrote them. If they're right, then we can't know if they're historically reliable! I'm really struggling

with this and starting to question if Christianity is true. This is really shaking my faith at its core!

Listening patiently, Gary said, "Mike, did Jesus rise from the dead?"

"Yes."

"And why do you believe that?"

"Because of what you call the 'minimal facts' approach. You take facts that are *so strongly* supported by the data, even *skeptical scholars* grant them! You can take *those facts alone* and build a very powerful case for the resurrection."

"And if Jesus rose from the dead, is Christianity true?"

"Absolutely!"

"Right. So, Mike, there are reasons for believing that Matthew, Mark, Luke, and John wrote the Gospels. But let's just say for a moment that we don't know who wrote them. Does that change the fact that Jesus rose from the dead?"

"No, because if Jesus rose from the dead, Christianity was true before the gospels were written."

"Then Mike, why are you letting the matter of Gospel authorship shake your faith?"

"You know, I never thought about that, doc. That's pretty good. BUT what do you do with all the alleged errors and contradictions in the Gospels!

"Mike, did Jesus rise from the dead?"

"Yes."

"Mike, there are so many ways to approach gospel differences, and most of them are *easily* resolved. But let's just say for the sake of argument that there are some errors in the gospels. Would that change the fact that Jesus rose from the dead?"

"No."

"Then why are you letting the matter of gospel differences shake your faith to its core?"

"All right, doc. I think I see where you're going with this now. BUT what do you do with the [alleged] genocide texts in the Old Testament! I mean…"

"MIKE... DID – JESUS – RISE – FROM – THE – DEAD?"

Commenting on the conversation with nostalgia, Licona states, "That was a life-changing phone call for me. I now understood that although these other matters are important, they don't change the answer to the ultimate question of whether Christianity is true. If Jesus rose from the dead, it's GAME-SET-MATCH. Christianity is true, PERIOD! And now, I felt a freedom to investigate these matters with an open mind, because even if the answers turned out differently than I had hoped, Christianity is still true."

Chapter 23

The Existence and Character of Jesus

Before examining the case for the resurrection, two preliminary contentions must be addressed: 1) the existence of Jesus and 2) the character of Jesus. The need for addressing the first is obvious; if Jesus didn't exist, then the resurrection didn't occur. Hence, for the resurrection to even *possibly be true*, Jesus must be a historical figure that actually existed. Concerning the second, this may be less obvious, but given our day and age, it's a popular point that needs to be addressed. Namely, who is Jesus, who did He claim to be, and more importantly, do His claims make Him a liar, a lunatic, or is He truly the Lord?

THE FIRST CONTENTION: DID JESUS EXIST?

There's a growing movement today among lay skeptics and nonbelievers known as **Jesus mythicism**—the view that *Jesus did not exist* as an actual historical figure. This is typically argued in one of two ways. The first claims that even if Jesus did exist, the accounts of His life were greatly exaggerated and copied from ancient pagan myths. The second outright claims that Jesus never existed to begin with.

It's quite unfortunate that trees must be sacrificed for the paper needed to respond to such fanciful objections. As we'll see, the Jesus mythicist view is widely regarded as patently false by expert historians. It's to historical scholarship what the flat Earth view is to science. It is nonsense. Nevertheless, given its rise in popularity, let's briefly address these views individually.

1. Jesus Is a Copy of Ancient Myths

According to this view, the account of Jesus' life, death, and resurrection is a copied amalgamation of ancient "dying and rising gods" from pagan myths such as Osiris, Dionysus, Mithras, Adonis, and so forth. Allegedly, the "deep parallels" between these accounts, such as a virgin birth, a following of twelve disciples, and being resurrected from the dead, prove that Jesus was merely the Christian "copycat" version.

Response

In response, the first thing to be said about such a view is that *no historical scholar holding a teaching position at an accredited university ever uses this argument.*[144] Why? Because *there are no substantial parallels* between the accounts of Jesus and these pagan "dying and rising gods." By way of example, mythicists claim that the story of Mithra includes a report of a virgin birth. Given that Jesus' account consists of a virgin birth, it must follow that Jesus' story was copied from this myth. This is demonstrably false.

According to the Mithra story, he was never *born* but emerged from a rock.[145] Sure, one could argue that rocks are "virgins," but not for reasons that are in any sense relevant to the word. Clearly, this is *not* an account of a "virgin birth." While much can be said for each alleged "parallel," a quick search on Google or YouTube easily provides detailed refutations (which I've included in the endnotes for reference).[146] [147] [148] As New Testament scholar Dr. Michael Licona explains, "Since the details of the stories are vague and unlike Jesus' resurrection, today's scholars would not regard these stories as parallels."[149]

Licona adds, "the first account of a dying and rising god that *somewhat* parallels the story of Jesus' resurrection appeared at least 100 years after the reports of Jesus' resurrection."[150] Hence, Jesus' account couldn't have been a copy of these ancient myths, given that reports of the resurrection came *before* these legends appeared, not after. Again, *no teaching scholar today uses such objections.* Instead, they are used by online bloggers or YouTubers merely parroting what they've heard some other blogger or YouTuber say on the internet.

Conceding for the Sake of Argument

As a final point to consider, let's concede for the sake of argument that there are mythical accounts of dying and rising gods *prior to* the life of Christ (tactical tool #3). Would this prove that the life, death, and resurrection of Jesus were copies of these ancient myths? Not any more than a counterfeit $20 bill disproves the existence of a real one. But to make this point as clear as possible, let's engage in a thought experiment and see what follows. I'm going to describe two events, and I want you to picture the event I'm describing.[151]

The Plane That Crashed into a New York Skyscraper

This first event is a historical account of a plane that took off from Massachusetts just after 9 am and, shortly after 10 am, flew into one of the tallest skyscrapers in New York City, hitting between the 78th and 80th floors of the building. Which historical event is this? Clearly, the B-25 bomber plane that crashed into the Empire State Building on July 28, 1945. Was this the historical event you were thinking of, or did you picture a different one?

Chances are, you imagined the more recent historical event that included similar details. Namely, the Boeing 767 plane that crashed into the Twin Towers on September 11, 2001, which came over half a century later. Is this an odd coincidence? Absolutely. But does this make one event "more historically true" than the other? Absolutely not. Just because one happened before the other with stark similarities, it wouldn't follow that 9/11 was a "copycat" version of the first, or that 9/11 didn't happen.

An Iceberg Sinks an Unsinkable Ship

This second story revolves around the "unsinkable ship" over a hundred years ago. While sailing over the Atlantic Ocean on an April evening, this ship hits an iceberg, sinks, and kills more than half of its passengers due to a lack of lifeboats. The name of the ship starts with a "T." Which story am I describing? Of course, the fictional story of the Titan written in a novel by Morgan Robertson in 1898 called *The Wreck of the Titan*. However, you were likely thinking of the historical event known as the sinking of the Titanic, which occurred in 1912.

Coincidentally, *the fictional* story of the Titan came fourteen years before *the factual* account of the Titanic. But does it follow from this that the sinking of the Titanic was a mythical "copycat" version of the novel? Of course not. Who would be so silly as to make such an inference? *Parallels of fiction do not disprove history.*

Therefore, even if we conceded parallel stories of "dying and rising gods" that came *before* the historical account of Jesus (which there are not), no alleged similarities change the truth of His life, death, and resurrection. So, in summation, 1) historical scholars regard these claims as patently false, 2) there are no substantial parallels, 3) any alleged "parallels" come at least 100 years *after* the reports of Jesus' resurrection, and 4) even if we granted the parallels, nothing is proven (or disproven) by them.

2. Jesus Did Not Exist

The second argument for mythicism amounts to the claim that Jesus of Nazareth never existed as an actual historical figure at all. Purportedly, the historical accounts of Jesus are only found in the Bible, and no extra-biblical sources reference His existence. The underlying assumption here is that Scripture cannot be used as a historical source to demonstrate that Jesus existed. Why not? Because using the Bible as a historical source commits the fallacy of begging the question by way of circular reasoning. Or so they argue.

Although this is mistaken on so many levels, we set the point aside for now and focus on the central claim of the objection. Namely, that Jesus is never mentioned in extra-biblical sources. This is false, and we have the evidence and scholarship to prove it.

Response

For the sake of space, we'll only survey three extra-biblical sources that reference the existence, life, and death of Jesus,[152] each of which comes from ancient historians that were either hostile to Christianity or outright opposed it. Given that these men were openly biased *against* Christianity, the impact of their historical testimonies weighs heavily in our favor.

1. Josephus (ca. A.D. 37-100)

The first is Josephus, a first-century Jewish historian that mentions Jesus on two occasions in the book, *Antiquities of the Jews*. Given that Josephus was a Jew, he would *not* have believed Jesus was the Messiah, much less the resurrected Son of God. Hence, we have a source that was naturally hostile toward Christianity.

Nevertheless, Josephus mentions that Jesus was (1) "a wise man… a doer of wonderful works—a teacher," (2) had Jewish and Gentile followers, (3) was "condemned by Pilate to the cross," and that (3) those who followed Him were called "Christians" who continued after His death. "The tribe of Christians, so named from him, are not extinct at this day."[153] On a separate occasion, he records that Jesus was (4) "considered to be the messiah by some and (5) had a brother named James."[154] Not only is this an *extra-biblical, non-Christian historical source* that mentions Jesus by name, but precisely describes what we find in the biblical records!

2. Tacitus (ca. A.D. 56-120)

A second, *more hostile*, extra-biblical source comes from Tacitus, a man considered "the greatest Roman historian"[155] who was no friend of Christianity. From his writings in *The Annals*, we know he thought of Christianity as "a most mischievous superstition," which he called "the evil." As before, his records regarding the details of Christianity bear much weight on its historical validity. Tacitus writes:

> To get rid of the report, Nero fastened the guilt and inflicted the most exquisite tortures on a class hated for their abominations, called Christians by the populace. Christus, from whom the name had its origin, suffered the extreme penalty during the reign of Tiberius at the hands of one of our procurators, Pontius Pilatus, and a most mischievous superstition, thus checked for the moment, again broke out not only in Judaea, the first source of the evil, but even in Rome.[156]

Consider the wealth of historical information that Tacitus provides about Jesus. (1) Christ was the origin of Christianity who (2) was put to death by the Roman procurator, Pontius Pilate, in (3) "the most exquisite tortures" and "suffered the most extreme penalty" (likely a reference to crucifixion), that (4) His death temporarily stopped the movement but (5) Christianity "again, broke out" and spread "not only in Judea but even in Rome." As Habermas observes, "This is strikingly consistent with the accounts in the Gospels and Acts of the transformation of the disciples, who were emboldened through seeing the risen Jesus to publicly proclaim him in all Judea and Samaria, and even to the remotest part of the earth (Acts 1:8)."[157]

3. Lucian (ca. A.D. 115-200)

Finally, we have the historian Lucian of Samosata, who thought little of Christ and His followers. As before, no accusation of bias in favor of Christianity could apply. In *The Death of Peregrine*, he writes:

> The Christians, you know, worship a man to this day–the distinguished personage who introduced their novel rites, and was crucified on that account... You see, these misguided creatures start with the general conviction that they are immortal for all time, which explains the contempt of death and voluntary self-devotion which are so common among them; and then it was impressed on them by their original lawgiver that they are all brothers, from the moment that they are converted, and deny the gods of Greece, and worship the crucified sage, and live after his laws. All this they take quite on faith, with the result that they despise all worldly goods alike, regarding them merely as common property.[158]

Note the mocking disdain, calling Christians "misguided creatures" and referring to Jesus as some "crucified sage." Habermas explains, "His point was to criticize Christians for being such gullible people that, with very little warrant, they would approve charlatans who pose as teachers."[159]

In his book, *The Historical Jesus: Ancient Evidence for the Life of Christ*, Habermas lists *sixteen points of data* that can be derived from Lucian's account. Consider just seven of these. (1) Christians worshipped Jesus, (2) He introduced new teachings, and (3) He was crucified because of these teachings. (4) All believers were brothers from the moment of conversion, (5) they believed in immortality, which (6) explained their contempt for death, and (7) they disregarded material possessions, putting the emphasis on the possession of the next life.[160] Once again, we have a historical report that remarkably matches what we see in The Gospels and Acts.

> They devoted themselves to the apostles' teaching and to fellowship, to the breaking of bread and to prayer... All the believers were together and had everything in common. They sold property and possessions to give to anyone who had need. Every day they continued to meet... They broke bread in their homes and ate together with glad and sincere hearts, praising God and enjoying the favor of all the people. And the Lord added to their number daily those who were being saved (Acts 2:42-47).

So, not only do we have *ancient, extrabiblical sources* referencing the life, followers, and crucifixion of Jesus, but sources that are hostile against Christianity and carry no bias in presenting these historic facts. The records are clear, Jesus existed, and the historical evidence is undeniably in our favor.

What the Current, Non-Christian Scholars Say

To reiterate, no historical scholar with a teaching position at an accredited university holds to the claims made by the Jesus mythicist movement. At the academic level, this isn't a debated topic—as if there's any credence to the view that Jesus never existed. To make this point as clear as possible, consider what the current *nonbelieving, non-Christian* historical scholars say about the mythicist view.

In his book, *Jesus: Evidence and Argument or Mythicist Myths?*, agnostic Maurice Casey states the following:

> I therefore conclude that the mythicist arguments are completely spurious from beginning to end. They have been mainly put forward by incompetent and unqualified people...who were not properly aware of critical scholarship then, and after conversion to atheism, are not properly aware of critical scholarship now... The mythicist view should therefore be regarded as verifiably false from beginning to end.[161]

Agnostic historian, R. Joseph Hoffmann:

> The disease these buggers spread is ignorance disguised as common sense. They are the single greatest threat, next to fundamentalism, to the calm and considered academic study of religion, touting the scientific method as their Mod Op while ignoring its application to historical study... While there is some very slight chance that Jesus did not exist, the evidence that he existed is sufficiently and cumulatively strong enough to defeat those doubts.[162]

Agnostic historian and New Testament Scholar Bart Ehrman:

> I do not discuss mythicists in the class since, as I've repeatedly indicated, the mythicist view does not have a foothold, or even a toehold, among modern critical scholars of the Bible.[163]
>
> [Jesus] certainly existed, as virtually every competent scholar of antiquity, Christian or non-Christian, agrees.[164]

Question Begging and Circular? A Response

Recall the accusation that using the Bible as an evidential historical source that Jesus existed commits the fallacy of begging the question through circular reasoning. Yet, here we have Bart Ehrman, an agnostic New Testament scholar writing an entire book defending the existence of Jesus and referencing Scripture as a historical source of knowledge. In

Ehrman's own words, "Whatever one thinks of them as inspired Scripture, they can be seen and used as significant historical sources."[165] But why would Ehrman (and scholars like him who don't believe in the inspiration of Scripture) not consider this to be question-begging or circular? The answer is simple.

When secular historians examine the historicity of the Bible, they aren't assuming it's some "holy book," much less the inerrant, inspired Word of God. Instead, they approach the text like any other ancient document to investigate whether the accounts are historically reliable. Why? *Because a text need not be "holy" or "inspired" to be historically reliable.* Therefore, using Scripture as a credible, historical source for the existence and life of Jesus is neither question-begging nor circular.[166] As Habermas observes:

> The vast, almost unanimous view among critical *scholars* across a wide theological spectrum, including atheists and other unbelievers, is that both New Testament and non-New Testament sources provide valuable information about Jesus.[167]

And as Craig explains,

> Today Jesus is no longer just a figure in a stained-glass window, but a real, flesh-and-blood person of history, just like Julius Caesar or Alexander the Great, whose life can be investigated by the standard methods of history. The writings contained in the New Testament can be scrutinized using the same historical criteria that we use in investigating other sources of ancient history.[168]

Moreover, although we have outside, extra-biblical sources referencing the existence of Jesus, it's important to note *they only confirm what our earliest documents already tell us* (i.e., the New Testament). Hence, we can set aside debates about inerrancy and focus on providing a case for the resurrection by using Scripture as any historian would: an ancient text that provides reliable, historical accounts surrounding the life and death of Jesus.

THE SECOND CONTENTION: THE CHARACTER OF JESUS

Jesus is undeniably the most influential historical figure that ever existed, and because of this, everyone wants a "piece of Jesus" to support their views. For instance, the Buddhist claims that Jesus was a "good moral teacher" who aligned Himself with Buddhist teachings and, thus, must've been a Buddhist. Disagreeing with the Buddhist, the Muslim claims that Jesus was a prophet of Allah, whereas the Mormon (claiming to be Christian) takes Jesus as a central figure but denies the orthodox Christian doctrine of His nature. Even nonbelievers rejecting Christianity often hold Jesus in high esteem, claiming He was "pro" this or that political position (which coincidentally always seems to be the exact position they have!).

As flattering as this may be, it reveals two things about our culture's perspective of Jesus. First, it reveals that most people still respect the life, character, and teachings of Jesus today. This is a good thing. Second, it reveals that most people do not understand the life, character, and teachings of Jesus to begin with, and this is the very point of contention we must address. Because see, if a person claims to hold Jesus in high esteem and yet rejects Him as Lord, then, ironically, they're only belittling the very life, character, and teachings of Jesus that they claim to revere in the first place.

Jesus: Liar, Lunatic, or Lord?

To grasp the problem, consider C. S. Lewis's "Liar, Lunatic, or Lord" trilemma. Given the life, character, and teachings of Jesus, only one of three conclusions could be true. Either Jesus was:

A) **A liar**: claiming to be the son of God incarnate (making Himself equal with God), when in reality *He knew* He was not.

B) **A lunatic**: claiming and *believing* to be the son of God incarnate (*believing* Himself to be equal with God), when in reality He was not.

C) **The Lord**: claiming to be the son of God incarnate, making Himself equal to God, because in reality He is Lord.

As Lewis explains in his book, *Mere Christianity*,

> I am trying here to prevent anyone saying the really foolish thing that people often say about Him: "I'm ready to accept Jesus as a great moral teacher, but I don't accept His claim to be God." That is the one thing we must not say. A man who was merely a man and said the sort of things Jesus said would not be a great moral teacher. He would either be a lunatic–on a level with the man who says he is a poached egg–or else he would be the Devil of Hell. You must make your choice. Either this man was, and is, the Son of God: or else a madman or something worse. You can shut Him up for a fool, you can spit at Him and kill Him as a demon; or you can fall at His feet and call Him Lord and God. But let us not come with any patronizing nonsense about His being a great human teacher. He has not left that open to us. He did not intend to.[169]

Lewis' Trilemma in Evangelism: Addressing the Second Contention

After an evening of speaking at a camp where students volunteered their summertime, I was informed that one student had recently come out as a nonbeliever. According to the staff, he was a self-proclaimed agnostic "on a spiritual journey and looking into Buddhism." Unfortunately, this student couldn't be present for the service, which was explained to me as I walked to my car with hours of driving ahead. It was late, I was tired, and eager to get home.

But, lo and behold, as if by divine providence, the young man walked in and joined the conversation. Within minutes, he confirmed what the staff said, and our conversation proceeded as follows:

Eric: So, why work at a Christian camp that promotes the teachings of Christ if you don't believe He's the Lord and Son of God?

Student: Because although I no longer consider myself a Christian, I still respect Jesus as a great moral teacher. He taught us to love and serve others and exemplified this in His own life.

Eric: A great moral teacher? You really think so? Because if He's not the Lord and Son of God, then He sounds like a lunatic to me.

Student: What do you mean?

Eric: Well, He told people to eat His flesh, drink His blood, and said, "whoever *feeds* on me will live *because of* me" (John 6:43-70). What sane person would ever say a thing like that?

Student: I don't know. But don't Christians have a way of explaining that?

Eric: Absolutely! He was claiming to be the bread of life. The sacrifice and atonement for our sins. That through His body and blood, we could find forgiveness and eternal life. However, this only makes sense *if He was truly the Son of God*.

Student: But I don't believe He was the Son of God.

Eric: Then He must be a liar. His teachings made it clear He was *claiming* to be the son of God, and everyone knew this was a claim to be *equal* with God. It was literally the reason they wanted to kill Him (John 5:18).

Student: Okay, but that doesn't make Him a liar. Maybe He really believed He was the Son of God, even if He wasn't.

Eric: Then we're back to Him being a lunatic. After all, if your brother claimed to be the Son of God, making Himself equal with God, would you believe it, or think He was a liar or lunatic?

Student: A liar or a lunatic, because I know my brother!

Eric: Right. And Jesus had brothers who knew Him too and thought He was crazy (Mark 3:21). But you don't seem to think this about Jesus.

Student: Oh, no, I wouldn't dare call Jesus a lunatic!

Eric: Neither would I. But let's recap. If Jesus *knew He was not* the Son of God, but said the kinds of things He did, then He was a liar. By contrast, if Jesus truly *believed* He was the Son of God but was not, then He was a lunatic in serious need of psychiatric help. Either way, a liar or lunatic is far from a "good moral teacher." However, if Jesus *is* the Son of God, then He had the unique authority to say what He did, but only because *He was and is*, in fact, the Lord. So, which is it? Liar, lunatic, or Lord?

Student: Well, I don't know. But I certainly don't think Jesus was a liar or lunatic.

Eric: Then He must be the Lord, and if He is Lord, then I see no other option than to surrender your life to Him.

For this reason, Lewis concludes the trilemma by stating:

> We are faced, then, with a frightening alternative. This man we are talking about either was (and is) just what He said or else a lunatic, or something worse. Now it seems to me obvious that He was neither a lunatic nor a fiend: and consequently, however strange or terrifying or unlikely it may seem, I have to accept the view that He was and is God.[170]

Chapter 24

A Case for the Resurrection

Part 1: What Are the Facts?

Our case for the resurrection of Jesus will be divided into two parts—each of which is an answer to two questions that any historian must ask when examining the historicity of an event:

1. What are the facts surrounding the event?
2. What is the best explanation for these facts?

In this chapter, we take up the first question by examining the historical facts surrounding the life, death, and resurrection of Jesus. Facts "so strongly attested historically that they are granted by nearly every scholar who studies the subject, even the rather skeptical ones."[171] In the next chapter, we'll take up the second by surveying competing theories that seek to explain these facts and determine which hypothesis provides the best explanation of the data. This is the task of the historian, and it becomes our task in presenting a case for the resurrection.

The Minimal Facts Approach

In accomplishing our first step, we adopt a variation of the approach developed by Dr. Gary Habermas (a scholar who is arguably the world's leading expert on the resurrection), known as the "**minimal facts**" **approach**. With this approach, a person only considers data that is 1) "so strongly evidenced historically that nearly every scholar regards them as reliable facts" and 2) are "backed by so much evidence that nearly every scholar who studies the subject, even the rather skeptical ones, accepts them."[172]

Five Criteria for Establishing Historically Credible Facts

When historians examine any ancient document, certain principles are employed to determine whether a historical account (or text) is credible and reliable. In their book, *The Case for the Resurrection of Jesus*, Habermas and Licona list five:[173]

1. **Multiple, independent sources**. When an event or saying is attested by more than one independent source (multiple accounts reporting on the same thing), there is a strong indication of historicity.
2. **Enemy attestation**. If your mother reports that you're an honest person, we take her claim with a grain of salt given that she loves you and is somewhat biased. However, if an enemy that hates you admits that you're an honest person, then we have a stronger reason to believe the claim since potential bias does not exist (there is no reason to lie about you in a positive way).[174]
3. **Criterion of embarrassment.** "An indicator that an event or saying is authentic occurs when the source would not be expected to create the story, because it embarrasses his cause and weakened its position in arguments with opponents."
4. **Eyewitness testimony.** When an event occurs publicly, we expect to find eyewitnesses. If not, we have strong reasons to doubt the claim. Similarly, if we have multiple eyewitness testimonies to a public event, we have strong reasons to believe the event occurred.
5. **Early testimony/sources**. Sometimes sources testifying about an event come a few hundred years *after* the event occurred. When dealing with ancient history, this may be our earliest source. The earlier the source, the more reliable and credible the testimony.

Suffice it to say that the New Testament meets all these criteria (and more) for establishing historical authenticity, and we'll utilize these for part one in our case for the resurrection.

PART ONE: PRESENTING THE FACTS

In other works, Habermas lists a minimum of twelve historical facts supporting the resurrection that are accepted by virtually all scholars who study the subject (atheists, agnostics, and skeptics included). For our purposes here, we focus on three:

1. The empty tomb of Jesus.[175]
2. The postmortem appearances of Jesus.
3. The origin of the Christian faith.

Although most scholars accept these as historically reliable facts, nonbelieving scholars (obviously) reject the resurrection as the best explanation. Hence, the focus of our first step is not to argue for the resurrection (that will be done in the next chapter—step two) but to present and establish *why* these are regarded as historically reliable facts by virtually all scholars who study the subject.

Fact #1: The Empty Tomb

To grasp the significance of the empty tomb as a historically reliable fact, consider this: had the tomb of Jesus *not* been empty, reports of the resurrection could easily be disproven by pointing to the body. However, if the tomb was empty, then we have a historical fact that requires an explanation. Here are three lines of evidence that attest to the historicity of the empty tomb.

1. Jesus Was Buried by a Member of the Jewish Sanhedrin

In Mark 15:43-47 (arguably, the earliest written gospel), we read Jesus was buried by Joseph of Arimathea, who is described as a rich man and prominent member of the Jewish Sanhedrin. As an argument in support of the empty tomb, this is important for a few reasons.

First, the Sanhedrin was the highest ruling council of the Jews that condemned Jesus to death. They were considered the enemies of Jesus, and there would've been understandable hostility toward this group by his followers. Despite this, the Gospels report that Joseph—a Sanhedrist, not the followers of Christ—took care of and buried the body of Jesus (this also falls under the criterion of embarrassment). Second, Joseph of Arimathea was a respected, well-known public figure who could've publicly denied the story had the burial account been fabricated.

Third, and most importantly, this would mean that "the location of Jesus' tomb was known in Jerusalem to both Jew and Christian alike, since both were present when Jesus was laid in the tomb."[176] To put this in perspective, the resurrection was being proclaimed *in the same city Jesus had been crucified and buried*. Thus, a quick visit to the *known location* of the tomb would've sufficed to disprove the resurrection claims the disciples were making. However, the Jewish and Roman authorities never argued against the claims of an empty tomb, but instead accused the disciples of stealing the body. This brings us to our second line of evidence: enemy attestation.

2. Enemy Attestation

According to this principle, "if testimony affirming an event or saying is given by a source who does not sympathize with the person, message, or cause that profits from the account, we have an indication of authenticity."[177] Consider the earliest response from the enemies of Jesus when the disciples began proclaiming He'd risen from the dead. Rather than try and argue the tomb was *not* empty, they sought to explain *why* it was empty by accusing the disciples of stealing the body.[178] But think about this for a moment, because such a point is easily overlooked.

Had the tomb of Jesus not been empty, there would have been *no reason* to accuse the disciples of stealing the body. But as Habermas explains:

> When the boy tells his teacher that the dog ate his homework, this is an indirect admission that his homework is unavailable for assessment. Likewise,

> the earliest Jewish claim reported regarding Jesus' resurrection was to accuse the disciples of stealing the body, an indirect admission that the body was unavailable for public display.[179]

In other words, we would expect the followers of Jesus to claim the tomb was empty, but we wouldn't expect this from their enemies. Therefore, if the enemies of Jesus provided an explanation for the empty tomb, then we know they're not denying it, but confirming it! Hence, enemy attestation provides us with firm, historical credibility for an empty tomb.

3. The Criterion of Embarrassment

If an author reports an account that includes embarrassing details about themselves or the story they want to promote (which would only hurt their case), then we have strong reasons to believe they're telling the truth. Relevant to this fact, the strongest example of this criterion is given when the Gospels report women being the first to discover the empty tomb. Now, to have women make this discovery isn't something to be embarrassed about—at least not in our culture. However, when historians examine a source, the consideration of credibility is not just based on what's said but, more pertinently, on what's said given the cultural, historical context.

To understand why scholars see this as falling under the criterion of embarrassment, consider the social status and credibility of a woman's testimony in first-century Judaism as expressed in these ancient Jewish writings:

> But let not the testimony of women be admitted, on account of the levity and boldness of their sex, nor let servants be admitted to give testimony on account of the ignobility of their soul; since it is probable that they may not speak truth, either out of hope of gain, or fear of punishment (Josephus, Antiquities 4.8.15).
>
> Any evidence which a woman [gives] is not valid (to offer), also they are not valid to offer. This is equivalent to saying that one who is Rabbinically accounted a robber is qualified to give the same evidence as a woman (Talmud, Rosh Hashannah 1.8).

> Sooner let the words of the Law be burnt than delivered to women (Talmud, Sotah 19a).

In line with this, consider the misogynistic view of women in this patriarchal society.

> Happy is he whose children are male, but unhappy is he whose children are female! (Talmud, Kiddushin 82b).

And a common, daily prayer of a Jewish male:

> Blessed are you, Lord our God, ruler of the universe, who has not created me a Gentile, a slave, or a woman (Berachos 60b).

I share these quotes only to demonstrate the historical perception that was prevalent in this Jewish culture. In this male-dominated society, women were comparable to Gentiles, dogs, slaves, and their testimony was given the same respect as that of a robber. But as Craig notes, "No such regulation is to be found in the Bible. It is rather a reflection of the patriarchal society of first-century Judaism."[180]

Now, if this was the average Jewish mindset concerning women and their testimony, and if the gospel was to be preached *first* to the Jew (Romans 1:16), then why would the Gospel writers invent a story that depicted women as the *first and principal* witnesses to the empty tomb? This would only hurt the receptibility and credibility of their case. Why not invent a story with the disciples (or any other male for that matter) as the brave ones to discover the empty tomb? Because, embarrassing or not, they were telling the truth. Commenting on this point, Turek observes:

> Who wrote all that down? Men–some of the men who were characters in the story. Now, what man is going to say that he was hiding for fear of the Jews while the women went down and discovered the empty tomb? If you were these men, would you depict yourselves as dim-witted, bumbling, rebuked, lazy, skeptical sissies, who ran away at the first sign of trouble, while the women were the brave ones who discovered the empty tomb and the risen Jesus?[181]

Reflecting on this, Turek imagines that a made-up story from the disciples would have probably gone "more like this:"

> While we assured the women that everything would turn out all right, they couldn't handle the crucifixion. Squeamish and afraid, they ran to their homes screaming to hide behind locked doors. But we men stood steadfast at the foot of the cross, praying for hours until the very end… That Sunday morning we marched right down to the tomb and overpowered those elite Roman guards. Then the stone (that took eleven of us to roll into place) rolled away by itself. A glowing Jesus emerged from the tomb and said, "I knew you'd come! My mission is accomplished." He praised Peter for his brave leadership and congratulated us on our great faith. Then we went home and comforted the trembling women.[182]

Now *this* is what a made-up story would sound like! And yet, we find the exact opposite in *all four gospel accounts* (with male witnesses appearing only *later* in two gospels!). Whether they liked it or not, women were the *first* and *primary witnesses* to the empty tomb, and the disciples had the integrity to write it down just as it happened. No fabrications. No exaggerations. Just a pure fact-of-the-matter history. On that third day, the men were still hiding, and the *women* were the first to discover the empty tomb and risen Jesus—*not the men*. Given the criterion of embarrassment, we have solid historical credibility for the fact of an empty tomb.

For these reasons and more, the empty tomb is "well evidenced for historical certainty."[183] In the words of John A. T. Robinson of Cambridge University, the burial of Jesus is "one of the earliest and best-attested facts about Jesus," and according to New Testament critic Jacob Kremer, "By far most scholars hold firmly to the reliability of the biblical statements about the empty tomb."[184]

Fact #2: The Postmortem Appearances

Our focus for this fact is simply to establish that the disciples claimed and believed the risen Jesus had appeared to them (and others) after His death. Remember that for this step, we're not trying to establish that Jesus *actually* resurrected and appeared to His disciples (again, we'll take up that task in the next chapter—step two), but that at the very least, they *claimed* and *sincerely believed* He had appeared to them after being crucified, dead, and buried in a tomb for three days. If this can be established historically, then we have another fact that requires an explanation.

Criteria #5: The Earliest Source–1 Corinthians 15:3-8

In 1 Corinthians 15:3-8, Paul provided a list of eyewitnesses to Jesus' resurrection appearances which presents a creed from the disciples dating within just two-to-five years of Jesus' crucifixion.[185] Hence, we have an *incredibly early source* for the events it describes, which, according to Dean Rodgers, "is the sort of data that historians of antiquity drool over."[186] Beginning with Peter (called *Cephas* in verse 5), let's briefly examine the historical significance of these eyewitnesses.

"And that he appeared to Cephas"

Recall that Peter didn't follow Jesus unto death but publicly denied Him three times.[187] However, something happened three days later that radically changed Peter's behavior to the point that he was not only willing to follow Jesus *after* His death (despite refusing to do so prior) but, more pertinently, he was willing to be persecuted and martyred for it. What explains this radical change? According to the earliest source, "he appeared to Cephas."

"After that, he appeared to more than five hundred"

In verse six, Paul states, "He appeared to more than five hundred brothers and sisters at the same time," and then says something odd: "... most of whom are still living, though some have fallen asleep." Essentially, Paul is putting his credibility on the line by insinuating that anyone could go and speak to these people for themselves. As New Testament scholar C. H. Dodd observes, "There can hardly be any purpose in mentioning the fact that most of the 500 are still alive, unless Paul is saying, in effect, 'The witnesses are there to be questioned.'"[188]

To put this in perspective, suppose someone ran up to you and said, "I just saw bigfoot running throughout downtown!" Like me, you wouldn't believe it. But suppose he further says, "If you don't believe me, go ask the five hundred people who were there. They saw it too!" Now, if each of these alleged witnesses denies it, no further inquiry is needed to write the person off as insane or seeking attention. However, if the eyewitnesses confirm the sighting, then it should give one pause to, at the very least, pursue further investigation. Perhaps it was a promotion for an upcoming movie or just a man in a costume. Whatever the reason, the point is this: if it can be verified the man was not lying, then *some explanation* is needed.

In the same way, Paul backs the credibility of his claim by pointing to five hundred witnesses, implying that if the event did not occur, then there would be no eyewitnesses to consult. But as Habermas explains, "Paul either knew some of these people or was told by someone who knew them that they were still walking around and willing to be interviewed" because it was "written at a time when people could still check them out if they wanted confirmation."[189] Therefore, if the event *did* occur and *hundreds* of eyewitnesses were available, then some explanation is required (criteria #4).

"Then he appeared to James"

Next, Paul said He appeared to James, the younger brother of Jesus. Why is this significant? Because in John 7:5 and Mark 3:21, we read that His brothers "did not believe him" and said, "He is out of his mind." Hence, they thought He was crazy, *not the divine Messiah* (criterion #3 also applies here). Yet, we later read that James not only became *a devout believer* and *follower* of Jesus but is listed as an "esteemed pillar" of the church (Galatians 2:9) and, according to the Jewish historian, Josephus, was eventually martyred for his faith (Antiquities 20.200). As Craig explains:

> What would it take to make you believe that your brother is the Lord, so that you would die for this belief, as James did? Can there be any doubt that the reason for this remarkable transformation is to be found in the fact that "then

he appeared to James"? Even the skeptical New Testament critic Hans Grass admits that the conversion of James is one of the surest proofs of the resurrection of Jesus Christ.[190]

"And last of all he appeared to me also"

Finally, Paul stated, "and he appeared to me also." To fully appreciate the significance of this appearance, consider Paul's background. He was a Rabbi, a Pharisee, and a respected Jewish leader that hated, persecuted, and killed Christians, regarding their beliefs as heretically blasphemous. Yet, virtually overnight, Paul gave this up and became a Christian missionary, leading to "a life of poverty, labor, and suffering. He was whipped, beaten, stoned, left for dead, shipwrecked three times, in constant danger, deprivation, and anxiety. Finally, he made the ultimate sacrifice and was martyred for his faith in Rome."[191] Why? Because, in Paul's own words, "he appeared to me also."

As atheist skeptic and historian Gerd Lüdemann observes, "It may be taken as historically certain that Peter and the disciples had experiences after Jesus' death in which Jesus appeared to them as the risen Christ."[192] Although Lüdemann doesn't grant these were appearances of the *physically risen* Jesus (he is a nonbeliever, after all), he objectively states it as "historically certain" that they at least *believed it* to be. Again, this is all we're trying to establish at this point.

In a similar vein, skeptic Paula Fredriksen of Boston University writes:

> I know in their own terms what they saw was the raised Jesus. That's what they say and then all the historic evidence we have afterwards attest to their conviction that that's what they saw. I'm not saying that they really did see the raised Jesus. I wasn't there. I don't know what they saw. But I do know that as a historian that they must have seen something.[193]

And in conclusion, Habermas observes:

> On the state of Resurrection studies today, I (Habermas) recently completed an overview of more than 1,400 sources on the resurrection of Jesus pub-

> lished since 1975. I studied and catalogued about 650 of these texts in English, German, and French… perhaps no fact is more widely recognized than that early Christian believers had real experiences that they thought were appearances of the risen Jesus. A critic may claim that what they saw were hallucinations or visions, but he does not deny that they actually experienced something.[194]

Fact #3: The Origin of the Christian Faith

Although we'll cover objections in the next chapter, it's relevant to point out that some have attempted to write off the claims of postmortem appearances as mere lies on the part of the disciples, possibly to gain power or make a name for themselves. Hence, the disciples didn't really believe in the resurrection but lied about their experiences.

Why is this relevant? Because today there's no doubt (even from nonbelieving scholars) that Christianity's rise, spread, and flourishing was grounded in and owed its origin to the *earliest disciples believing* God had raised Jesus from the dead. Had they not *sincerely believed* it, Christianity would've never gotten off the ground, much less flourished. But as Habermas and Licona explain:

> There is a virtual consensus among scholars who study Jesus' resurrection that, subsequent to Jesus' death by crucifixion, his disciples really believed that he appeared to them risen from the dead. This conclusion has been reached by data that suggest that (1) the disciples themselves claimed that the risen Jesus had appeared to them, and (2) subsequent to Jesus' death by crucifixion, his disciples were radically transformed from fearful, cowering individuals who denied and abandoned him at his arrest and execution into bold proclaimers of the gospel of the risen Lord. They remained steadfast in the face of imprisonment, torture, and martyrdom. It is very clear that they sincerely believed that Jesus rose from the dead.[195]

Therefore, if the origin and spread of Christianity depended on these early disciples' belief in the resurrection, then once again, an explanation for this fact is needed.

To grasp the significance, let's briefly compare the expectations and understanding of Jesus as the Messiah *before* His death and the expectations and understanding of Jesus as the Messiah *after* His death.

Pre-Death: Expectations and Understanding of the Messiah

The chart below summarizes three expectations of the coming Messiah in contrast to the life and ministry of Jesus.

The Messiah was believed to be:	But Jesus:
1. A triumphant figure.	Claimed to be a servant.
2. The one to establish the throne. of David.	Said His kingdom was not of this world.
3. Someone who would command respect from everyone.	Was publicly humiliated from and killed by His enemies.

1. Jesus Was Not a "Triumphant Figure"

The Jews believed the Messiah would be a triumphant figure that would overthrow the government and liberate them from dictatorial oppression.[196] As Craig explains:

> Israel labored under the oppressive military dictatorship of a pagan nation. The Jews chafed under the yoke of Roman rule... Jews yearned for a messianic deliverer who would once and for all restore to Israel the throne of David and establish God's Kingdom in the land."[197]

In Mark 11:1-11, we see a glimpse of this expectation in the "Triumphal Entry" on Palm Sunday. In making this grand entrance, Jesus is "deliberately and provocatively claiming to be the promised king of Israel who will re-establish the throne of David,"[198] and the Jews would have interpreted this event as such.

Seeing this prophecy fulfilled before them, they lay down their cloaks and palm branches in excitement, ushering in this promised Messiah who, in their mind, would overthrow the government and establish a political reign on earth. But imagine the look of confusion as they see Jesus riding in, not on a horse, but a donkey! Why would this matter? Because when a military leader wanted to declare war or overthrow the government, they rode into the city on a horse. This served as a visual "symbol of warfare" and was "the choice of conquerors."[199]

However, Jesus doesn't enter the city on a horse or mule ("the steed of Jewish kings like David himself")[200] but on a donkey, "a pack animal, a lowly beast of burden, as his royal mount."[201] In doing so, Jesus intentionally portrays Himself, not as a conqueror or king, but a servant. As Craig remarks:

> The Kingdom of God which he preached and inaugurated was not an earthly, political kingdom, but the rule of God in the hearts of people who know and serve Him. But this was not the kingdom which the people expected or wanted, and so they rejected Jesus as their Lord.[202]

In Matthew 20:20-28, James and John echo this expectation by asking if they can "sit, at your right and at your left when you are king."[203] In their minds, Jesus was going to establish an earthly throne, and they wanted in on the power. When the other disciples heard this, they became angry, likely because they didn't think to make the request first! But again, imagine their confusion when Jesus responds by saying, "You don't know what you are asking," explaining that they'll have to suffer as He will suffer.

> Whoever wants to become great among you must be your servant, and whoever wants to be first must be your slave–just as the Son of Man did not come to be served, but to serve, and to give his life as a ransom for many.

Servant? Slave? What kind of king serves others as opposed to being served himself? This clearly went against their expectations of Jesus as the promised Messiah.

2. Jesus Claimed His Kingdom Was Not of This World

Despite this, the disciples held this expectation up to the point of his arrest. Willing to fight, they shout, "Lord, should we strike with our swords?" and without hesitation, Peter swings at a soldier's neck but misses and cuts off his ear.[204] After all, how could Jesus establish His earthly kingdom if He was arrested? But rather than resist arrest or fight back, Jesus does the exact opposite. He chastises Peter, heals the soldier's ear, and openly admits He's not fighting back, claiming that if He wanted to, He could call on God to provide more than twelve legions of angels (roughly 72,000) to fight for Him.[205]

At this point, disappointment finally dawns on them as they realize that Jesus was *not* the Messiah they expected, and "all the disciples deserted him and fled."[206] Finally, when Pilate asks, "Are you the king of the Jews?" Jesus responds, "My kingdom is not of this world."[207] Undoubtedly, this was all a devastating blow to their hope, confidence, and, most importantly, their faith in Him as the Messiah.

3. Jesus Was Publicly Humiliated and Killed by His enemies.

When we read about the brutal accounts of Jesus' torture, humiliation is an understatement. He was spat on, slapped in the face, mocked, and brutally beaten.[208] Given that He was deemed a prophet, they blindfolded Him and began to "strike him with their fists," shouting, "Prophesy to us, messiah! Who hit you?" In addition to the physical abuse, various insults were lodged at Him that were so unimaginably demeaning that the Bible intentionally refrains from listing them.[209]

Having committed no crimes, He was tried and punished as a criminal. When He gives an answer they don't like, He's slapped in the face and asked, "Is this the way you answer the high priest?" Confused by the abusive treatment, Jesus responds by asking, "If I said something wrong, ... testify as to what is wrong. But if I spoke the truth, why did you strike me?"[210] From here, they virtually strip Him naked and nearly flog Him to death.

Given that He was deemed a king, they twisted a crown of thorns, forced it onto His head, knelt together, and sarcastically shouted, "Hail, king of the Jews!" With deep wounds exposed, they placed a scarlet robe on His back, a staff in His right hand, and continued spitting on Him. After the mockery, they snatched the staff and repeatedly beat Him over the head with it.[211] After all this, they forced Him to carry His own cross, crucified Him between two criminals, and placed a patronizing sign above His head that read, "This is Jesus, the King of the Jews."[212]

Given the method of execution, the Jews knew this meant He was a cursed man; as it is written, "cursed is everyone who is hanged on a tree."[213] And there He hung—bare, beaten, and bloody on public display for all to see. And yet, *this* was the Messiah? The One who, in their minds, was supposed to command respect from everyone? It's no wonder that all but one abandoned Him at the cross. He was no triumphant figure, He was no respected authority, and He was certainly no earthly king. Instead, He was publicly humiliated and killed by His enemies. As Craig explains:

> A Messiah who failed to deliver and to reign, who was defeated, humiliated, and slain by His enemies, is a contradiction in terms. Nowhere do Jewish texts speak of such a "Messiah." Therefore, it's difficult to overemphasize what a disaster the crucifixion was for the disciples' faith. Jesus' death on the cross spelled the humiliating end for any hopes they had entertained that He was the Messiah.[214]

Post-Death: A Changed Expectation and Understanding of Jesus as the Messiah

Again, without these early disciples believing Jesus was the promised Messiah and Lord, Christianity would have never begun, much less spread and flourished. Yet at this point, the disciples retreated in despair, hid in fear, and even publicly denied they ever knew Him to begin with.[215] He was not what they expected, so they abandoned all hope and belief in Him as the Messiah.

However, three days after His death, we find a radical shift in their mindset, behavior, and understanding of Jesus as the promised Messiah. No longer are they hiding away in fear, but instead, are boldly proclaiming the gospel, even to the point of suffering persecution and, for some, agonizing death. But why? According to the historical records, *they believed God had raised Jesus from the dead*, and this simultaneously vindicated His claims to be the Messiah and Lord (Acts 2:23-36). As Habermas explains:

> After Jesus' death, the lives of the disciples were transformed to the point that they endured persecution and even martyrdom. Such strength of conviction indicates that they were not just claiming that Jesus rose from the dead and appeared to them in order to receive some personal benefit. They really believed it...they willingly endangered themselves by publicly proclaiming the risen Christ. These facts are validated by multiple accounts, both from early sources in the New Testament as well as outside of it.[216]

While this doesn't establish that what they believed about the resurrection was true, it does establish that—contrary to their initial hopes and expectations, *they now believed it to be true*. And no one dies for what they *believe* to be false. Therefore, if Christianity's origin, rise, and spread hinges on this historical fact, then an explanation for it is needed. As R. H. Fuller remarks, "even the most skeptical critic must posit some mysterious X to get the movement going. But what was that X?"[217] In the next chapter, we take up this task for part two of our case: seeking the best explanation of the facts.

Chapter 25

A Case for the Resurrection

Part 2: What Is the Best Explanation?

In the last chapter, we presented three historically established facts accepted by virtually all scholars who study the subject (even the skeptical ones) surrounding the death and resurrection of Jesus. 1) The empty tomb, 2) The postmortem appearances, and 3) The origin of the Christian faith. In this chapter, we aim to find the best explanation for them.

To do this, we begin by laying out the standard criteria historians use when assessing a hypothesis that seeks to explain the data. Using these standard criteria, we'll examine three of the most popular hypotheses opposing the resurrection: 1) The conspiracy hypothesis, 2) The apparent death hypothesis, and 3) The hallucination hypothesis. From here, we'll apply the same criteria to the resurrection hypothesis and see how it compares as an explanation of the data.

Five Standard Criteria for Weighing Historical Hypotheses

In his book, *The Resurrection of Jesus*, Licona provides a list of five criteria used by historians for weighing a hypothesis, stating that "these five important criteria define how a fair-minded critical examination of the data may be conducted."[218] Whatever the best explanation, it must satisfy the following five criteria better than any other competing hypothesis.

1. ***Explanatory scope***. "This criterion looks at the *quantity* of facts accounted for by a hypothesis."[219] The best hypothesis will explain the majority of the evidence and account for all the relevant facts.
2. ***Explanatory power.*** "This criterion looks at the *quality* of the explanation of the facts."[220] The best hypothesis makes the observable data *more probable* than its rivals (the facts aren't "*forced*" to fit the theory).
3. ***Plausibility***. The best hypothesis must be more *plausible* than competing explanations (it fits best with all the data).
4. ***Less ad hoc/contrived***. The best hypothesis won't require adopting *new beliefs* that have *no independent evidence* (it won't have to "make up" new theories to support its conclusion).[221]
5. ***Disconfirmed by fewer accepted beliefs***.[222] The best hypothesis will *not be disconfirmed by what we already know to be true* (e.g., our knowledge of psychology or background about a culture).

To grasp these five criteria, Licona provides a helpful illustration demonstrating how this assessment is not unique to historiography.[223]

Suppose a teenager reports the following three symptoms to his doctor: fever, vomiting, and pain in the lower-right side of his abdomen. Taking this as a teaching opportunity, the doctor asks three of his medical students to offer a diagnosis. The first student hypothesizes that the flu is the best explanation given the fever. However, the doctor remarks that the flu doesn't cause vomiting and abdominal pain. Thus, it lacks *explanatory scope* for *all* the facts (criteria #1). The second student retorts by arguing that it's the flu season, giving this hypothesis stronger plausibility.

Acknowledging this, the doctor explains that in all his years of medicine and surveying the medical literature, there's never been a case of the flu causing those three symptoms. This lowers the *probability* of the flu diagnosis (failing to meet criteria #2). So, it's best to seek another diagnosis with greater explanatory power, making the data more probable.

To salvage the flu hypothesis, the third student suggests it could still be the flu and that perhaps the other two symptoms are unrelated. The student proposes that the boy is a martial artist who was kicked in the abdomen during practice (explaining the pain in the lower right side) and later ate a bad meal (explaining the vomiting from food poisoning). Amused by this, the doctor points out how this would only force two new assumptions that have no independent evidence, making it an *ad hoc, contrived* explanation (failing criteria #4). Therefore, a better hypothesis is needed.

Rather than allow his students to conjure new theories, the doctor announces that all three symptoms are a textbook case of appendicitis. This diagnosis explains all the evidence (#1 *explanatory scope*), accounts for all the symptoms (#2 *explanatory power*), accurately fits the condition (#3 *plausibility*), does not require forced assumptions (#4 *not ad hoc*), and is *not disconfirmed* by the established medical knowledge (#5). Given this meets all five criteria, the appendicitis diagnosis is the best explanation of the data.

In the same way, when historians examine the established data for a historical event, they look for a hypothesis that offers the *best explanation by meeting all five criteria mentioned above*. Going forward, we'll utilize these to accomplish part two of our case: seeking the best explanation of the facts.

PART TWO: WHAT IS THE BEST EXPLANATION OF THE FACTS?

We begin our assessment by examining three of the most popular opposing hypotheses to the resurrection that seek to explain the data. We then end by applying the same standard criteria to the resurrection hypothesis that God raised Jesus from the dead. As Licona states, "The hypothesis that best meets the criteria is to be preferred and regarded as most likely to represent what occurred."[224]

Competing Hypothesis #1: The Conspiracy Hypothesis (Stolen Body Theory)

Ironically, this theory offers the same explanation the Jewish and Roman authorities gave in response to the apostle's proclamation of the resurrection. According to this view, God did not raise Jesus from the dead. Instead, it postulates that the disciples stole the body (explaining fact #1) and lied about the postmortem appearances (explaining fact #2). It then attributes the origin, rise, and spread of Christianity to some "conspiratorial motive" by the apostles (allegedly explaining fact #3). This is often referred to as **the conspiracy hypothesis**. Using the five standard criteria for weighing a historical hypothesis, let's assess the view accordingly.

1. √ Explanatory scope. Being unbiased historians, we can objectively say this theory meets the first criteria. As presented, it can account for all data. Nevertheless, four criteria remain, so conceding this point comes at no loss. Remember, the best hypothesis is the one that adequately meets all five criteria, not just one or two.

2. *X* Explanatory power. Recall that the best hypothesis must not force the facts to fit a theory, "as if trying to push a round peg through a square hole."[225] For several reasons, the conspiracy hypothesis fails this criterion.

First, even if the disciples stole the body, it wouldn't make sense to invent women finding the tomb because it would only hurt the reception and credibility of their alleged conspiracy. Second, consider the problem of Roman soldiers guarding the tomb. Are we seriously to believe that these disciples, who fled and hid in fear after Jesus was arrested, suddenly mustered the courage to fight off armed Roman soldiers—just to steal the body and preach a message they'd already abandoned? Why fight for a message they didn't believe in after Jesus died when we know they didn't do so when He was alive?

Finally, this hypothesis implicitly denies the evidence for the third historical fact—the origin of the Christian faith. The disciples *genuinely believed* God raised Jesus from the dead. As Craig remarks:

> But as critics have universally recognized, you can't plausibly deny that the earliest disciples at least sincerely *believed* that Jesus was risen from the dead. They staked their very lives on that conviction. The transformation in the lives of the disciples is not credibly explained by the hypothesis of a conspiracy. This shortcoming alone has been enough in the minds of most scholars to sink the old conspiracy hypothesis forever.[226]

3. *X* _Plausibility_. Once again, this hypothesis fails. To reiterate, if the disciples had no motivation to follow Jesus to His death while He was alive, why would they do so now that He was dead? Given what we know historically concerning the disciple's mentality about the Messiah, this conspiracy becomes utterly implausible.

4. *X* _Less ad hoc/contrived_. The phrase ad hoc entails the notion of unjustifiably making up a solution to save a theory from being false. For example, if a person posited the existence of mischievous aliens to explain the empty tomb (and yes, I have heard this before!), then such a "solution" would be ad hoc, attempting to salvage some naturalistic theory to avoid the resurrection.

Similarly, the conspiracy hypothesis becomes incredibly contrived as it forces us to posit alleged motives, ideas, and actions for the disciples for which *there is no evidence*. What incentive would they have to make up such a conspiracy? Imagine what this proposed "conspiracy pitch" would've sounded like as the disciples huddled together in secret:

> *Okay, guys, look, I know we all gave up and ran when he was arrested, but I've got an idea! Let's fight off the guards at the tomb, steal the body, stash it somewhere, and then come back and tell a story that will probably get us all beaten, tortured, and killed. Who's with me?*[227]

As cold-case homicide detective, Christian apologist, and former atheist J. Warner Wallace explains, there are three reasons people commit crimes or engage in conspiracies: money, sex, or power.[228] And which of these did the apostles receive? None. Looking just at the life of Paul, he was whipped, beaten, stoned, left for dead, shipwrecked three times, in constant danger, deprived, imprisoned, and martyred for his faith. Are we honestly expected to disregard history and imagine he was in on the conspiracy?

Moreover, consider the appearances to the women, the five hundred witnesses, and the conversion of hostile antagonists like James and Paul. Such a hypothesis must also posit arbitrary motives for these eyewitnesses, leading to further *ad hoc* explanations. Hence, the conspiracy hypothesis is deeply contrived and, thus, fails at meeting this fourth criterion.

5. *X* *Disconfirmed by fewer accepted beliefs*. Given that the conspiracy hypothesis contradicts first-century Jewish beliefs, it fails our final criterion. As we learned in the previous chapter, there was no expectation of a Messiah who would be publicly humiliated and executed by His enemies. Hence, no Jew would've bought into such a conspiracy, nullifying the rapid rise and spread of Christianity (fact #3). Yet, historically speaking, this is precisely what happened, all because these witnesses claimed to have seen the risen Lord (fact #2).

Furthermore, claims to be the messiah were not unheard of in Judaism. A person could claim to be the messiah, convince others, and grow a devout following. But as New Testament Scholar N. T. Wright explains, "If a messiah was killed by the pagans, especially if he had not rebuilt the Temple or liberated Israel, that was the surest sign that he was another in the long line of false messiahs... if you're a first-century Jew, and your favorite Messiah got himself crucified, then you've basically got two choices: Either you go home or else you get yourself a new Messiah."[229] [230]

Conclusion

Although the conspiracy hypothesis checks the first criterion, it failed spectacularly at the latter four. For this reason, it's a virtually dead view widely rejected by modern scholarship.

Competing Hypothesis #2: The Apparent Death Hypothesis (The "Swoon Theory")

According to this view, Jesus never actually died on the cross but was in some unconscious, comatose state when placed in the tomb. Over three days, Jesus awakened from His coma, escaped the tomb, appeared to His disciples, and presented Himself as "the risen Lord."

In the Journal of the Royal College of Physicians of London, the following proposal was given for how Jesus may have survived His execution on the cross:

> At his crucifixion, Jesus was in shock and hypotensive, and lost consciousness because of diminished blood supply to the brain. His ashen skin and immobility were mistaken for death and there is no doubt that the bystanders believed he was dead... Oxygen supply to the brain remained minimal, but above a critical level, until the circulation was restored when he was taken down from the Cross and laid on the ground. Chill during the eclipse of the sun helped to maintain the blood pressure.[231]

Taking a different approach, Australian historian Barbara Thiering suggests that:

> [a] drink was brought, of 'vinegar,' wine that had been spoiled... It was snake poison, taking a number of hours to act. But its first effect, together with that of the trauma he had suffered, was to render him unconscious... Jesus did not die on the cross. He recovered from the effects of the poison, was helped to escape from the tomb by friends, and stayed with them until he reached Rome.[232]

Continuing the explanation, Thiering imagines that within the tomb was:

> ... a container holding one hundred pounds of myrrh and aloes, a very large quantity. The juice of the aloe plant acts as a purgative, and when given in large quantities acts quickly. Myrrh is a soothing ingredient, acting on mucous membrane. The medicines only had to be administered to effect the expulsion of the poison.[233]

Regardless of the explanation, proponents of this view are essentially claiming that Jesus never actually died on the cross but was "swooning" in some unconscious state and later resuscitated in the tomb. Hence, the "**swoon theory**." God did not raise Jesus from the dead because He was never dead to begin with.

Therefore, the tomb was empty because, after being in a comatose state, Jesus resuscitated and escaped (explaining fact #1), the postmortem appearances weren't "postmortem" because, again, Jesus was never dead to begin with (explaining fact #2), and thus, the origin of the Christian faith was not based on a *resurrection*, but a *resuscitation* that was mistakenly believed to be a resurrection (explaining fact #3). Using our five criteria, let us unpack **The Apparent Death Hypothesis**.

1. √ *Explanatory scope*. Surprisingly, this hypothesis meets the first criteria by explaining all three facts.

2. *X* *Explanatory power*. Unsurprisingly, however, the view fails miserably at the second. To begin with, some apparent death theories allege that the disciples helped Jesus fake His death. This not only suffers the same problems as the conspiracy hypothesis, but we're now forced to imagine that Jesus was in on the lie! Setting this version aside, numerous other problems arise.

First, even if we granted that Jesus somehow survived the cross (more on this later), it doesn't *adequately* explain how a bloody, beaten, wounded Jesus escaped the tomb and appeared to His disciples (facts #2 and #3). To illustrate, Jesus was embalmed in about seventy-five pounds of bandages and spices.[234] Hence, before leaving the tomb, He must first escape His burial bandages by unwrapping them with no help at all.

Second, we must imagine that, after surviving extreme torture (along with three days without food or water), He used His *nail-pierced hands* to press against a two-ton stone (causing unimaginable pain) and move it by Himself. Third, after his escape, He must now deal with Roman soldiers guarding the tomb. Upon realizing Jesus was still alive, they would've wanted to finish the job. Hence, a bloody, beaten, wounded Jesus must now overpower trained soldiers armed with weapons.

Fourth, assuming all this was accomplished, He now must walk miles on *bare, nail-pierced, wounded feet* in search of where the disciples were hiding. Upon arrival, Jesus knocks on the door and, as Licona imagines:

> Peter opens only to see a severely wounded and dehydrated Jesus who is hunched over and looks up at Peter and through his extreme pain grimaces and says, "I'm the firstfruits of the general resurrection!" Such a Jesus would never have convinced his disciples that he was the risen prince of life. Alive? Barely. Resurrected? Never.[235]

Commenting on this, Habermas states,

> Upon seeing a swooned Jesus who was limping, bleeding, pale, and stooped over in pain, Peter would not have responded, "Wow, I can't wait to have a resurrection body just like that!" Rather the disciples would have said, "Let's get you a doctor. You need help!" One of my acquaintances chuckles as he imagines Jesus grimacing when Thomas touches him and responds, "Wait! That still hurts! Ouch![236]

Additionally, consider His appearance to Paul, which he described as a "glorious body" (Philippians 3:21). However, a disfigured face and mutilated body of Jesus would not have been something "glorious." Thus, even if we grant the central claim of this theory, Jesus wouldn't have appeared to them as "the risen Lord" who conquered death, but as a beaten, bloodied, half-dead person in need of desperate medical attention. As New Testament scholar and historian Dale Allison remarks, "how a flagellated, halfdead victim of the hideous torture of crucifixion could impress others as triumphant over death is hard to envisage."[237]

3. *X* *Plausibility*. Given that this view claims Jesus survived crucifixion, the apparent death hypothesis becomes *astronomically implausible*. Roman soldiers were professional executioners who could ensure a victim was dead, and historically speaking, this was done in one of two ways.

The first is **crurifragium**—breaking the knees or bones in the legs of the victim.[238] In crucifixion, being nailed to a cross isn't what killed the person. Instead, it was a slow, agonizing death by asphyxiation. As Dr.

Alexander Metherell, a medical professional who specializes in bio-muscular physics (the study of what happens to muscles when they are under stress), explains:

> His arms would have immediately been stretched, probably about six inches in length, and both shoulders would have become dislocated–you can determine this with simple mathematical equations...Once a person is hanging in the vertical position, crucifixion is essentially an agonizingly slow death by asphyxiation. The reason is that the stresses on the muscles and diaphragm put the chest into the inhaled position; basically, in order to exhale, the individual must push up on his feet so the tension on the muscles would be eased for a moment. In doing so, the nail would tear through the foot, eventually locking up against the tarsal bones. After managing to exhale, the person would then be able to relax down and take another breath in. Again he'd have to push himself up to exhale, scraping his bloodied back against the coarse wood of the cross. This would go on and on until complete exhaustion would take over, and the person wouldn't be able to push up and breathe anymore... If they wanted to speed up death...the Romans would... shatter the victim's lower leg bones. This would prevent him from pushing up with his legs so he could breathe, and death by asphyxiation would result in a matter of minutes.[239]

The second method of expediting death involved thrusting a spear into the victim's side, which Licona describes as "death insurance." Habermas explains, "The Roman author Quintilian (A.D. 35-95) reports of this procedure being performed on crucifixion victims. No question remained concerning the status of the victim afterward."[240] Coincidentally, this is precisely what we find in the Gospel accounts.[241] Metherell concludes:

> I'll grant you that these soldiers didn't go to medical school. But remember that they were experts in killing people–that was their job, and they did it very well... Besides, if a prisoner somehow escaped, the responsible soldiers would be put to death themselves, so they had a huge incentive to make absolutely sure that each and every victim was dead when he was removed from the cross.[242]

Therefore, to suggest that a man—after being brutally beaten, tortured, nailed to a cross, speared, and left for three days in a tomb without the best medical attention—could survive crucifixion is pure fantasy, making this hypothesis historically *implausible*.

4. X *Less ad hoc/contrived*. Given what we've discussed thus far, it's easy to see how this hypothesis becomes incredibly ad hoc, forcing us to believe things for which there is no evidence and, more pertinently, things for which there is evidence against them. Moreover, for the theory to even get off the ground, one must contrive speculative, arbitrary motives for why Jesus would want to fake His death in the first place (given that He claimed to be the risen Lord). Additionally, how the disciples could regard a beaten, bloodied, half-dead Jesus as the "glorious" risen Lord who conquered death. Not to mention—how they started an entirely new religious movement by proclaiming that we could someday have a body like His!

5. X *Disconfirmed by fewer accepted beliefs*. Again, the apparent death hypothesis requires us to believe that Jesus survived His execution on the cross. And with this criterion, the theory truly shines in its absolute failure. For our purposes here, we'll look at an expert medical analysis regarding the physiological condition of Jesus in the garden, at the flogging, and on the cross to demonstrate how this theory is massively disconfirmed by modern medical science.

In the Garden. To understand the state that Jesus would've been in coming off of the cross, we begin at the Garden of Gethsemane. Why? Because before the physical torture began, the mental anguish was clearly present. In the Gospel of Luke, we find an odd description of Jesus' condition, suggesting that His blood and sweat mingled as it seeped through His pores (Luke 22:44).

It's known today that severe mental stress can manifest through physiological ailments, but could it actually lead to sweating blood? Put differently, is such a condition biologically possible, and more pertinently, would such a description be medically accurate? In his book, *The Case for Christ*, Lee Strobel interviews the credentialed medical expert, Dr. Alexander Metherell. A man described as a "distinguished medical authority" who "speaks with scientific precision" as "a board-certified" diagnostician.[243] So, rather than attempt to explain the condition myself, consider the following excerpts from their interview as Metherell provides a detailed medical analysis of the situation:[244]

> "Since he knew the amount of suffering he was going to have to endure, he was quite naturally experiencing a great deal of psychological stress."
>
> I [Strobel] raised my hand to stop him. "Whoa–here's where skeptics have a field day," I told him. "The gospels tell us he began to sweat blood at this point. Now, c'mon, isn't that just a product of some over-active imaginations? Doesn't that call into question the accuracy of the gospel writers?"
>
> Unfazed, Metherell shook his head. "Not at all," he replied. "This is a known medical condition called hematidrosis. It's not very common, but it is associated with a high degree of psychological stress. What happens is that severe anxiety causes the release of chemicals that break down the capillaries in the sweat glands. As a result, there's a small amount of bleeding into these glands, and the sweat comes out tinged with blood."

Coincidentally, without modern medical knowledge, Luke describes this rare medical condition (**hematidrosis**) accurately, and this set the context for grasping the intense amount of pain Jesus would experience in the next stage: flogging.

> "Did this have any other effect on the body?" [Metherell responds] "What this did was set up the skin to be extremely fragile so that when Jesus was flogged by the Roman soldier the next day, his skin would be very, very sensitive."

At the Flogging. Describing the historical records of flogging, Licona writes:

> *The Martyrdom of Polycarp* reports of people whose flesh were "so torn by whips" that their "veins and arteries" became visible. Josephus tells of a man who… was whipped to the bone by one of Pilate's successors in Jerusalem. He also reports that a group was whipped until their intestines were exposed. In the first century, Seneca described crucified victims as having "battered

> and ineffective carcasses," "maimed," "misshapen," "deformed," "nailed" and "drawing the breath of life amid long drawn-out agony."[245]

Explaining the process, Merethell states:

> Roman floggings were known to be terribly brutal...The soldier would use a whip of braided leather thongs with metal balls woven into them. When the whip would strike the flesh, these balls would cause deep bruises or contusions, which would break open with further blows. And the whip had pieces of sharp bone as well, which would cut the flesh severely. The back would be so shredded that part of the spine was sometimes exposed by the deep, deep cuts. The whipping would have gone all the way from the shoulders down to the back, the buttocks, and the back of the legs... One physician who has studied Roman beatings said, "As the flogging continued, the lacerations would tear into the underlying skeletal muscles and produce quivering ribbons of bleeding flesh." A third-century historian by the name of Eusebius described a flogging by saying, "The sufferer's veins were laid bare, and the very muscles, sinews, and bowels of the victim were open to exposure." We know that many people would die from this kind of beating even before they could be crucified. At the least, the victim would experience tremendous pain and go into hypovolemic shock.[246]

Mind you, this was merely the preparation for crucifixion, and these Roman soldiers would've been very careful not to kill Jesus. This required accurate precision for each blow, knowing where to strike to cause the most pain while keeping Him alive, prolonging the suffering as much as possible for further agony on the cross.

> "...hypovolemic shock means the person is suffering the effects of losing a large amount of blood... This does four things. First, the heart races to try to pump blood that isn't there; second, the blood pressure drops, causing fainting or collapse; third, the kidneys stop producing urine to maintain what volume is left; and fourth, the person becomes very thirsty as the body craves fluids to replace the lost blood volume."
>
> "Do you see evidence of this in the gospel accounts?"

"Yes, most definitely...Jesus was in hypovolemic shock as he staggered up the road to the execution site at Calvary, carrying the horizontal beam of the cross. Finally Jesus collapsed... Later we read that Jesus said, 'I thirst...' Because of the terrible effects of this beating, there's no question that Jesus was already in serious to critical condition even before the nails were driven through his hands and feet."[247]

On the Cross. We know from history and archeology that Romans would drive large spikes through the wrist between the two bones: the radius and ulna. This would ensure the victim stayed fastened to the cross despite the body's weight. As Metherell explains:

This was a solid position that would lock the hand; if the nails had been driven through the palms, his weight would have caused the skin to tear and he would have fallen off the cross. So the nails went through the wrists, although this was considered part of the hand in the language of the day. It's important to understand that the nail would go through the place where the median nerve runs. This is the largest nerve going out to the hand, and it would be crushed by the nail that was being pounded in. Let me put it this way...Do you know the kind of pain you feel when you bang your elbow and hit your funny bone? That's actually another nerve, called the ulna nerve. It's extremely painful when you accidentally hit it. Well, picture taking a pair of pliers and squeezing and crushing that nerve," he said, emphasizing the word squeezing as he twisted an imaginary pair of pliers. "That effect would be similar to what Jesus experienced."[248]

This was done to both the hands and feet of Jesus. Hence, the nerves in His feet would've been crushed by the impaling nail, resulting in the same type of pain.

"The pain was absolutely unbearable. In fact, it was literally beyond words to describe; they had to invent a new word: excruciating. Literally, excruciating means 'out of the cross.' Think of that: they needed to create a new word, because there was nothing in the language that could describe the intense anguish caused during the crucifixion."[249]

Finally, we come to John's account of the spear thrust into Jesus's side, leaving no question that He was dead. But as with the garden account in Luke, we find another unusual report:

> ...Because the Jewish leaders did not want the bodies left on the crosses during the Sabbath, they asked Pilate to have the legs broken and the bodies taken down. The soldiers therefore came and broke the legs of the first man who had been crucified with Jesus, and then those of the other. But when they came to Jesus and found that he was already dead, they did not break his legs. Instead, one of the soldiers pierced Jesus' side with a spear, bringing a sudden flow of blood and water. The man who saw it has given testimony, and his testimony is true. He knows that he tells the truth, and he testifies so that you also may believe. These things happened so that the scripture would be fulfilled: "Not one of his bones will be broken," and, as another scripture says, "They will look on the one they have pierced" (John 19:31-37).

At least three observations can be made here. First, recall that, historically speaking, the Romans would expedite the death of crucifixion by either crurifragium (breaking the legs) or thrusting a spear into the victim's side. Not only is this practice confirmed through the historical records, but it's precisely what we find in the Gospel accounts, giving further *historical credibility* to the text. Second, we find several prophecies being fulfilled here (Psalm 22:16; Zechariah 12:10; Psalm 34:20), providing additional *theological credibility* to the text as well. Now consider how at this point, history and prophecy come together.

Quintilian (A.D. 35-95) states, "As for those who die on the cross, the executioner does not forbid the burying of those who have been pierced."[250] Although crurifragium was most common, this seems to imply that, *historically speaking*, Jesus would not have been buried and, *theologically speaking*, would leave prophecy (that none of His bones would be broken) unfilled. Yet, Jesus was pierced and, thus, allowed a burial, giving the account both *theological and historical credibility* simultaneously.

Our third observation concerns John's "blood and water" report flowing from Jesus' side. As with the situation in Luke, no explanation is given for this physiological anomaly. In fact, John recognizes the oddness of this report and assures the reader this is what happened. "The man who saw it has given testimony, and his testimony is true. He knows that he tells the truth." The early church fathers didn't know what to make of this either, often trying to allegorize what they *thought* John was trying to convey. Nevertheless, given our modern medical knowledge, we now understand the diagnosis. Metherell explains:

> Even before he died–and this is important, too–the hypovolemic shock would have caused a sustained rapid heart rate that would have contributed to heart failure, resulting in the collection of fluid in the membrane around the heart, called a pericardial effusion, as well as around the lungs, which is called a pleural effusion...The spear apparently went through the right lung and into the heart, so when the spear was pulled out, some fluid–the pericardial effusion and the pleural effusion–came out. This would have the appearance of a clear fluid, like water, followed by a large volume of blood, as the eyewitness John described in his gospel.[251]

Strobel states:

> "John probably had no idea why he saw both blood and a clear fluid come out–certainly that's not what an untrained person like him would have anticipated. Yet John's description is consistent with what modern medicine would expect to have happened... At this juncture," I said, "What would Jesus' condition have been?" Metherell's gaze locked with mine. He replied with authority, "There was absolutely no doubt that Jesus was dead."[252]

Conclusion

Given the medically attested evidence and historical knowledge of Roman flogging and crucifixion, there was *no possibility that Jesus could've survived the cross.* According to the *Journal of the American Medical Association*, "interpretations based on the assumption that Jesus did not die on the cross appear to be at odds with modern medical knowledge."[253]

As Licona observes, "few have ventured to suggest that Jesus may not have died as a result of his crucifixion. Their proposals have not received a following from either the academic or medical communities."[254] Hence, atheist historian and skeptic Gerd Lüdemann writes, "Jesus' death as a consequence of crucifixion is indisputable."[255] By all accounts, the apparent death hypothesis is dead, and the historical, scientific, and medical evidence provides no hope for its resurrection.

Competing Hypothesis #3: The Hallucination Hypothesis

This hypothesis concedes that the disciples sincerely believed they saw Jesus *alive and well* after His death (explaining fact #2) with the caveat that these weren't physical appearances but hallucinations. Take Peter, for example. This theory purports grief-induced hallucinations, which are not uncommon for those who've recently experienced the death of a loved one. Moreover, assuming Peter's guilt for denying Jesus, the combination of grief and guilt produced a high probability of hallucinations. Applying this to the other disciples explains their genuine belief in the resurrection (fact #3).

1. X *Explanatory scope*. Conspicuous by its absence is an explanation regarding fact #1: the empty tomb. Had the appearances been mere hallucinations, the tomb would've remained occupied, and the disciples would not have believed in a physical resurrection. This fails fact #3.

Additionally, the disciples report postmortem appearances that included touching the body of Jesus (John 20:24-29) and eating with him (Luke 24:39-43). Hence, even if we granted hallucinations, explaining the empty tomb (fact #1) and their belief in a physical, flesh, and blood resurrection (fact #3) is left unaccounted for.

2. X *Explanatory power*. Ironically, this theory cannot account for *all* the postmortem appearances. For instance, even if Peter's appearances were grief and guilt induced, it cannot explain Jesus' appearance to large groups of people at once (the five hundred witnesses) or to opposing,

hostile enemies (James and Paul). With the possible exception of James (more on this later), grief and guilt would not apply.

Nevertheless, we have no reason to believe Peter experienced guilt-induced hallucinations. Instead, we have evidence against it. Given what we know about his mentality before Jesus' death, Peter would've only felt ashamed and embarrassed that he'd been deceived into believing Jesus was the Messiah—not guilt or shame for rejecting Him. As Craig explains:

> The true problem Peter faced ... was not so much that he had failed his Lord as that his Lord had failed him! ... Any mockery and contempt he would face would be not for his failure to go to his death with Jesus–after all, everyone else had deserted him too–but rather for his having followed the false prophet from Nazareth in the first place. Some Messiah he turned out to be! Some kingdom he inaugurated! The first sensible thing Peter had done since leaving his wife and family to follow Jesus was to disown this pretender! ... Ignoring the disaster of the cross, Goulder imagines without a shred of evidence a self-preoccupied Peter wrestling with his own guilt and shame rather than struggling with dashed messianic expectations. Lest anyone say that such shattered expectations led to Peter's hallucinating Jesus alive from the dead, let me simply repeat that no such hope existed in Israel, either with respect to the Messiah or to the final resurrection.[256]

3. X *Plausibility*. To see the failure for this criterion, consider the postmortem appearance to the five-hundred witnesses. In psychology, hallucinations are defined as seeing, smelling, or hearing something that's not there in reality. Moreover, hallucinations are not shared among groups of people but, like dreams, only occur in the minds of the individual.

To illustrate, if I dreamt of being in Hawaii, I could not awaken my wife, ask her to join the dream, and then expect a free vacation as we returned to sleep. Why not? Because the dream would only be occurring in my mind, not hers. Likewise, hallucinations are individual experiences, not collective ones.[257] As clinical psychologist, Gary. R. Collins explains:

> Hallucinations are individual occurrences. By their very nature only one person can see any given hallucination at a time. They certainly are not some-

> thing which can be seen by a group of people. Neither is it possible that one person could somehow induce a hallucination in somebody else. Since a hallucination exists only in this objective, personal sense, it is obvious that others cannot witness it.[258]

Expanding on this, Gary A. Sibcy writes:

> I have surveyed the professional literature (peer-reviewed journal articles and books) written by psychologists, psychiatrists, and other relevant health-care professionals during the past two decades and have yet to find a single documented case of a group hallucination, that is, an event for which more than one person purportedly shared in a visual or other sensory perception where there was clearly no external referent.[259]

So given the medical literature, we know that hallucinations are 1) an experience of something not actually there and 2) individual experiences, not collective ones. Therefore, the hallucination hypothesis becomes an *implausible* (if not outright impossible) explanation for the five-hundred witnesses. Furthermore, given that the disciples reported *group experiences* where they *collectively interacted* with Jesus (walking, eating, touching, etc.), an explanation other than hallucinations is required. As medical professional S. J. Leinster remarks, "the circumstantial details given suggest a real presence and not a psychological experience; hallucinations do not commonly prepare breakfast for those experiencing them."[260]

4. X *Less ad hoc/contrived*. For this criterion, consider the hostile eyewitnesses, James and Paul. For the hallucination hypothesis to apply, one must imagine some hidden motives or agendas sufficient to induce grief or guilt hallucinations. Not only is this highly implausible (evidenced by history and psychology), but ad hoc and contrived. As with the case of Peter, we have evidence against such an explanation.

Beginning with James, recall that Jesus' brothers thought He was "out of his mind" (Mark 3:21). Hence, they would've seen Jesus' death as something brought about by His own insanity, feeling sorry for His fate, *not guilty*. One could imagine them saying, "We tried to tell Him, but He just wouldn't listen!" Although James may have mourned His brother's brutal death, we have no reason to believe He felt guilty about it. As Licona explains, "it seems more likely that Jesus' execution as a criminal and blasphemer would have supported their continued unbelief rather than their conversion to a faith that the especially pious James would have regarded as apostasy."[261]

Concerning Paul, the hallucination hypothesis becomes a greater failure. Would Paul have grieved over the death of Jesus? No. Far from it. Paul was publicly orchestrating the murder of Christians and regarded Jesus as a blasphemous false prophet. He would've rejoiced over His death, not grieved it! But would he have felt guilty? Again, far from it. Paul described himself as "blameless" under the law and saw his persecution of the church as zealous, believing it to be the very will of God before his conversion (Galatians 1:13-14; Philippians 3:4-6). Commenting on this, Swedish scholar Krister Stendahl writes:

> Contrast Paul, a very happy and successful Jew, one who can say "As to righteousness under the Law (I was) blameless" (Phil. 3:6). That is what he says. He experiences no troubles, no problems, no qualms of conscience. He is a star pupil.... Nowhere in Paul's writings is there any indication ... that psychologically Paul had some problem of conscience.[262]

Therefore, the guilt aspect is nowhere evident in the records of these men, and given their own words, the exact opposite was true. This shows the *ad hoc* implausibility of such a hypothesis, attempting psychoanalysis to fit a theory for which there is no evidence. And as Craig observes:

> Psychoanalysis is difficult enough to carry out even with patients on the psychoanalyst's couch, so to speak, but it's next to impossible with historical figures. For that reason the attempt to write psychobiography is rejected by historians today.[263]

Licona concludes, "it is pure speculation, significantly lacking in evidence. It is therefore ad hoc... and all without an ounce of solid evidence. It appears to be an attempt to salvage a favored but failing hypothesis."[264]

5. X *Disconfirmed by fewer accepted beliefs.* But suppose we granted, against all historical and psychological evidence, that these appearances

were mere hallucinations. The question remains—are mere hallucinations sufficient to invoke belief in a resurrected Jesus given the cultural, Jewish understanding of the afterlife, and a final resurrection? The answer is a resounding no.

First, the Jewish belief concerning resurrection didn't consist of *individual* resurrections but only a *final* resurrection at the end of time. Take the death of Lazarus as an example (John 11:17-44). When Jesus tells Martha, "Your brother will rise again," her response is, "I know he will rise again in the resurrection at the last day." She took his comment as someone saying, "Don't worry, you'll see him again *one day*." Recognizing her misunderstanding, Jesus tells her plainly, "I am the resurrection and the life." Still, her deeply engrained Jewish beliefs of a *singular, final resurrection* kept her from realizing His point.

When He requests for the stone to be moved, she says, "But Lord, by this time there is a bad odor, for he has been there for four days." Apparently, she thought he just wanted to see the body, but certainly not resurrect him. Despite her belief in Jesus as the Messiah, the thought would've never crossed her mind because, again, t*here was no Jewish concept of a resurrection prior to the final one.*

Second, if the disciples had a hallucination of Jesus, their immediate interpretation would've been that of a ghost or disembodied soul, *not of a physically resurrected person*. In this culture, seeing a vision of someone who recently died didn't prove they were alive but dead![265] As Craig explains:

> Given the current Jewish beliefs about life after death, the disciples, if they were to project hallucinations of Jesus, would have seen Jesus in Heaven or in Abraham's bosom, where the souls of the righteous dead were believed to abide until the final resurrection. And such visions would not have led to belief in Jesus' resurrection. At the most, it would have only led the disciples to say that Jesus had been assumed into heaven, not raised from the dead.[266]

Consider two instances that provide evidence of this belief.

In Luke 24:36-40, Jesus appears to them, and they automatically assume He's a ghost. Jesus corrects this by saying, "Look at my hands and feet. It is I myself! Touch me and see; a ghost does not have flesh and bones, as you see I have." Additionally, recall the "mount of transfiguration" where Elijah and Moses appear before them. Note that they don't interpret the situation by saying, "Oh wow! Elijah and Moses must have resurrected, too!" Instead, they interpret it as a disembodied existence, *not a physical one.*

In other words, if seeing a vision of someone dead was sufficient to produce a belief in a resurrection, then we'd expect it to apply here, and yet, it does not. Therefore, given our background knowledge of the Jewish mindset, the hallucination hypothesis fails to account for the disciple's belief in a physical, bodily resurrection (fact #3)—failing this fifth criterion and, thus, failing as a plausible explanation.

Conclusion

Unlike the previous, the hallucination hypothesis failed to satisfy *any* of the five criteria. Even if we granted the theory, it doesn't explain the empty tomb, nor could it explain the disciple's belief that Jesus had *physically risen* from the dead (facts #1 and #3). Concerning group hallucinations, we saw how this was psychologically implausible, no different than sharing a dream with my wife.

Additionally, grief and guilt were proposed to explain why the disciples hallucinated. Not only is there no evidence for this, but there is historical evidence against it. Finally, visions of the dead would not illicit beliefs in a resurrection but would only confirm the belief that the person was dead. Therefore, the hallucination hypothesis fails, and another explanation is needed.

THE RESURRECTION HYPOTHESIS AS THE BEST EXPLANATION

Our final hypothesis is the view that the disciples provided and is, historically speaking, the reason for the rise and spread of Christianity. Namely, that God bodily raised Jesus from the dead. But is it true? Can it accurately account for all the data?

Using the same standard criteria as before, let's examine the resurrection hypothesis (showing why it's the best explanation of the facts) and briefly respond to possible objections. In some sense, the previous chapter serves as a positive case for this view, and the previous hypotheses are typically given as objections against it. Nevertheless, we can defend and expand on the data.

1. √ _Explanatory scope._ With the resurrection hypothesis, all three facts are adequately accounted for with great explanatory scope. If God raised Jesus from the dead, then this explains why the tomb was empty (fact #1), how He was able to appear alive and well after His brutal execution (fact #2), and explains the origin of the Christian faith—the disciples genuinely believed God raised Jesus from the dead (fact #3). Hence, the resurrection was "God's vindication of Jesus' radical personal claims for which He was condemned as a blasphemer."[267]

2. √ _Explanatory power._ Not only does the resurrection hypothesis explain the facts, but unlike the previous theories, does so with greater explanatory power.

For instance, although the apparent death hypothesis explains an empty tomb, it fails to account for why the disciples believed that a beaten, bloody Jesus was the "glorified" risen Lord who conquered death. Conversely, although the hallucination hypothesis explains why they believed Jesus was alive and well, it fails to explain why the tomb was empty. Concerning the conspiracy hypothesis, although it provided an explanation for the facts (the disciples lied about everything), it becomes utterly implausible and *ad hoc* as to why these men would willingly suffer persecution, torment, and agonizing death for what they *would have known to be a lie.*

But with the resurrection hypothesis, all three facts (along with the supporting historical evidence in chapter 24) are adequately accounted for with no further speculation. Therefore, it has both *explanatory scope* and *explanatory power* that far outweighs the rest.

Objection: People Die for Their Beliefs All the Time

At this point, a popular objection is that religious zealots die for what they *believe* all the time and the disciples are no exception. For instance, the 9/11 Muslim terrorists died for what they *believed* to be true, which is not uncommon in Islam. Yet, no Christian takes this as proof for Islam being true. What makes Christianity any different?

Response

First, the fact that someone is willing to die for what they believe doesn't prove their belief is true (although it does prove they *believed it to be true*). And we've conceded this point all along. Recall that we didn't present this as evidence for the truth of the resurrection, but as evidence for the truth of fact #3. Hence, the objection is a strawman that confuses Part 1 of our case (presenting the historical facts) with Part 2 (defending the resurrection as the best explanation of these facts).

Second, the objection-by-comparison is not analogous to the martyrdom of the apostles. Why not? Because I can lie to someone today *and have them die for what I know to be false*, but whether I'm willing to die for that false belief is an entirely different story. I don't doubt that devout, religious followers willingly die for what they *were told or convinced* to be true, but this is not the case for the apostles. As Habermas explains:

> The apostles died for holding to their own testimony that they had personally seen the risen Jesus. Contemporary martyrs die for what they believe to be true. The disciples of Jesus died for what they knew to be either true or false.[268]

In other words, not only did the disciples believe this to be true *but were in the unique position to know if it was true. That* is the fundamental difference. Without benefit or gain, *no one dies for what they know to be false*.

3. √ Plausibility. In terms of plausibility, the resurrection hypothesis accounts for all the data in a way that far outweighs the rest.

For instance, recall the Jewish concept of the Messiah and a *singular, final* resurrection. Unless Jesus had *actually resurrected and physically appeared* to His disciples, their belief in a resurrected Messiah becomes implausible. Not only did He fail to meet their expectations, but more pertinently, the Messiah would've never been crucified in the first place (seen as a curse hanging on a tree). So why did they drastically change their cultural beliefs and follow Jesus to their death *after* His crucifixion? Because, according to their reports, God raised Jesus from the dead, and this vindicated His radical claims to be the Messiah—shifting their understanding of both the Messiah and the resurrection.

Additionally, the previous hypotheses couldn't account for the appearances and conversions of the hostile eyewitnesses, James and Paul. Again, what would it take to convince and convert these men—one who thought Jesus was insane and the other who killed Christians, thinking it was the will of God? In their own words, because God raised Jesus from the dead, and they saw the evidence for themselves.

4. √ *Less ad hoc/contrived*. The resurrection hypothesis accounts for all the data, and no *ad hoc*, contrived explanations are needed.

Objection: God of the Gaps Fallacy

At this point, a common objection is that the resurrection hypothesis depends on an additional belief without evidence. Namely, the belief that God exists. Allegedly, this commits a "God of the gaps" fallacy (see chapter 14) and thus, a natural explanation for the facts must be preferred over a supernatural one.

Response

First, recall that this criterion calls for the hypothesis with *fewer* prior assumptions, eliminating explanations for which no evidence exists. The explanation that God raised Jesus from the dead only requires *one* additional belief (that God exists), as opposed to the numerous, contrived assumptions of the previous theories (e.g., conspiratorial lies, psychoanalysis of grief and guilt, and purported motives and agendas) for which there is not a shred of evidence. Hence, the resurrection hypothesis far surpasses these in meeting this criterion.

Second, not only is there strong evidence for the belief that God exists, but this book provided (at least) four independent, logically deductive arguments for it. Therefore, it's not *ad hoc*, and the "God of the gaps" fallacy doesn't apply.

Third, the objection itself becomes an "argument from ignorance fallacy," which we can call a "**naturalism of the gaps**" fallacy. Why? Because this objection wishes to "plug in" a natural explanation in the face of a supernatural explanation that has already provided the philosophical, cosmological, scientific, metaphysical, teleological, epistemic, logical, historical, and medical evidence to support it. Hence, without a shred of evidence for the objection, it becomes nothing more than a "naturalism of the gaps" argument from ignorance fallacy.

Objection: The Resurrection Requires a Miracle

Despite this, some accuse the resurrection hypothesis of being *ad hoc* or contrived by arguing the impossibility of miracles. However, this presupposes a naturalistic worldview (which is both question-begging and circular) and suffers from the same problems as before. Remember, we're not asking, "what is the best *natural* explanation of the data," but rather, what explanation of the data is best supported by the historical evidence—*irrespective of our presuppositional biases* (e.g., naturalism or scientism).

Moreover, note the ironic hypocrisy within the objection. The competing natural theories call for astoundingly contrived miracles: such as a "psychological miracle" (causing people to become liars and conspirators without reason) or a "biological miracle" (that Jesus survived the cross despite having a spear thrust into His side, or miraculously reviving in a tomb after suffering a brutal, tortuous execution without food or water). Talk about implausible, *ad hoc*, contrived miracles! I certainly don't have enough "faith" to believe such things. As Craig observes:

> The conspiracy hypothesis requires us to suppose that the moral character of the disciples was defective, which is certainly not implied by already existing knowledge; the apparent death hypothesis requires the supposition that the centurion's lance thrust into Jesus' side was just a superficial poke or is an unhistorical detail in the narrative, which again goes beyond existing knowledge; the hallucination hypothesis requires us to suppose some sort of emotional preparation of the disciples which predisposed them to project visions of Jesus alive, which is not implied by our knowledge. Such examples could be multiplied… It is *these* miraculous hypotheses that strike us as artificial and contrived, not the resurrection hypothesis… the resurrection hypothesis cannot be characterized as excessively contrived.[269]

Furthermore, if the resurrection is the best explanation that accounts for all the data, then it serves as another line of evidence that God exists, miracles are possible, and, more pertinently, that Christianity is true.

5. √ *Disconfirmed by fewer accepted beliefs*. Given all we've discussed, there are no historical or medically accepted facts that one must deny in affirming the resurrection. At best, one could object by saying that dead men don't *naturally* rise from the dead. But we aren't denying this, and even people in Jesus' time knew that! Nevertheless, there's no contradiction in believing that dead men don't *naturally* rise from the dead and that God *supernaturally* raised Jesus from the dead. As atheist philosopher Peter Slezak explains, "For a God who is able to create the entire universe, the odd resurrection would be child's play!"[270]

Therefore, if God exists (chapters 18-21), then we have no reason to deny the possibility that God was able to raise Jesus from the dead. If anything, we have profound evidence to affirm that He did! As New Testament scholar, N. T. Wright states, "That is why, as a historian, I cannot explain the rise of early Christianity unless Jesus rose again, leaving an empty tomb behind him."[271]

Conclusion: Therefore, Christianity Is True

Recall that in 1 Corinthians 15:12-19, Paul provided a test for the truth of Christianity, stating that if Christ had not been raised, then our faith is in vain, and Christianity is false. This meant the truth of Christianity hinges on the truth or falsity of the resurrection.

Using the standard historical method, we've evaluated the resurrection hypothesis that God raised Jesus from the dead and analyzed it with the same scrutiny as before. Given all the data, this hypothesis far outweighed the rest, accounting for all the facts, requiring no speculation, no implausibility, and no *ad hoc*, contrived explanations. All five standard criteria were met, and not only is the resurrection the best explanation of the data, but all the historical, medical, and scientific evidence is on our side.

Therefore, given the truth of the resurrection, we can rationally, justifiably, and confidently proclaim the good news. He is risen, He is risen indeed! As the apostle Paul concludes:

> But Christ has indeed been raised from the dead, the firstfruits of those who have fallen asleep. For since death came through a man, the resurrection of the dead comes also through a man. For as in Adam all die, so in Christ all will be made alive (1 Corinthians 15:20-22).

This is the hope of our salvation, the assurance of our faith (Ephesians 2:8-9, Romans 10:9-13). God exists, Christianity is true, and no arguments, objections, or complaints could ever change this fact. We have the truth, and I pray this book has equipped you to share this good news with a nonbelieving world.

> *Beloved, while I was very diligent to write to you concerning our common salvation,* ***I found it necessary to write to you exhorting you to contend earnestly for the faith which was once for all delivered to the saints****.*
>
> – Jude 1:3 (NKJV)

Endnotes

CHAPTER 1

1 Barna Group, "Atheism Doubles Among Generation Z," January 24, 2018, www.barna.com/research/atheism-doubles-among-generation-z/.

2 Sean McDowell and J. Warner Wallace, *So the Next Generation Will Know: Preparing Young Christians for a Challenging World* (Colorado Springs: David C Cook, 2019), Kindle, 34.

3 Richard Dawkins, *The God Delusion* (Boston: First Mariner Books, 2008), 51.

4 https://www.beliefnet.com/columnists/scienceandthesacred/2009/08/why-i-think-the-new-atheists-are-a-bloody-disaster.html.

5 Front cover of *The Dawkins Delusion.*

6 J. Gresham Machen, address delivered on September 20, 1912, at the opening of the 101st session of Princeton Theological Seminary.

7 Alan Axelrod and Charles Phillips, editors, "Religious Wars," *Encyclopedia of Wars* (Vol.3). Facts on File, (2004): 1484-1485.

CHAPTER 2

8 Melinda Penner, *The Doctrine of the Trinity at Nicaea and Chalcedon.* https://www.str.org/w/the-doctrine-of-the-trinity-at-nicaea-and-chalcedon.

9 Ibid.

10 J. P. Moreland, *Love Your God With All Your Mind: The Role of Reason in the Life of the Soul* (Colorado Springs: NavPress, 2012), 115.

11 C. S. Lewis, *God in the Dock* (Grand Rapids: Eerdmans, 1970), 48.

12 J. P. Moreland and William Lane Craig, *Philosophical Foundations for a Christian Worldview* (Westmont: InterVarsity Press, 2nd edition) 6.

CHAPTER 4

13 Moreland and Craig, *Philosophical Foundations for a Christian Worldview,* 142

14 Ibid, 80.

15 Ibid, 81.

16 This was similar to my approach in example #1.

CHAPTER 5

17 Moreland, *Love Your God with All Your Mind,* 89.

18 Barna Group, *Gen Z: The Culture, Beliefs and Motivations Shaping the Next Generation* (Ventura: Barna Group, 2018), 25.

19 Ibid.

20 https://www.barna.com/research/resilient-disciples/.

21 https://crossexamined.org/church-beliefs/.

22 https://www.barna.com/research/five-myths-about-young-adult-church-dropouts/.

23 Moreland, *Love Your God With All Your Mind,* 219.

CHAPTER 6

[24] Moreland and Craig, *Philosophical Foundations for a Christian Worldview*, 118, 132-133, 419, 427-428.

[25] https://www.barna.com/research/millennials-oppose-evangelism/.

[26] Ibid.

[27] Ibid.

[28] Ibid.

[29] Ibid.

[30] Moreland, *Love Your God With All Your Mind*, 112.

[31] Allen Carden, *Puritan Christianity in America* (Grand Rapids: Baker, 1990), 186.

[32] As quoted in Donald J. Grout and Claude V Palisca, *A History of Western Music* (New York: W. W. Norton, 1973).

[33] Moreland and Craig, *Philosophical Foundations for a Christian Worldview*, 432-433.

CHAPTER 7

[34] Moreland and Craig, *Philosophical Foundations for a Christian Worldview*, 370.

[35] J. P. Moreland, *Scientism and Secularism: Learning to Respond to a Dangerous Ideology* (Wheaton: Crossway, 2018), 26.

[36] Moreland, *Love Your God With All Your Mind*, 21.

[37] As Craig explains, "On none of these theories, then, should miracles be understood as violations of the laws of nature. Rather they are naturally (or physically) impossible events, events which at certain times and places cannot be produced by the relevant natural causes. Craig, William Lane. *Reasonable Faith* (3rd edition) (p. 263). Crossway. Kindle Edition.

[38] J. P. Moreland, *Kingdom Triangle: Recover the Christian Mind, Renovate the Soul, Restore the Spirit's Power* (Grand Rapids: Zondervan, 2009), 42.

CHAPTER 8

[39] 1 Corinthians 5:6-8, Phillippians 1:21-24. At the resurrection, it is not merely a body that will be resurrected, but me, the self/soul (see endnotes 97 and 99). As John Cooper has pointed out, Paul makes a distinction between himself and the body (presupposing what is known as substance dualism). See, John Cooper, "Absent from the Body . . . Present with the Lord" Is the Intermediate State Fatal to Physicalism?" in *Christian Physicalism? Philosophical Theological Criticisms*, ed R. Keith Loftin and Joshua R. Farris (United States: Lexington Books, 2017), 322.

[40] It's been argued that we have more than five senses. https://bigthink.com/surprising-science/think-you-have-only-5-senses-its-actually-a-lot-more-than-that/

[41] Moreland, *Love Your God with All Your Mind*, 21.

[42] https://www.medicalnewstoday.com/articles/322539#The-future-of-neurotheology-and-religion.

[43] J. C. Lennox, (2021). *God and Stephen Hawking: Whose Design Is it Anyway?* (Oxford: Lion Hudson, 2011), 24.

[44] https://www.thoughtco.com/worth-of-your-elements-3976054

CHAPTER 9

[45] Moreland, *Love Your God With All Your Mind*, 151.

[46] Ibid, 151-152.

CHAPTER 10

[47] Gregory Koukl, *Tactics, 10th Anniversary Edition: A Game Plan for Discussing Your Christian Convictions* (Grand Rapids: Zondervan, 2019), 46.

[48] Ibid, 69.

CHAPTER 11

[49] Ibid, Koukl, 57.

[50] Hugh Hewitt, *In, But Not Of: A Guide to Christian Ambition* (Nashville: Nelson, 2003), 173.

[51] Matthew 22:17

[52] Mark L. Strauss, *Jesus Behaving Badly: The Puzzling Paradoxes of the Man from Galilee* (United States, InterVarsity Press, 2015), 25-26.

[53] Matthew 22:15-22; Mark 12:13-17.

[54] David A. Reed and John R. Farkas, *Mormons Answered Verse by Verse* (Grand Rapids: Baker Books, 1992).

[55] As a side note, consider the oddity of the claim. If Christians are hypocrites, does this prove Christianity is false? No. Just as students failing a math test doesn't entail that math is false and should be given up, Christians being hypocritical doesn't entail that Christianity is false and should be dismissed. The former only means the principles of math haven't been adequately applied to the test, and the latter only means that the principles of Christ haven't been adequately applied to one's life.

[56] Thomas Nagel, *The Last Word* (Oxford: Oxford University Press, 1997), 130.

[57] Romans 12:2.

[58] Reed, 113.

[59] Timothy A. Stratton, *Human Freedom, Divine Knowledge, and Mere Molinism: A Biblical, Historical, Theological, and Philosophical Analysis* (Eugene: Wipf and Stock, 2020), 179.

CHAPTER 12

[60] 1 Corinthians 15:6.

CHAPTER 13

[61] Allan Bloom, *The Closing of the American Mind* (New York: Simon & Schuster, 1987).

[62] Moreland, *Love Your God with All Your Mind*, 33.

[63] Matthew 7:1-5, John 7:24, Romans 2:1.

[64] Koukl, *Tactics*, 101.

[65] Ibid, 54-55.

66 Ibid.

67 Ibid, 99-100.

68 Ibid.

CHAPTER 14

69 Robert B. Reich, "Bush's God," *The American Prospect Online*, July 17, 2004, 40.

70 Excerpt from Dr. Moreland's lecture on *Scientism vs. Christianity* video https://www.youtube.com/watch?v=tQYuCIOjuTQ&t=500s.

71 Moreland, *Scientism and Secularism*, 52.

72 Frank Turek, *Stealing From God: Why Atheists Need God to Make Their Case* (Colorado Springs: NavPress, 2014), 159-160.

73 Moreland and Craig, *Philosophical Foundations for a Christian Worldview*, 372.

74 Daniel C. Dennett, *Darwin's Dangerous Idea: Evolution and the Meaning of Life* (London: Simon & Schuster, 2014), 21.

75 Norman L. Geisler and Frank Turek, *I Don't Have Enough Faith to Be an Atheist* (Wheaton: Crossway, 2004), 37.

76 Moreland, *Scientism and Secularism*, 55.

77 Moreland and Craig, *Philosophical Foundations for a Christian Worldview*, 413.

78 Moreland, *Scientism and Secularism*, 68,156.

79 https://rationallyspeaking.blogspot.com/2012/04/curates-eggo-alex-rosenberg-and-meaning.html.

80 C. S. Lewis, *Miracles* (London: Simon and Schuster, 1996), 140.

81 John C. Lennox, *Can Science Explain Everything?* (Oxford: The Good Book Company, 2019), Kindle, 13.

82 Turek. *Stealing From God*, 150.

83 John C. Lennox, *God's Undertaker: Has Science Buried God*? (London: Lion Books, 2009), 20.

84 Ibid, 21.

85 Melvin Calvin, *Chemical Evolution* (Oxford: Oxford University Press, 1969), 258.

86 Lennox, *Can Science Explain Everything?*, 13.

87 Lennox, *God's Undertaker*, 44-50, 87.

88 Turek, *Stealing From God*, 155-156.

89 Richard Swinburne, *Is There a God* (Oxford: Oxford University Press, 1996), 68.

90 Lennox, *God's Undertaker*, 45.

CHAPTER 15

91 *Darwinism: Science or Naturalistic Philosophy? The Debate at Stanford University*, William B. Provine (Cornell University) and Phillip E. Johnson (University of California, Berkeley), videorecording © 1994 Regents of the University of California.

92 Video: *Does the Soul Exist?* Debate between Eric Hernandez and Matt Dillahunty, highlight reel, https://youtu.be/ZhW4SYbR6vc.

93 In philosophy, this syllogism is known as a *modus tollens* argument.

94 For responding to objections concerning quantum indeterminacy, see Moreland, *Body & Soul*, 105.

95 Sam Harris, *Free Will* (New York: Free Press, 2012), 16.

96 To see why determinism (both theistic and non-theistic) is incompatible with thinking freely, see Timothy A. Stratton and J. P. Moreland, "An Explanation and Defense of the Free-Thinking Argument," *Religions* 13, no. 10 (2022): 988. https://doi.org/10.3390/rel13100988.

CHAPTER 16

97 "...future resurrection included affirmation of the intermediate state." John W Cooper, *Body, Soul, and Life Everlasting: Biblical Anthropology and the Monism-dualism Debate*, (United Kingdom: Leicester, 2000) 136.

98 Brandon J. O'Brien, and Randolph E. Richards, *Misreading Scripture with Western Eyes: Removing Cultural Blinders to Better Understand the Bible* (United States, InterVarsity Press, 2012), 129, 135.

99 Cooper calls this a "two-stage eschatology." John W. Cooper, "Scripture and Philosophy on the Unity of Body and Soul" in *The Ashgate Research Companion to Theological Anthropology,* Routledge Accessed on: 30 Mar 2023 https://www.routledgehandbooks.com/doi/10.4324/9781315613673.ch2

100 As in earlier endnote, O'Brien, Richards, 129, 135. Also, see Strauss, 36, 45, 155.

101 Strass, 44.

102 This was a verse they would've *all* been familiar with (much like us quoting John 3:16), which adds a funny twist to his statement, "Have you not read?"

CHAPTER 17

103 Jesus is pointing at the evidence of fulfilled OT promises that validate his identity. Isa 35:5-6; 26:19; 29:18-19; 61:1

104 Richard Dawkins, *The Selfish Gene* (Oxford: Oxford University Press, 1976), 198.

CHAPTER 18

105 William Lane Craig, *On Guard: Defending Your Faith With Reason and Precision* (Colorado Springs: David C Cook, 2010), 53.

106 More specifically, metaphysically necessary.

107 W. L. Craig and J. P. Moreland, editors, *The Blackwell Companion to Natural Theology*. (Chichester, West Sussex: Wiley-Blackwell, 2012), 332.

108 Craig, *On Guard*, 55-56.

109 Moreland, Craig, *Philosophical Foundations*, 478. "Therefore, there must exist an ultramundane being that is metaphysically necessary in its existence, that is to say, its nonexistence is impossible. It is the sufficient reason for its own existence as well as for the existence of every contingent thing." Also, 511.

110 J. P. Moreland and Scott B. Rae, *Body & Soul: Human Nature & the Crisis in Ethics* (Downers Grove: InterVarsity Press, 2000), 20.

111 Craig, *On Guard*, 55-56.

CHAPTER 19

[112] https://youtu.be/gtfVds8Kn4s.

[113] For a full defense of the argument, see the one-hundred-page chapter in *The Blackwell Companion to Natural Theology*, 101.

[114] Moreland and Craig, *Philosophical Foundations for a Christian Worldview,* 159.

[115] Craig, *On Guard*, 76-77.

[116] https://www.npr.org/2012/01/13/145175263/lawrence-krauss-on-a-universe-from-nothing.

[117] https://youtu.be/7ImvlS8PLIo.

[118] Ibid. Emphasis mine.

[119] https://www.nytimes.com/2012/03/25/books/review/a-universe-from-nothing-by-lawrence-m-krauss.html.

[120] Ibid.

[121] Delia Perlov and Alex Vilenkin, *Cosmology for the Curious* (Heidelberg: Springer International Publishing, 2017), 329.

[122] Craig, *On Guard*, 92.

[123] John Maddox, "Down With the Big Bang," *Nature*, 340, (1989): 425.

[124] https://thevillagechapel.com/friday-night-chats/friday-night-chats-seven-days-that-divide-the-world-with-professor-john-lennox-2/.

[125] Alexander Vilenkin,. *Many Worlds in One* (New York: Hill and Wang, 2006).

[126] J. P. Moreland and Kai Nielsen, *Does God Exist? The Debate Between Theists & Atheists* (New York: Prometheus, 1993), 37.

[127] Craig, *On Guard*, 77.

CHAPTER 20

[128] Ibid, Craig, 129.

[129] See, Adam L. Johnson, *Divine love theory: How the Trinity is the Source and Foundation of Morality* (Kregel Academic, 2023), 8-9.

[130] Ibid, 83-84.

[131] See Johnson, *Divine Love Theory,* 93. "moral obligation is inherently personal and social. It's personal because we're obligated only to persons, not facts, principles, or natures...obligations arise in the context of social relationships between persons." Also, Vern S. Poythress, *Knowing and the Trinity* (Phillipsburg, NJ: P&R, 2018), 335-336. "Persons are ultimately responsible only to persons.... moral authority is personal. And to have moral absolutes, the moral authority must be absolute. So we must have a personal absolute."

[132] Ibid, 134.

[133] Michael Ruse, Michael. "Evolutionary Theory and Christian Ethics," in *The Darwinian Paradigm* (London: Routledge, 1989), 262, 268-89.

[134] Johnson, *Divine Love Theory,* 11, 14-16.

[135] In other words, the source of objective morality is grounded in God's necessarily good ***nature***, not his will or desires. Though his commands to us reveal his will

and desires, they are not grounded in them. They are grounded in his nature, and his will, desires, and commands will never go against his perfectly good nature. Thus, God, being perfectly moral and good, could never command something immoral. See Johnson, *Divine Love Theory,* 95-96, 146.

136 "God is the ontological ultimate because he, as a causal agent, could have caused everything else to come into existence." Johnson, *Divine Love Theory,* 134-135, 194.

CHAPTER 21

137 This is similar to the principle that we discussed in chapter 15 regarding epistemic chains.

138 Richard Dawkins, *River Out of Eden: A Darwinian View of Life* (New York: Basic Books, 1995), 133.

139 Moreland, Craig, *Philosophical Foundations,* 449.

140 https://www.kare11.com/article/news/girl-who-cant-feel-pain-battling-insurance-company/89-557702857.

141 Norman L. Geisler, *Chosen But Free: A Balanced View of God's Sovereignty and Free Will* (Grand Rapids: Baker Publishing Group, 2010), 35.

142 See, Alvin Plantinga, *God, Freedom, and Evil* (United States, Eerdmans, 1989).

CHAPTER 22

143 Licona shared details with me in a private a conversation and allowed me to use them here. This can also be heard in his opening statement in the debate, Is the Bible Inherent. https://youtu.be/rLwnjx6-5dc.

CHAPTER 23

144 Bart Ehrman (agnostic historian and New Testament scholar) makes this point in response to a question about mythicism here: https://youtu.be/43mDuIN5-ww

145 Joseph Holden, editor, *The Harvest Handbook of Apologetics* (Eugene: Harvest House Publishers, 2019), 154.

146 See video playlist by Michael Jones of Inspiring Philosophy. *Was Jesus a Copycat Savior?* https://www.youtube.com/playlist?list=PL1mr9ZTZb3TVOYpPpjYhTUHXycJrY6P2I.

147 Zeitgeist *Debunked: Jesus Is Not A Copy Of Pagan Gods.* https://www.youtube.com/watch?v=30AunYXtYDg.

148 Online article. *Is Jesus a Copy of Other Pagan Myths?* https://www.discipledojo.org/blog/pagan-jesus.

149 Gary R. Habermas and Michael R. Licona, *The Case for the Resurrection of Jesus* (Grand Rapids: Kregel Publications, 2004), 90.

150 Ibid. Emphasis mine.

151 Licona has used these examples in various lectures and talks.

152 An exhaustive analysis of the scholarship on the topic can be seen in the work of Dr. Robert Van Voorst, Jesus Outside the New Testament: An Introduction to the Ancient Evidence, and the work of Dr. Gary Habermas, The Historical Jesus: Ancient Evidence for the Life of Christ.

[153] Holden, 126.

[154] Flavius Josephus, *The Antiquities of the Jews*, 20.9.

[155] Habermas and Licona, 45.

[156] Tacitus, *Annals*, 15.44.

[157] Habermas and Licona, 273.

[158] Lucian of Samosata, *The Death of Peregrine,* 11-13 (c. mid-second century).

[159] Gary R. Habermas, *The Historical Jesus: Ancient Evidence for the Life of Christ* (Joplin: College Press Publishing Company, 1996), 206.

[160] Ibid, 206-207.

[161] Maurice Casey, *Jesus: Evidence and Argument Or Mythicist Myths?* (London: Bloomsbury Publishing, 2014), 245.

[162] Online article by R. Joseph Hoffmann. *Mythic Pizza and Cold-Crooked Scholars.* https://rjosephhoffmann.wordpress.com/2012/04/23/mythtic-pizza-and-cold-cocked-scholars/.

[163] Bart D. Ehrman, *Did Jesus Exist? The Historical Argument for Jesus of Nazareth* (New York: HarperOne, 2012), 268.

[164] Bart D. Ehrman, *The New Testament: A Historical Introduction to the Early Christian Writings* (Oxford: Oxford University Press, 1999), 248.

[165] Erhman, *Did Jesus Exist?,* 74.

[166] There are two instances where Ehrman defends this point brilliantly but were omitted for the sake of space. Both can be found in video form here: https://youtu.be/43mDuIN5-ww and here: https://www.youtube.com/watch?v=u9C-C7qNZkOE.

[167] Holden, 125.

[168] Craig, *On Guard*, 184.

[169] C. S. Lewis, *Mere Christianity.* (London: Collins, 1952), 52.

[170] Ibid, 53.

CHAPTER 24

[171] Habermas and Liconia, 44.

[172] Ibid, 47-48.

[173] Ibid. 37-40.

[174] Ibid, 71.

[175] Ibid, 70. Habermas reports that "roughly 75% of scholars accept the empty tomb as a historical fact" (in a recent 2023 interview, he reports that this number has gone up to 80% https://youtu.be/lXEAZw9Oz-s?t=3674). Though this is a large majority, it is not above the ninety-something percent threshold for what he labels a "minimal fact." Nevertheless, in his book with Licona, he presents and defends this as a "+1" "fact that is "granted by an impressive majority." 149.

[176] Craig, *On Guard,* 221.

[177] Habermas and Licona, 37-38.

[178] Matthew 28:13.

[179] Habermas and Licona, 71.

[180] Craig, *On Guard*, 228.

[181] Turek, *Stealing From God*, 199-200.

[182] Ibid, 200-201.

[183] Habermas and Licona, 73.

[184] Jacob Kremer, *Die Osterevangelien—Geschichten um Geschichte* (Stuttgart: Katholisches Bibelwerk, 1977), 49-50.

[185] Habermas and Licona, 52, 212, 222.

[186] Ibid, 53.

[187] Matthew 26:69-75; Luke 22:54-62.

[188] C. H. Dodd, *More New Testament Studies* (Manchester: University of Manchester, 1968), 128.

[189] Lee Strobel, *The Case for Christ* (Nashville: Zondervan, 1998), 231-232.

[190] Craig, *On Guard*, 233-234.

[191] Ibid, 235.

[192] Gerd Lüdemann, *What Really Happened to Jesus*?, trans. John Bowden (Louisville: Westminster John Knox Press, 1995), 80.

[193] In an interview by Peter Jennings in *The Search for Jesus* (American Broadcasting Corp. [ABC], July 2000).

[194] Habermas and Licona, 60.

[195] Ibid, 50.

[196] Strauss, 19-23.

[197] https://www.reasonablefaith.org/writings/popular-writings/jesus-of-nazareth/the-triumphal-entry.

[198] Ibid.

[199] Ibid.

[200] Ibid.

[201] Ibid.

[202] Ibid.

[203] Good News Translation.

[204] Luke 22:49-50.

[205] John 20:18; Luke 22:51; Matthew 26:53.

[206] Matthew 26:56.

[207] John 18:33, 36.

[208] Matthew 26:67.

[209] Luke 22:64-65.

[210] John 18:22-23.

[211] Matthew 27:27-31.

[212] Matthew 27:37.

[213] Galatians 3:13.

[214] Craig, *On Guard*, 241.

[215] Luke 22:54-62.

[216] Habermas and Licona, 56,93.

[217] Craig, *On Guard*, 242.

CHAPTER 25

[218] Michael R. Licona, *The Resurrection of Jesus: A New Historiographical Approach* (Downers Grove: InterVarsity Press, 2010), 111-112.

[219] Ibid, 109. Emphasis mine.

[220] Ibid.

[221] Craig, *On Guard,* 244.

[222] This criterion was modified for the sake of simplicity. In Licona's book, his fifth criteria is "illumination," which occurs when one piece of data strengthens other areas of inquiry. For our purposes here, we will use the criterion of a hypothesis being disconfirmed by fewer accepted beliefs, which can be seen as coinciding with Licona's illumination criterion. See, Craig, *On Guard*, 244.

[223] Licona, 112.

[224] Licona, 108-109.

[225] Ibid.

[226] Craig, *On Guard*, 247.

[227] Ibid, 246.

[228] From his website: https://coldcasechristianity.com/writings/why-understanding-criminal-motive-is-so-important-to-christians/.

[229] N.T. Wright *Sewanee Theological Review* 41.2, 1998. Online article: https://ntwrightpage.com/2016/07/12/christian-origins-and-the-resurrection-of-jesus-the-resurrection-of-jesus-as-a-historical-problem/.

[230] Craig, *On Guard*, 247.

[231] Lloyd Davies and Lloyd Davies (1991), 168. As cited in Licona, 314.

[232] Thiering (1992), 120. As cited in Licona, 316.

[233] Ibid.

[234] Geisler and Turek, *I Don't Have Enough Faith to be an Atheist*, 305.

[235] Licona, 313.

[236] Habermas and Licona, 103.

[237] Dale Allison, *Resurrecting Jesus: The Earliest Christian Tradition and Its Interprets* (New York: t&t Clark, 2005).

[238] As Licona states, "readers understood that the crurifragium was employed in order to expedite death," 309.

[239] Strobel, 198-200.

[240] Habermas and Licona, 102.

[241] John 19:31-37.

[242] Strobel, 201.

[243] Ibid, 194.

[244] Ibid, 194-195.

[245] Licona, 303.

[246] Strobel, 195-196.

[247] Ibid.

[248] Ibid, 197.

[249] Ibid, 198.

[250] Quintilian. *Declamationes Maiores.* 6.9

[251] Strobel, 199.

[252] Ibid, 200.

[253] Edwards, Gabel and Hosmer (1986), 1463. As cited in Licona,313.

[254] Licona, 312.

[255] Gerd Lüdemann, *The Resurrection of Christ: A Historical Inquiry* (Amherst: Prometheus Books, 2004), 50.

[256] Paul Copan and Ronald K Tacelli, editors, *Jesus' Resurrection: Fact or Figment? A Debate Between William Lane Craig & Gerd Lüdemann* (Downers Grove: InterVarsity Press, 2000), 194.

[257] Habermas and Licona, 106.

[258] Gary R. Habermas and J. P. Moreland, *Beyond Death* (Wheaton: Crossway, 1998), 119-20.

[259] An email exchange between Licona and Sibcy, as reported in Licona's book and footnotes, 484.

[260] Comments by S.J. Leinster in "Letters" (1991), 269. Licona, 314.

[261] Licona, 517.

[262] Kristen Stendahl, *Paul Among Jews and Gentiles* (Philadelphia: Fortress, 1976), 12-13.

[263] Craig, *On Guard*, 257.

[264] Licona, 483, 518.

[265] Craig, *On Guard*, 255.

[266] Ibid.

[267] Ibid, 220.

[268] Habermas and Licona, 59.

[269] Craig, *On Guard*, 261.

[270] Debate between Peter Slezak and William Lane Craig. Craig, 240.

[271] N. T. Wright, "The New Unimproved Jesus," *Christianity Today* (September 13, 1993), 26.

Made in United States
Orlando, FL
03 March 2024